Mental Health Aspects of Autism
and Asperger Syndrome

of related interest

Asperger's Syndrome
A Guide for Parents and Professionals
Tony Attwood
Foreword by Lorna Wing
ISBN 1 85302 577 1

Children, Youth and Adults with Asperger Syndrome
Integrating Multiple Perspectives
Edited by Kevin P. Stoddart
ISBN 1 84310 319 2

Health Care and the Autism Spectrum
A Guide for Health Professionals, Parents and Carers
Alison Morton-Cooper
ISBN 1 85302 963 7 95

The Development of Autism
A Self-Regulatory Perspective
Thomas L. Whitman
ISBN 1 84310 735 X

Pretending to be Normal
Living with Asperger's Syndrome
Liane Holliday Willey
Foreword by Tony Attwood
ISBN 1 85302 749 9

Autism: An Inside-Out Approach
An Innovative Look at the 'Mechanics' of 'Autism'
and its Developmental 'Cousins'
Donna Williams
ISBN 1 85302 387 6

Mental Health Aspects of Autism and Asperger Syndrome

Mohammad Ghaziuddin

Jessica Kingsley Publishers
London and Philadelphia

First published in 2005
by Jessica Kingsley Publishers
116 Pentonville Road
London N1 9JB, UK
and
400 Market Street, Suite 400
Philadelphia, PA 19106, USA

www.jkp.com

Library of Congress Cataloging in Publication Data
Ghaziuddin, Mohammad.
    Mental health aspects of autism and Asperger Syndrome / Mohammad Ghaziuddin.— 1st american pbk.
ed.
        p. cm.
    ISBN-13: 978-1-84310-727-9 (pbk.)
    ISBN-10: 1-84310-727-9 (pbk.)
    ISBN-13: 978-1-84310-733-0 (hardback)
    ISBN-10: 1-84310-733-3 (hardback)
    1. Autism. 2. Asperger's syndrome. 3. Comorbidity. 4. Autism—Patients—Mental health. 5. Asperger's
syndrome—Patients—Mental health. 6. Psychology, Pathological. I. Title.
    RC553.A88G485 2005
    616.85'8832—dc22

                                                                2004029854

British Library Cataloguing in Publication Data
A CIP catalogue record for this book is available from the British Library

ISBN-13: 978 184310 727 9 (pbk)
ISBN-10: 1 84310 727 9 (pbk)

ISBN-13: 978 184310 733 0 (hb)
ISBN-10: 1 84310 733 3 (hb)

Printed and Bound in Great Britain by
Athenaeum Press, Gateshead, Tyne and Wear

Contents

List of Figures, Tables and Boxes

Preface

The aim of this book is to present an overview of the mental health aspects of autism and Asperger syndrome. It is not generally known that several types of behavioral and emotional problems occur in persons with autism spectrum disorders, of which autism and Asperger syndrome are the main categories. In fact, there is a common misperception among professionals and care-givers alike that people with these disorders do not develop additional psychiatric conditions. The purpose of this book is to dispel this myth. Although written primarily for parents and care-givers, specialists working in the field, such as psychiatrists and pediatricians, will also find it useful.

It is somewhat of an irony that, while autism is classified as a psychiatric disorder, not much is known about its psychiatric aspects. The same is true of Asperger syndrome. Although autism was first described in the 1940s, it is only now that attention is being paid to the psychiatric symptoms that often accompany it. Quite often, the presenting symptoms of autism are not the core deficits of social interaction and communication, but superimposed psychiatric problems such as anger outbursts, depression, and hyperactivity. Unfortunately, these problems are usually either ignored by professionals or dismissed as being part of the disorder of autism (and Asperger syndrome). While several good books have described the causes and treatment of autism spectrum disorders, none has specifically focused on the occurrence of psychiatric disorders in this population. This book aims to describe the presentation, diagnosis, and treatment of common psychiatric disorders in persons with autism and Asperger syndrome. Its objective is not to give an extensive account of each psychiatric disorder, but to provide a broad overview of the various disorders and underscore the need for treatment in persons with autism spectrum disorders.

There is no consensus as to what exactly constitutes a psychiatric disorder. However, for the purpose of this book, a psychiatric disorder is defined as any behavioral or emotional disorder which causes a significant degree of distress or impairment to the individual, the family, or to the community. The key requirement is that the behavior should cause a significant degree of impairment or dysfunction. If there is no impairment, there is no disorder, at least in the psychiatric sense. This issue is important because maladaptive behaviors and traits are present in all of us. For the problem to be called a psychiatric disorder, however, it must be accompanied by a certain degree of distress and disability. The focus of this book, therefore, is not to examine the hassles of daily living, and the transitory periods of distress that we all go through now and then. Rather, its goal is to give an account of the co-occurrence of distinct and clearly defined psychiatric disorders, such as depression and schizophrenia, in persons with autism and Asperger syndrome.

An increasingly popular view among some professionals is the notion that psychiatric disorders are not specific categories but dimensions that are normally distributed in the general population. While this argument makes sense in some cases, we do not yet have sufficient information to abandon the categorical method of psychiatric diagnosis, which is the one that is followed in this book. In addition, the diagnostic categories used here are broadly based on those given in the International Statistical Classification of Diseases and Related Health Problems (ICD) and the Diagnostic and Statistical Manual of Mental Disorders (DSM) systems of classification.

There are several reasons why so little is known about the prevalence of psychiatric disorders in children and adults with autism spectrum disorders. First, there is the perception that psychiatric disorders, in general, are uncommon, when, in reality, the reverse is true. Several studies have repeatedly confirmed the high prevalence of psychiatric disorders in the general population. For example, in the US, at least 20 per cent of the population shows some form of a psychiatric illness at any point in time. Studies from other industrialized countries also show similar estimates. Research performed on select populations, such as those who are medically ill, consistently shows higher figures. Second, there is a general shortage of trained professionals who know how to diagnose and treat psychiatric conditions in persons with autism spectrum disorders. This applies to all those professionals who work with people who are mentally or physically disabled, including psychiatrists and pediatricians. Third, some people believe that giving a psychiatric label is inherently stigmatizing. The purpose of reaching a correct diagnosis is not to stigmatize the patient, but to provide help and services. It would be extremely difficult to plan for services for people with disabilities if we do not know what those difficulties are. Fourth, the vagaries of the current systems of classification discourage giving more than one psychiatric diagnosis to people with autism. For example, according to the DSM-IV system of classification, the diagnosis of Attention Deficit Hyperactivity Disorder (ADHD) should not be given 'during the course of a PDD [pervasive developmental disorder].' Finally, some professionals tend to minimize the prevalence of psychiatric disorders by arguing that any disturbance that is precipitated by the environment is not a disorder but a response, when, in fact, research shows that this is not always the case.

What is the importance of treating psychiatric disorders in autism? Why does it matter if a teenager with autism also happens to be depressed? The answer lies in the fact that the treatment of superadded conditions of autism results in a substantial degree of improvement in the general level of functioning. In other words, while it may not be possible in the near future to cure autism, identification and treatment of the various behavioral and psychiatric symptoms that often occur in autistic patients leads to an improvement in their quality of life, and facilitates learning in school and adjustment in the community. And this impacts positively not only on the patient, but also on the family, and other care-givers. Any teacher who takes care of children with autism will agree that teaching a fidgety and hyperactive youngster is much more difficult than one who is calm and cooperative.

The focus of the book is on autism, and to a lesser extent on Asperger syndrome. At present, autism and Asperger syndrome are conceptualized as falling within the spectrum of pervasive developmental disorders (PDDs). However, other subtypes of the PDD spectrum, such as Rett's syndrome, disintegrative disorder, and Pervasive Developmental Disorder Not Otherwise Specified (PDDNOS), are also discussed briefly. Since the term autism spectrum disorder (ASD) is increasingly being used as a synonym for PDD, both these labels are used interchangeably here. Also, since the book is concerned mainly with medical and psychiatric conditions, the word 'patient' or 'subject' is used, rather than 'client' or 'customer.' In addition, the masculine pronoun 'he' is preferred because of the high rates of autism spectrum disorders among males.

Another point that needs to be clarified is that most of the information reviewed here pertains to children and not to adults with autism. This is unfortunate but reflects the current state of the field. Relatively little is known about the problems of adults with autism and Asperger syndrome. In part this is because the disorder itself is not very 'old': some of the patients first described by Leo Kanner in 1943 are probably still alive today. However, a more important reason relates to the lack of a systematic effort to study older persons with autism spectrum disorders. Children with autism are often seen by child psychiatrists, or pediatricians, or child neurologists. Once they turn

18 years of age, they are largely forgotten by the 'system,' and their care is transferred to people who do not often have a background in mental or physical health care. This makes it more difficult to identify and treat psychological problems from which many of them suffer in their adult years. It is important to remember that the symptoms of autism do not disappear when the child turns into an adult because autism is a life-long disorder.

The book is divided into chapters which closely follow the DSM and the ICD systems of classification. While these systems are not perfect, they do provide us with a template of the common types of mental disorders that exist in the general population. Not every disorder given in the DSM is reviewed. This is because some of the topics often do not apply to people with autism (e.g. pathological gambling). However, every effort has been made to include as many topics as possible. While the emphasis is on common psychiatric syndromes, such as depression and ADHD, uncommon conditions such as selective mutism have also been included. Case vignettes are provided where appropriate to help understand the clinical features. These short case histories are derived from the author's notes, although the names and identities of the patients have been altered to protect their confidentiality. A brief introduction about each psychiatric disorder is given at the beginning of each chapter for those readers who may not be familiar with psychiatric diagnoses.

Although the book is written from a psychiatric perspective, it is not intended to promote a particular viewpoint or a specific form of intervention. Medical doctors, including psychiatrists, are often accused of pill-pushing: that certainly is not the objective of this book. In fact, there is no medication that is universally effective in cases of autism. Yet medications are often prescribed both for the control of maladaptive behaviors and for the treatment of other medical conditions, such as seizures. Each chapter gives a brief summary of the medications commonly used, and underscores the importance of combining medications with other forms of interventions. The mainstay of treatment of autism spectrum disorders is educational and behavioral, combined with social skills training. Medications are used only for the treatment of additional symptoms. This point is repeatedly emphasized throughout the book.

Care has been taken not to propose a direct link between autism and any of the psychiatric disorders discussed here (although this may well prove to be the case in the future). Instead, I have sought to present the clinical and treatment aspects of the different conditions as they occur in autism, emphasizing the special features of these associations where applicable. Likewise, I have tried to avoid controversial issues as much as possible; the purpose is to focus on what is known about comorbidity of autism, and to suggest suitable strategies of intervention, rather than to discuss controversies about specific types of interventions.

The central theme, and the main message, of the book is that people with autism and Asperger syndrome suffer from a wide range of behavioral problems and psychiatric disorders at various stages of their lives, and that treatment of these disorders is critical to a good outcome. Some of these disorders are common, such as depression and ADHD, and some are not so common, such as school refusal and anorexia nervosa. It is hoped that this book will facilitate the early recognition and treatment of these conditions in persons with autism and Asperger syndrome, and help improve their quality of life and that of their loved ones.

Note

The terms 'mental retardation' and 'intellectual disability' are used interchangeably in this book.

CHAPTER 1

Autism and Pervasive Developmental Disorders: An Overview

Introduction

Autism is a severe, handicapping disorder of early childhood characterized by a distinct pattern of social deficits, communication impairment, and rigid ritualistic interests. These symptoms, however, are not specific to the disorder. They occur not only in other psychiatric conditions but also in the normal population. Several people in the community show autistic traits, but they do not meet the diagnostic criteria of autism because either their symptoms are not severe enough to cause impairment or they do not cluster together. The key to the diagnosis, therefore, lies in the clustering together of the three different types of symptoms – reciprocal social problems, communication deficits, and restricted interests – all of which start early in life, usually before the age of 3 years.

Historical background

Leo Kanner (1943), a child psychiatrist at Johns Hopkins University in Baltimore, USA, first described this condition based on his observations in eleven children. These children, he believed, were born without the usual ability to form relationships with others. They all had problems in relating, difficulties in communicating, and a tendency to perform routines and rituals. Kanner believed that these problems stemmed from two basic deficits: aloofness and a desire for sameness. His description of the clinical features of autism has stood the test of time. Widely regarded as the most clearly defined psychiatric disorder of childhood, autism occurs in all cultures and countries.

Classification

Although autism was described in the 1940s, it was introduced as a formal diagnostic category much later. Over the years, its diagnostic criteria have gone through several changes and revisions. Currently, it is classified as a pervasive developmental disorder (PDD), although the term 'autism spectrum disorder' is being increasingly used. These disorders are characterized by a distinct pattern of deficits involving multiple areas of functioning, namely, socialization, communication, and imagination. Some authorities have questioned the rationale of labeling these conditions 'pervasive' because there are other conditions, such as mental retardation, which may also be placed under this category. However, at this time, the official position of both the American DSM (APA, 1994) and the WHO's ICD (1993) is to regard autism as the main category within the group of PDDs. Before the early 1990s, there were only two main categories in the PDDs: autistic disorder and Pervasive Developmental Disorder Not Otherwise Specified (PDDNOS). Patients who met the required criteria for autism were called autistic, and those who fell short of meeting the full criteria were grouped together under the residual category of PDDNOS. Later, three new disorders were split off from PDDNOS, namely, Asperger syndrome, Rett's syndrome, and disintegrative disorder. These disorders are discussed in Chapters 2 and 3.

Prevalence

Recent reports have suggested a marked increase in the prevalence of autism (see Chakrabarti and Fombonne, 2001). While it is not yet clear as to why this is the case, several theories have been proposed. These range from an increasing awareness of the diagnosis to a broadening of the diagnostic criteria. While clinical evidence suggests that the increase is widespread, data are limited only to western countries. A recent study in California found a threefold increase in the number of autistic cases from 1987 to 1998 that did not seem to be the result of changes in diagnosis or of such external factors as immunization and birth injuries (Blakeslee, 2002). Traditionally, the estimate of autism is given as four or five per 10,000 children. However, several reports now suggest estimates as high as one per 500 children or even more, when conditions such as Asperger syndrome and PDDNOS are included in the broad definition of autism. For example, a British survey gave a prevalence rate of 26 per 10,000 in children aged between 5 and 15 years (Fombonne *et al.*, 2003).

Causes of autism

There is no single cause of autism. It is described as a multifactorial disorder in which both genetic and environmental factors play a role. While the extent to which each of these factors operates in any single case depends on the individual case, there is a consensus that autism is a neuropsychiatric disorder that is caused by some as yet undefined biological factor. This factor, perhaps in combination with a pre-existing genetic vulnerability, results in the clinical syndrome of autism.

Genetic factors

The association of genetic factors in the etiology of autism is well established. Several family and twin studies have shown that the disorder is strongly influenced by genetic factors. The chances of having a child with autism are significantly increased if the couple already has one such child. In line with research done in other branches of medicine, it is now generally believed that what is transmitted is not autism itself, but a tendency to it.

People with autism not only have an increased family history of autism, but also of autistic traits. These traits are collectively referred to as the 'broader autistic phenotype' (BAP). Also sometimes referred to as the lesser variant of autism, this concept describes a condition in which a person shows many of the features of autism without meeting its full diagnosis. Thus, there may be an excess of such personality traits as rigidity and awkwardness (Bolton et al., 1994). That the parents of autistic children show an excess of such characteristics was known even at the time of Kanner (1943). However, at that time it was widely believed that the presence of those traits supported a psychogenic, rather than a biologic, origin of the disorder.

In addition to the increase of autism and autistic-like traits in the family members, there is also an increase of a variety of psychiatric disorders. Thus, parents of autistic children show an increase in depression and anxiety disorders. Compared to a group of parents with Down syndrome, parents of autistic children show an increased prevalence of psychiatric disorders, thus underscoring the fact that these disorders do not result from the burden of care inherent in raising a handicapped child (Piven et al., 1991). Sometimes, the presence of psychiatric disorders, such as depression, in the parents of autistic children is correlated with the prevalence of similar disorders in the autistic children themselves (Ghaziuddin and Greden 1998). The last decade has witnessed an enormous surge of knowledge in molecular genetics.

Findings at this time suggest that autism probably results from at least three to twenty genes and that there is no single gene for autism. Promising as these studies are, they are preliminary in nature, and need to be replicated.

Environmental factors

While autism is characterized by a strong genetic component, the dramatic increase in recent years, if accurate, raises the possibility that environmental factors may also be at work. Some of the environmental agents that have been implicated are briefly discussed below.

- *Viruses*: Some researchers believe that viruses can cause autism. While several viral disorders have been associated with autism, it is unclear to what extent they directly result in the symptoms of autism. For example, herpes virus attacks the brain directly. Case reports have described the emergence of autistic symptoms after herpes encephalitis both in children (Ghaziuddin, Al-Khouri and Ghaziuddin, 2002) and in adults (Gillberg, 1991). In addition to herpes, other viruses that have been implicated in the etiology of autism include the measles virus and the cytomegalovirus.

- *Valproate and thalidomide*: Reports have described the association of autism with fetal valproate syndrome (Williams *et al.*, 2001). The exposure occurs when the mother is exposed to valproate during the first trimester of pregnancy. Similar associations have also been proposed between autism and thalidomide. Of a population of 100 Swedish thalidomide embryopathy cases, at least four met the criteria for autism. The authors proposed that thalidomide embryopathy of the kind encountered in these cases affects fetal development early in pregnancy, probably on days 20 to 24 after conception (Stromland *et al.*, 1994).

- *Mercury*: Hazards of mercury have been linked to a variety of behavioral and cognitive problems in children. There are some reports of its association with lower IQ, Attention Deficit Hyperactivity Disorder (ADHD), and autism. The mercury-containing preservative thimerosal, contained in some vaccines, has been linked to autism. However, a recent study that examined infants who received vaccines containing thimerosal found that the levels of mercury in their blood were within safety limits (Pichichero *et al.*, 2002).

Neurobiology of autism

- *Neurochemistry:* About one third of patients with autism show increased levels of the neurotransmitter serotonin in the blood. However, many mentally retarded persons also show this abnormality. It is, therefore, unclear to what extent serotonin dysfunction is responsible for all the symptoms of autism.

- *Post-mortem studies:* Because of practical reasons, few post-mortem studies have been done. Although there are no gross alterations in the appearance of the brain, subtle changes have been seen in the way cells are packed in some regions (Bauman, 1991). Abnormalities in the temporal lobes and the cerebellum have also been described.

- *Neuroimaging studies:* A wide variety of abnormalities has been shown in persons with autism on computerized tomography (CT) scan and magnetic resonance imaging (MRI) studies. Some of these include enlargement of the cerebral ventricles, and abnormalities of the cerebral cortex and the basal ganglia (Piven *et al.*, 1990). However, these findings are not specific to autism, and may reflect the consequences of the disorder, rather than its cause.

Neuropsychology of autism

Several neuropsychological abnormalities characterize autism. Intellectual deficits are common, with at least half of all people with autism showing an IQ below 70. However, if milder variants of autism are included, perhaps fewer autistic patients have mental retardation than is generally believed. Most autistic patients show problems with abstraction, and on IQ tests most have a better ability to focus on parts of a puzzle rather than the whole. Likewise, verbal IQ scores are often suppressed in comparison with performance IQ scores. In addition, there are abnormalities in the ability to read other peoples' emotions and feelings. Often described as Theory of Mind (TOM) deficits, these explain why autistic persons find it difficult to make judgments about others (Baron-Cohen, 1989). However, TOM deficits do not explain other symptoms of autism, such as ritualistic behaviors. Other theories, such as the Central Coherence Theory[1] (Frith, 1996), attempt to explain how intense focus on certain areas can interfere with social and communication functioning. Deficits in executive functioning also occur which interfere with the individual's ability to plan and execute actions satisfactorily. A selective impairment of the ability to recognize human faces has also been described (Schultz et al., 2000).

Clinical features

Behavioral abnormalities

Although the boundaries of autism remain fuzzy, there is a general consensus that all autistic people share certain qualities that set them apart from others: they are rigid, mechanical, and emotionally distant.

SOCIAL INTERACTIONS

People with autism have reciprocal social deficits. They lack the ability to interact in a to-and-fro manner with others. Their quality of interactions lacks flexibility and spontaneity. Although autistic persons are able to form relationships, it is the way those relationships are formed that is distinctly different from normal human relationships. At times, these deficits are so mild, especially in adults with autism, and in those who do not suffer from mental retardation, that they may be missed at first glance.

COMMUNICATION

Perhaps the most common symptom that arouses parental concern is the child's inability to communicate. According to some estimates, at least a quarter of all children with autism fail to develop meaningful speech. Many a time, the autistic child will communicate his needs by leading the parent by the arm, and using the arm as if it were an extension of his (the child's) body, for example, using the parents arm to open a door or get an object. Speech is often delayed, and those who eventually speak, show a variety of abnormalities both in the form as well as in the content of speech. Several types of speech abnormalities may occur, including a tendency to repeat the speech of others, and sometimes to repeat phrases and sentences heard in the recent

---

1   According to this theory, a person with autism processes excessive information focusing on parts and details, and ignores the meaning of the whole.

past. Problems with eye contact, facial expression, and other aspects of nonverbal communication are often present. The tone and pitch of the voice may also be different. Sometimes the child may speak in a loud voice; at other times, the voice may have a sing-song quality.

RESTRICTED INTERESTS

Restricted and ritualistic interests form the third main clinical feature of autism. These depend on the level of intelligence (Bartak and Rutter, 1976). Patients who have mental retardation often show fixation on simple routines. These may consist of lining up objects, such as pencils or sticks; arranging pieces of furniture; insisting on performing routines in a certain way, etc. Those who are higher-functioning are often focused on more sophisticated activities and interests, such as following the weather, reading and collecting maps, charting out the course of the planets, etc.

Physical abnormalities

There are no common physical signs in autism. However, features that have been described are discussed below.

INCREASED HEAD SIZE

Some people with autism have large heads. Kanner himself commented on this feature in his paper (Kanner, 1943). Several recent studies have re-ignited the interest in this topic. It has been suggested that the increase in head size occurs immediately after birth in the first few years of life, suggesting that it can be used as a possible marker for early diagnosis. However, several issues remain unclear at this time. First, the increase in head size is not seen in all patients with autism but only in about a third of the cases and it is not clear whether it is present at birth or soon after. Second, it is not specific to autism; many patients with other psychiatric conditions, such as ADHD, may also show this feature (Ghaziuddin et al., 1999). Third, the trait for increased head size may run in families, and have little to do with autism. Fourth, the increase in the head size does not correlate with the severity or the type of autism.

FACIAL APPEARANCE

No facial features are typical of autism or related disorders. Indeed, autistic children have been traditionally described as being attractive and good-looking. Features of accompanying disorders may, however, be present. For example, those autistic children who also suffer from Down syndrome may show the facial appearance of that condition. Some children who also have Fragile X syndrome may show low-set ears and a prominent lower jaw. While no chromosome abnormalities are characteristic of autism, some, such as tetrasomy 15, may show features such as a high-arched palate. Those with deletion of chromosome 2 and autism may show distinct facial features, such as a flat nasal bridge, and dark circles under the eyes. (Ghaziuddin and Burmeister, 1999). Likewise, patients with tuberous sclerosis (a disorder that affects the brain and other organs of the body) and autism may show the typical butterfly rash on the face.

SKIN LESIONS

Various types of skin lesions can be seen in persons with autism, although no single lesion is specific to the disorder. These include the shagreen patches of tuberous sclerosis, the typical *café au lait* patches of Von Recklinghausen's disease (neurofibromatosis), and the lesions of hypomelanosis of ito (a disorder of the nervous system characterized by hypopigmented patches, seisures, and mental retardation).

MOTOR CLUMSINESS

Problems with motor coordination are often seen in persons with autism and related disorders. Sometimes, these deficits are referred to as clumsiness. Although some studies have claimed that clumsiness is more common in some types of PDDs, such as Asperger syndrome, there is little evidence to support this at this stage. Rather, the deficits seem to occur across the entire range of autistic disorders, and not specifically in Asperger syndrome or any other disorder. Abnormalities of gait are also seen. Patients may show a tendency to walk with an awkward gait, or swing their arms in an abnormal manner while walking. Some patients walk on their tiptoes while others come across as being stiff.

SENSORY ABNORMALITIES

Sensory deficits are sometimes found in autism. These consist of altered pain tolerance, increased sensitivity to certain sounds (such as a dog barking, a baby crying), and altered sensory response to touch. For example, the patient may refuse to wear certain types of clothing. A tendency to the 'lazy eye syndrome' is also seen occasionally.

SAVANT SYNDROME

Some people with autism, called 'savants,' are gifted in a particular field beyond their general level of ability, and can perform super-specialized mental feats. Common areas of giftedness include musical abilities (e.g. to play any tune by ear); photographic memory (e.g. to reproduce from memory in drawing any picture having seen it once); and calculation (e.g. to correctly identify the day given a certain date in the past or the future). People with autism who are so gifted usually become less capable as they grow older. Their ability to perform extraordinary mental feats does not seem to increase with practice. While various theories have been proposed, the exact mechanism underlying the savant syndrome is not clear. The fact that some aspects of normal 'thinking' are distorted or delayed in autism may itself contribute to the overgrowth of other abilities.

Diagnosis

Psychological and social assessment

The first task is to establish the diagnosis. This is not always easy because there is no blood test or a biologic marker for autism. Despite the emergence of a wide variety of diagnostic instruments and structured interviews, the diagnosis remains clinical. Although the process differs with the age of the patient, in general, it is based on the same principles. The diagnosis of autism is multidisciplinary in nature. The assessment depends on collecting information in all areas of functioning and from all available sources, including schools, social agencies, and community mental health centers. Milder forms of the disorder are likely to be missed if the patient is seen in a structured setting such as a pediatrician's office with no input from other professionals. Quite often, patients do not show, in one setting, all the behaviors necessary to make a valid diagnosis. For example, a diagnosis of autism is difficult to make in a busy outpatient clinic where the clinician has about an hour to complete the evaluation.

In addition to obtaining a good developmental history focusing on the core features of autism, rating scales and interviews can be used to strengthen the diagnosis. One of the most commonly used rating scales is the Autism Behavior Checklist (Krug, Arick and Almond, 1980). This is a screening instrument that reliably separates out subjects with autism from those with other handicapping conditions. Another scale that is commonly used is the Childhood Autism Rating Scale (CARS: Schopler et al., 1980). This is an observer-rated instrument which takes about 30 minutes to complete. It has been widely used all over the world. Other rating scales include the Checklist for Autism in Toddlers (CHAT: Baird *et al.*, 2000) and the Social Communication Questionnaire (Rutter *et al.*, 2003). Another observation scale that is increasingly being used, especially in research settings, is the Autism Diagnostic Observation Scale (ADOS: Lord *et al.*, 2000). It provides a semi-structured standardized assessment of the patient's social interaction, play, and imagination. It consists of four 30-minute modules, each designed to be administered according to the patient's level of expressive language. Structured interviews are also sometimes used. These interviews provide more detailed information about the symptoms and the level of functioning, and include the Autism Diagnostic Interview (ADI: Lord, Rutter and Le Couteur, 1994), and the Diagnostic Interview for Social and Communication Disorders (DISCO: Wing *et al.*, 2002).

Biological assessment

Every child with autism should undergo a detailed physical examination. The skin should be examined, preferably with an ultraviolet lamp, for spots of discoloration seen in disorders such as tuberous sclerosis. The head circumference should also be measured. Features of genetic syndromes, such as Fragile X syndrome, should be noted.

Blood tests that should be done include thyroid and liver function tests. This is because in some cases, especially those with marked hyperactivity and impulsivity, thyroid dysfunction may be present. Cytogenetic examination to rule out chromosome abnormalities should be performed, along with a DNA analysis for Fragile X syndrome, especially if mental retardation is present. More advanced tests should be decided on a case-by-case basis, and only if clinically indicated. For example, in a youngster who presents with severe regression of behavior, a brain imaging study (brain MRI) may be indicated.

Differential diagnosis

Mental retardation

It is important to differentiate global mental retardation from autism. This is the most common differential diagnosis when preschool children are referred for a diagnostic evaluation. In mental retardation, there is global delay affecting all areas of functioning, as opposed to autism, where the classical feature is deviance. It is the altered nature of behavior that is important for a diagnosis of autism rather than delay in itself. People with mental retardation do not show the typical social deficits of autism. An example is Down syndrome: people with Down syndrome, despite their mental retardation, are able to form relationships and are often friendly and sociable.

Specific language disorder

Patients with Specific Language Impairment should be differentiated from those with autism. Again, these patients do not show the reciprocal social deficits typical of autism, or, more importantly, the restricted range of interests of autism. However, despite this distinction, it is not always possible to differentiate between these two conditions. Some children with language disorders show mild autistic features. When followed up in the long term, however, they generally show a better outcome than those with traditional autism.

Schizophrenia

Autism is sometimes confused with schizophrenia. This is likely to occur when patients with mild forms of autism are referred for diagnostic evaluation for the first time during adolescence. Also, adults with autism are sometimes misdiagnosed as suffering from schizophrenia. Initially, autism and schizophrenia in childhood were regarded as belonging to the same group of disorders. However, the two disorders are now regarded as distinct and schizophrenia is further discussed in Chapter 9.

Reactive attachment disorder

The essential feature of this disorder is developmentally inappropriate social relatedness beginning before 5 years of age in the context of gross neglect and deprivation. It is an uncommon condition sometimes seen in children reared in orphanages and residential settings. Children with this disorder may sometimes develop features resembling autism. However, they improve when they are placed in a more nurturing environment.

Shyness

Sometimes autism is mistaken for normal shyness. Many children are shy by temperament, and some are more clinging and withdrawn than others. Normal shyness gradually begins to decrease by the time a child is 4 years of age. However, if the child remains shy and withdrawn beyond this age, and especially if the play is marked by routines and rituals, autism or one of the pervasive developmental disorders should be considered. This is especially true if deficits of communication are also present.

Treatment

There is no specific *cure* for autism, and no single treatment works for all cases. Treatment is symptomatic, and is aimed at fostering normal development and improving the likelihood of independent living. Although several methods of intervention exist, the mainstay of treatment continues to be behavioral and educational. Almost all these methods employ elements of social skills training and speech and language therapy. The key to successful treatment lies in devising a plan that takes into account not only the strengths and weaknesses of the affected person, but also the severity and the subtype of the disorder, the age of the individual, the presence of associated medical and psychiatric conditions, the needs of the family, and the availability of resources in the community. Most children with autism benefit from receiving educational services meant for them. In most industrialized countries, children with autism are eligible by law to receive special services from the state. For example, it is customary for a child with autism in the US to be classified appropriately, such as being labeled 'autistic impaired.' This allows the child to receive a range of services through the school that are otherwise difficult to access. These services can be delivered in a mainstream classroom or in a special classroom. The decision where to place a child is made after taking his level of intelligence, degree of communication, and accompanying behavior into consideration. Although treatments can be divided into two broad categories – non-medication and medication – in practice, they are often combined.

Social skills training

Training in social skills is based on the premise that social interactions can be successfully accomplished in a positive manner. Techniques include modeling, coaching, and role-playing. Deficits in social skills form an integral part of autism, and promoting appropriate social interaction remains a central feature of any educational treatment program. In fact, the diagnosis of an autism spectrum disorder is not complete without the presence of social deficits. Among factors that contribute to these deficits are a biologically based abnormal development, a tendency to fixations and preoccupations, and a range of communication abnormalities. People with autism often present with additional symptoms that impact negatively on social interaction such as hyperactivity, impulsivity, and depression. Improving in social skills, therefore, constitutes an important component of interventions for autism and related disorders.

Social skills training is often school-based. Skills that are targeted include greeting others, sharing of objects, and engaging in reciprocal conversation. As part of the treatment program, autistic children are taught to use these skills in sessions lasting 10–20 minutes several times during the week. Sometimes, normally developing children are involved as peer-facilitators, and are taught skills to help them interact better with autistic children. Social skills training can also occur in community settings such as mental health clinics and hospital clinics. This sort of training is often longer, lasting for an hour or two, and typically occurs once a week. Although community-based social skills training programs of autistic children are gaining in popularity, information about their efficacy is limited.

Before starting a social skills training program, target skills should be clearly identified. Goals, both short-term and long-term, should be defined at the outset, depending on the level of functioning. A program that focuses on the acquisition of a few clearly defined skills, such as greeting or improving eye contact, is preferable to one that addresses socialization in a more general way. Improvement in social skills is more likely to occur in those who are more verbal and higher-functioning than in those who suffer from severe cognitive deficits.

Despite their popularity, social skills programs suffer from two inherent weaknesses. First, the gains made are not permanent. Intervention research in autism has focused primarily on short- or medium-term effects, generally less than a year. Second, new skills are not generalized across different situations. Thus, a child who learns a new social skill at school may not use it appropriately in a different setting, such as a grocery store.

Despite these caveats, training in social skills is necessary to improve the chances of independent living. It increases positive social interactions and decreases inappropriate behaviors, such as temper tantrums. Also, social engagement directly affects other important behaviors like language, even when these behaviors are not specifically targeted by the teaching program. In addition, improvement in social skills contributes to a general sense of well-being and protects against depression. Research has shown that in people with autism, deficits in social skills cause loneliness which, in turn, increases the risk of depression and other psychiatric disorders (see Barry *et al.*, 2003; Rogers, 2000; Weiss and Harris, 2001).

Speech and language intervention

Impairment of communication is one of the three main symptoms of autistic spectrum disorders. A range of communication abnormalities occur in persons with autism spectrum disorders, ranging from a failure to develop any functional speech in about 30–50 per cent of cases to almost normal but idiosyncratic and pragmatically impaired speech in others. While the degree of impairment varies, problems in the social use of language are present in all cases. The nature and goal of intervention, therefore, depends on a variety of factors including the age of the patient, the level of intelligence, and the severity of deficits. Several treatment approaches are used with the aim of improving both verbal and nonverbal aspects of speech.

The goal, when working with nonverbal autistic children, is to facilitate meaningful spontaneous verbalizations across different settings. Techniques such as the Picture Exchange Communication System (PECS: Bondy and Frost, 1998) are commonly used. Other methods include time delay procedures and video modeling. Computer-assisted methods have also been used to teach vocabulary and language to children with autism (Bosseler and Massaro, 2003). Compensatory strategies, such as sign language and visual symbols, can be used with children who do not acquire functional language.

The goal when working with verbal and higher-functioning children with autism is to promote spontaneous and socially appropriate speech, minimize deviant responses, and improve the social use of language. People with autism have a tendency to fixate on certain topics in their conversations. Perseverations focusing on schedules and timetables, for instance, are not uncommon. These can be decreased, to a certain extent, by differential reinforcement of appropriate verbal behavior and by extinction of verbal responses to the perseverations. Techniques have also been devised to reduce stereotyped utterances and echolalia. These include giving simple instructions and supplementing these with pictures, written instructions, and other cues (Prizant and Rydell, 1984).

While speech and language interventions are important, they cannot be delivered satisfactorily when additional behavioral symptoms complicate the disorder. These include aggression, extreme hyperactivity and impulsivity, and lack of motivation. These symptoms may index the presence of superimposed psychiatric disorders, such as ADHD and depression, and need to be addressed independently.

Behavioral intervention

Autistic children typically do not have the ability to learn from others and, therefore, need to be taught even simple tasks repeatedly. Most experts recommend early intervention, starting when the child is around 3 years of age, and involving a minimum of 25 hours a week. By law, autistic children in the US, like other special needs children, are entitled to public education. All types of behavioral treatments incorporate elements of structure and consistency, and are based on the premise that positive or desirable behaviors can be built, and negative or undesirable behaviors eliminated. These treatments include extinction, differential reinforcement, and modeling. Some of the better-known treatments used in persons with autism spectrum disorders include those described below.

Applied behavioral analysis

Applied behavioral analysis involves intensive behavior therapy being given to the child for prolonged periods of time. Sessions of up to 40 hours a week are not unusual. The therapist asks the child to perform small tasks and then offers feedback to reinforce correct responses. Some researchers have suggested that the more intensive the intervention, the better the outcome. Prominent among these researchers is Lovaas (1987) and his colleagues. These researchers have suggested that the child should receive intensive training, consisting of 40 hours of one-on-one exposure. They have reported success rates as high as 47 per cent (McEachin, Smith and Lovaas, 1993). However, it seems the key to successful outcome does not lie in one single method employing a fixed number of hours, but on a wide variety of educational and behavioral techniques that incorporate repeated training and consistency.

Treatment and Education of Autistic and related Communications Handicapped Children (the TEACCH method)

This treatment was popularized by Eric Schopler, Gary Mesibov, and their colleagues at the University of North Carolina at Chapel Hill, in the US. It focuses on communication training, developing play skills and facilitating social interaction using a highly structured and visually based approach. The program adopts a holistic approach to the care of persons with autism that incorporates parent–professional collaboration, assessment for individualized treatment, skill enhancement and acceptance of deficits, and a community-based service. It views maladaptive behaviors within an 'iceberg' conceptualization model with visible behaviors depicted as occurring 'above the water line' and hypothesized causes hidden 'below the water line' of the iceberg. It has been shown to be effective in reducing inappropriate behaviors and increasing vocational skills (Schopler, Mesibov and Hearsey, 1995).

Occupational therapy

Occupational therapy (OT) often forms an important part of a comprehensive treatment package for children with autism spectrum disorders. Two main reasons justify this. First, coordination problems are common in these conditions. If the criteria for Developmental Coordination Disorder (DCD) are strictly applied, most children with autism/Asperger syndrome would be labeled as suffering from it. Second, problems of sensory integration are common in persons with PDD. Even when compared with subjects with other forms of developmental disorders, such as Fragile X syndrome, children with autism spectrum disorders show a wide range of sensory problems, including those affecting the sense of taste and smell. Neither the developmental level nor the IQ seems to be responsible for the spectrum of sensory abnormalities (Rogers, Hepburn and Wehner, 2003). Similar results have also been seen in samples of children with Asperger syndrome. OT is also helpful in vocational training and job placement of adults. Several techniques and methods of intervention have been described as discussed elsewhere (see Watling et al., 1999).

Pharmacotherapy of autism spectrum disorders

Medications are widely used in the treatment of autism spectrum disorders. About 23 per cent of autistic children and adolescents between 3 and 14 years of age are placed on medications (Aman, 1995). Clinical experience suggests that over their lifetime, about 60–80 per cent of patients with these conditions receive psychotropic medications. The use of medications is based on the rationale that a decrease in behavioral symptoms reduces the level of overall impairment, and improves the chances of success with other forms of treatments. While the core features of the disorder do not respond to medications, additional symptoms such as hyperactivity and depression often improve. Medications commonly used to control these symptoms are summarized in Table 1.1.

Table 1.1 Indications of pharmacotherapy
in autism spectrum disorders

Symptoms	Medications
Hyperactivity, impulsivity, distractibility	Stimulants (Ritalin, Adderall etc.), non-stimulants (Strattera, tricyclic antidepressants), antipsychotic agents (occasionally)
Aggression	Antipsychotic drugs, mood stabilizers, beta blockers (rarely)
Self-injurious behavior	Mood stablizers, antipsychotic drugs, naltrexone
Extreme difficulty with transitions	Clomipramine, SSRI antidepressants
Extreme compulsive behaviors	Clomipramine, SSRI antidepressants
Irritability	Antidepressants
Depressive symptoms	Antidepressants
Mood swings	Mood stabilizers (lithium), anticonvulsants (depakoate), antipsychotics
Anxious and phobic symptoms	Antidepressants
Psychotic behavior	Antipsychotic drugs
Sleep disturbance	Benadryl, trazodone, clonidine, antipsychotics
Tics and Tourette syndrome	Antipsychotic drugs, clonidine
Seizures	Anticonvulsants

Principles of pharmacotherapy

The main principles of pharmacotherapy include clarifying the target symptoms, documenting baseline behaviors, and monitoring the side-effects and drug interactions. Polypharmacy should be avoided if possible. Parents and care-givers should be informed about the rationale for using medications, and no attempt should be made to raise unrealistic expectations. Medications should always be prescribed as part of a comprehensive package of treatment. Medications commonly used in the treatment of persons with autism include those discussed below.

Antipsychotic medications

Antipsychotic drugs are widely used in the treatment of autism and related disorders. Indications for their use are both symptom-based and condition-based. The main symptoms that justify their use are *extreme* hyperactivity, impulsivity, aggressive behavior, and intractable self-injurious behavior. The main syndrome-based indications are psychotic disorders of any kind, such as psychotic depression and schizophrenia. It is sometimes wrongly believed that response to these medications proves the presence of psychosis. They are used with patients with schizophrenia because of their effects on the thought disorder. On the other hand, in patients with autism and related disorders, these drugs are used for their effect on behavioral disinhibition and disorganization. In fact, antipsychotic drugs have a calming effect on any person who is agitated and anxious. They tend to calm the patient, decrease the level of hostility and aggression, and decrease stereotypic behaviors. There are two main groups: typical (older) antipsychotic drugs and atypical (newer) antipsychotic drugs.

TYPICAL ANTIPSYCHOTIC DRUGS

Typical antipsychotic drugs act by knocking off the dopamine receptors of the brain and are used in the treatment of schizophrenia and related psychotic disorders. With the advent of newer antipsychotic drugs, which have fewer side-effects, their use has been steadily decreasing. However, they are still used for persons with autism spectrum disorders, especially those who cannot tolerate the newer atypical drugs or those who live in group homes and long-term residential centers. Some of these drugs include haloperidol (Haldol), chlorpromazine (Thorazine), and thiordidazine (Melleril).

Haloperidol has been widely used in the treatment of children and adults with autism. Earlier studies conducted by Magda Campbell and her colleagues established its efficacy and safety (Campbell *et al.*, 1982). It is a reasonably safe and effective medication that decreases the level of impulsivity, hyperactivity, and aggressive behavior. However, it can also cause side-effects such as tremors, rigidity, and movement disorders. Because of this reason, its use has decreased over the years. Chlorpromazine and thioridazine are rarely used, except in those adults with autism who have been labeled as suffering from schizophrenia or mental retardation. They are more sedating than the other antipsychotic medications, and are also associated with other side-effects.

ATYPICAL ANTIPSYCHOTIC DRUGS

Few drugs have generated as much interest in the treatment of autism as the atypical antipsychotic medication *risperidone* (Risperdal). Drawing on studies of schizophrenia, researchers have advocated its use in patients with autism. Case reports and a few preliminary studies suggest that the medication reduces aggressive behavior and irritability; however, the side-effects include an increase in weight, which poses a serious problem, and an increased vulnerability to diabetes. A recent systematic multisite study suggested that the medication was effective and safe in the treatment of children with autism aged between 5 and 17 years of age. A positive response was observed in 23 out of 34 subjects with autism by eight weeks of a double-blind trial and the results were maintained at follow-up after six months (McCracken *et al.*, 2002). Risperidone is likely to be approved by the FDA in the US for the treatment of behavioral symptoms in children with autism.

Experience with the drug *ziprasidone* (Geodon) is limited, although claims have been made about its efficacy. In an open trial, McDougle, Kem and Posey (2002) found that ziprasidone was effective in a group of 12 patients with autism or PDDNOS. No significant side-effects were noted. This medication holds some promise for the treatment of both mood symptoms and aggressive behavior because of its action on the neurotransmitters. While it does not cause the weight gain that is usually associated with other atypical antipsychotic agents such as Risperdal, its effects on the conduction system of the heart need to be monitored closely.

Other atypical antipsychotic medications include clozapine, olanzapine, and quetiapine. Clozapine is not commonly used because of the risk of agranulocytosis, a condition in which there is an insufficient number of white blood cells. In addition, it may precipitate seizures which constitute a risk factor in autism spectrum disorders. Another atypical antipsychotic agent, aripripazole (Abilify), has recently been introduced in the treatment of schizophrenia. It possesses a unique ability to modulate dopamine and may be of use in some patients with autism and Asperger syndrome (Staller, 2003).

Antidepressants

Antidepressants are commonly used in persons with autism spectrum disorders (Martin *et al.*, 1999). They are grouped into two basic categories: older antidepressants belonging to the tricylic class, and the newer antidepressants belonging to the serotonin receptor uptake inhibitor (SSRI) class. The tricyclic antidepressants, such as imipramine and amitriptyline, are rarely used because of the effects of the medications on the heart. A few cases of sudden death in children and adolescents with depression highlighted the problem. Older tricyclic agents, such as imipramine and amitriptyline, are still sometimes used when other medications fail or for enuresis (urinary incontinence).

Clomipramine belongs to the tricyclic group of antidepressants that has been shown to be effective in the treatment of Obsessive-Compulsive Disorder (OCD). The rationale for its use in PDD stems from the fact that many patients show rigid ritualistic and compulsive behaviors. If these behaviors increase in intensity they interfere with educational and behavioral interventions. Under such circumstances, a drug such as Clomipramine may be used (Gordon *et al.*, 1993). Some reports have described the emergence of seizures in persons with PDD who are treated with this agent (McDougle *et al.*, 1992). Younger patients may be more prone to the side-effects of this medication than older ones. Because of these reasons, enthusiasm for the use of this drug has waned in recent years.

Along with stimulants, the SSRIs are probably the most commonly used medications in this population. These drugs are generally safe and effective, although long-term studies have not been done. The most commonly used medications in this category are fluoxetine (Prozac) and sertraline (Zoloft). Other medications include citaloprim and paroxetine. All these agents are currently used for treating persons with autism spectrum disorders not only for depression but also for a variety of other psychiatric and behavioral problems such as OCD, impulse control disorder, and anxiety disorder (Cook *et al.*, 1992). An increasing indication of the use of the SSRI group of antidepressants is the presence of severe aggression.

Trazodone (Desyrel) is an atypical antidepressant. Because its main side-effect is sedation, it is sometimes used as a hypnotic. Although it is a reasonably good antidepressant, it is not used as frequently as the SSRIs such as fluoxetine and sertraline. In the child and adolescent population, it is commonly used for disruptive behaviors, including severe aggressive outbursts, temper tantrums, and irritability. It also helps in the control of hyperactivity and impulsivity and is sometimes combined with stimulants for the control of severe symptoms of ADHD in children with PDDs. Its main side-effect, apart from sedation, is on the conduction system of the heart. Rarely, it causes a state of sustained painful erection (priapism). Other antidepressants that are sometimes used in persons with autism and Asperger syndrome include venlafaxine (Effexor) and buprupion (Wellbutrin).

Stimulants

Stimulants, such as methylphenidate (Ritalin), remain the drugs of choice for the treatment of hyperactivity and impulsivity in children with autism spectrum disorders. They are used in both high- and low-functioning patients, although their use in the latter group has traditionally been discouraged. This is because of the fear of increased side-effects which is not borne out by research. Persons with autism and Asperger syndrome seem to respond to these medications the same way as those who do not have these conditions, that is, without any increased risk of side-effects. Problems that occur as a result of these medications appear to be related more to the accompanying mental retardation rather than to the diagnosis of autism. While Ritalin continues to be commonly used, other more recently introduced drugs include Adderall and Concerta. These are longer-acting agents that increase drug compliance. Common side-effects include problems with sleep and appetite. A recently introduced medication for the control of hyperactivity and impulsivity is atomoxetine (Strattera). This drug is not a stimulant (like Ritalin) and works through a different mechanism (by decreasing the reuptake of norepinephrine). Its effect, however, is not as rapid as that of stimulants such as Ritalin.

Anticonvulsants

About 30 per cent of persons with autism suffer from seizure disorder. The prevalence rates in those with Asperger syndrome and PDDNOS are not clear. Anticonvulsants are used in autism spectrum disorders not only for the control of seizures but also for the treatment of associated psychiatric symptoms such as aggressive outbursts, temper tantrums, mood instability, and depression. At times, they are administered 'routinely' when abnormalities are detected on an EEG (electroencephalogram) even in the absence of clinical seizures. They belong to two groups: traditional anticonvulsants and newer anticonvulsants.

TRADITIONAL ANTICONVULSANTS

Traditional anticonvulsants include medications such as depakote and carbamazapine (Tegretol). Depakote is increasingly being used to control mood instability and aggressive outbursts. It is also used as an antimanic agent in patients with bipolar disorder. Some open label studies have suggested its potential for use in patients with autism spectrum disorders (Hollander *et al.*, 2001). However, reports have suggested that ingestion of depakote during pregnancy increases the risk of having a child with autism (Williams *et al.*,

2001). Carbamazepine is also used in patients with autism as a mood stabilizer and an anticonvulsant. Both the medications have side-effects, such as effects on the liver, excessive sedation, and problems with coordination, that need to be monitored closely.

NEWER ANTICONVULSANTS

Several newer anticonvulsants have recently been introduced. While few systematic data are available, many of these anticonvulsants are being used to treat children with autism spectrum disorders, not only for the control of seizures, but also for the treatment of mood and behavior symptoms. Gabapentin (Neurontin) is sometimes used in the treatment of children and adolescents with autism, although there are few published reports. The medication acts through its effect on the GABA neurotransmitter system. Reports on its use with mentally retarded children and adults have yielded mixed results. Although it is generally well tolerated, the drug can sometimes aggravate certain types of seizures, such as absence and myoclonic seizures. Anger outbursts and temper tantrums have also been reported. Other newer anticonvulsants that have sometimes been used in patients with developmental disabilities and autism include felbamate and lamotrigine.

Other medications

NALTREXONE

Naltrexone is a pure opioid antagonist used in the treatment of substance abuse. It is sometimes used for the control of self-injurious behavior in persons with autism and mental retardation. The mechanism of action is based on the theory that a patient with self-injurious behavior gets 'addicted' to it, and that naltrexone acts by reducing this addiction. Reports about the efficacy of this medication are mixed. In some cases, it reduces the self-injurious behavior dramatically, but on the whole, it does not appear to be as effective as often believed. In addition, it causes irritability and impulsivity in some individuals. Contrary to some earlier claims, it does not increase verbal output or improve communication.

LITHIUM

Lithium is a tried and tested medication for the control of bipolar disorder. It has been successfully used for the control of aggression in people with autism and mental retardation. Although its use has often been replaced by anticonvulsants, such as depakote, it remains a useful medication in the treatment of mood instability of any kind, especially when it is characterized by a cyclical pattern. While its use as a single agent in the control of symptoms of PDD has not been very encouraging, it is often used in combination with other drugs such as antidepressants or antipsychotic medications. Some reports have suggested that it works better when there is a family history of bipolar disorder (Kerbeshian, Burd and Fisher, 1987). The blood levels of those to whom it is prescribed should be monitored closely to prevent damage to the heart and the kidneys.

CLONIDINE

Clonidine, a medication used for the control of blood pressure, was accidentally found to calm children with hyperactivity and impulsivity, and is sometimes used in children with autism for this purpose. It is an alpha-2 noradrenergic receptor agonist that has been shown to be modestly effective in the control of hyperactivity and impulsivity associated with some children with autism (Jaselskis et al., 1992). It is also sometimes used for the control of tics, especially in those children who have ADHD and tics when stimulants, such as methylphenidate (Ritalin), are contraindicated. However, it causes two main side-effects: a fall of blood pressure leading to faints and falls, and excessive drowsiness. Some reports also suggest that when used for long periods of time, Clonidine loses its efficacy and increases the risk of irritability and depression.

PROPRANOLOL

This is a beta-blocker that is sometimes used in the control of aggression. Its more common use is as an antihypertensive agent because it reduces the blood pressure. However, studies have found that it can control aggressive outbursts and temper tantrums in some patients with developmental disabilities. Sometimes it is combined with anticonvulsants and benzodiazpines for this purpose. The latter are a group of drugs widely used in the treatment of anxiety disorders in the general population. However, when prescribing for persons with PDD, extra caution is indicated because they may cause disinhibition and temper outbursts.

Care of the family

Autism is a family disorder in the sense that it affects all members of the family in varying ways. Family support and cohesion are critical to a favorable long-term outcome of patients with autism. Yet relatively little is known about the problems which families with autistic children face and the strategies that are needed to help them.

Parents

Parents with autistic children experience a variety of problems. For decades following Leo Kanner's description of the disorder, it was wrongly believed that they (especially mothers) were responsible for causing the disorder. It is not uncommon to find parents today who still blame themselves. In addition, many parents are at an increased risk of developing psychiatric disorders. Compared to parents of other handicapping conditions, such as Down syndrome, parents of autistic children are more vulnerable to a variety of psychiatric disorders, particularly anxiety and depression. In addition, some of them suffer from milder features of the condition themselves. Therefore, parents should be advised to seek treatment when necessary. Belonging to a family support group and membership in the local autism society may help with practical issues, such as advocacy and help with school and social services. A combination of psychotherapy and medications may be required.

Siblings

Little attention has been paid to the mental health and adjustment of siblings of patients with autism. Siblings often experience a range of emotions ranging from grief to anger and guilt. At times, they are required to assume responsibilities beyond their age which often causes resentment and guilt. If the autistic patient suffers from additional behavioral problems, such as aggression, this places extra difficulties on the siblings. For example, they may find it embarrassing to invite friends home. Any treatment program, therefore, must involve the siblings. Individual therapy may be needed. Participating in sibling groups may also help brothers and sisters of children with autism work through their feelings and conflicts. Clinical experience suggests that the prevalence of formal psychiatric disorders, such as depression and anxiety, is increased in the siblings of autistic children. It is important, therefore, not to dismiss the behaviors and feelings of siblings as normal responses; instead, they should be actively treated.

Other treatments

In addition to standard treatments such as social skills training, speech training, and the use of medications, other less conventional treatment strategies have also been described. While most of these have not been studied systematically, they seem to be increasing in popularity. Parents expect help and answers, and are often willing to try 'just about anything that works.' Some treatments are better validated than others. The list is long and increasing because newer treatments are added almost every six to eight months. Some of these treatments are based on theories and hypotheses; others on faith and intuition. Well-known but unconventional methods include the use of massive doses of vitamins, treatment with intravenous secretin, avoidance of certain foods and adherence to certain diets, auditory integration and other sound therapies, and administration of a wide variety of herbs and over-the-counter medicinal supplements. Music therapy, conventional play therapy, and facilitated communication have also been used, with mixed results. It is the author's view that parents have the right to try anything that they believe may work for their child. However, it is the responsibility of the professionals to interpret the available research, make sense of the information, and be as objective and honest as possible. In the final analysis, parents have the right to decide what is best for their child, and the professional's responsibility is to provide support and advice, and refrain from doing any harm.

Outcome

It is important to emphasize that autism is a life-long condition (Rutter, 1970). In general, the earlier the disorder is diagnosed and treated, the better the prognosis. While many people with autism improve over time, the symptoms of autism often persist. The degree of improvement depends on two main factors: the person's level of intelligence and level of verbal skills. Patients who are intelligent and who possess reasonably good communication skills generally do better. However, to a certain extent, the outcome also depends on the presence of additional medical and psychiatric conditions. This issue has not received adequate attention in the literature. Thus, an adult with autism who suffers from chronic and severe depression has a worse outcome than one who is not depressed.

An important measure of outcome of a disability is the extent to which the individual can function independently in the community and assume normal expected roles. This often means raising a family and holding on to a suitable job. Although there are a few anecdotal reports of autistic people getting married and raising families, no systematic studies have explored this issue. People with autism are often able to hold on to jobs. Their success depends not only on the type of the job, but also on their level of functioning, and the degree of support available at work.

Conclusion

Autism is a life-long disorder. Contrary to what is sometimes claimed, most patients do not grow out of their symptoms. Yet, it is important to emphasize that almost all children with autism develop skills and behaviors as they grow up. While there is no known cause of autism, several factors influence its presentation. Both genetic and environmental factors are involved in its causation, although the bulk of the evidence supports a major role of genetics. Autism often occurs with a variety of medical and psychiatric disorders. While there is no cure for autism, and although the thrust of the treatment is psychoeducational, a wide variety of medications are used in clinical practice. The outcome of the disorder is determined by the level of IQ, the degree of verbal skills, and on the presence of medical and psychiatric complications.

References

Aman, M.G., Van Bourgondien, M.E., Wolford, P.L. and Sarphare, G. (1995) 'Psychotropic and anticonvulsant drugs in subjects with autism: Prevalence and patterns of use.' *Journal of the American Academy of Child and Adolescent Psychiatry, 34,* 12, 1672–81.

APA (American Psychiatric Association) (1994) *Diagnostic and Statistical Manual of Mental Disorders: Fourth Edition* (DSM-IV). Washington: APA.

Baird, G., Charman, T., Baron-Cohen, S., Cox, A., Swettenham, J., Wheelwright, S. and Drew, A. (2000) 'A screening instrument for autism at 18 months of age: A 6-year follow-up study.' *Journal of the American Academy of Child and Adolescent Psychiatry, 39,* 6, 694–702.

Baron-Cohen, S. (1989) 'The autistic child's theory of mind: A case of specific developmental delay.' *Journal of Child Psychology and Psychiatry, 30,* 2, 285–97.

Barry, T.D., Klinger, L.G., Lee, J.M., Palardy, N., Gilmore, T. and Bodin, S.D. (2003) 'Examining the effectiveness of an outpatient clinic-based social skills group for high-functioning children with autism.' *Journal of Autism and Developmental Disorders, 33,* 6, 685–701.

Bartak, L. and Rutter, M. (1976) 'Differences between mentally retarded and normally intelligent autistic children.' *Journal of Autism and Childhood Schizophrenia, 6,* 109–120.

Bauman, M.L. (1991) 'Microscopic neuroanatomic abnormalities in autism.' *Pediatrics, 87,* 791–6.

Blakeslee, S. (2002) 'Increase in autism baffles scientists.' *New York Times* 18 October.

Bolton, P., Macdonald, H., Pickles, A., Rios, P., Goode, S., Crowson, M., Bailey, A. and Rutter, M. (1994) 'A case-control family history study of autism.' *Journal of Child Psychology and Psychiatry, 35,* 5, 877–900.

Bondy, A.S. and Frost, L.A. (1998) 'The picture exchange communication system.' *Seminars in Speech and Language, 19,* 4, 373–88.

Bosseler, A. and Massaro, D.W. (2003) 'Development and evaluation of a computer-animated tutor for vocabulary and language learning in children with autism.' *Journal of Autism and Developmental Disorders, 33,* 6, 653–72.

Campbell, M., Anderson, L.T., Small, A.M., Perry, R., Green, W.H. and Caplan, R. (1982) 'The effects of haloperidol on learning and behavior in autistic children.' *Journal of Autism and Developmental Disorders, 12,* 2, 167–75.

Chakrabarti, S. and Fombonne, E. (2001) 'Pervasive developmental disorders in preschool children.' *Journal of the American Medical Association, 285,* 24, 3093–9

Cook, E.H. Jr., Rowlett, R., Jaselskis, C. and Leventhal, B.L. (1992) 'Fluoxetine treatment of children and adults with autistic disorder and mental retardation.' *Journal of the American Academy of Child and Adolescent Psychiatry, 31,* 4, 739–45.

Fombonne, E., Simmons, H., Ford, T., Meltzer, H. and Goodman, R. (2003) 'Prevalence of pervasive developmental disorders in the British nationwide survey of child mental health.' *International Review of Psychiatry, 15,* 158–65.

Frith, U. (1996) 'Cognititive explanations of autism.' *Acta Paediatrica Supplement, 416,* 63–8.

Ghaziuddin, M., Al-Khouri, I. and Ghaziuddin, N. (2002) 'Autistic symptoms following herpes encephalitis.' *European Child and Adolescent Psychiatry, 11,* 3, 142–6.

Ghaziuddin, M. and Burmeister, M. (1999) 'Deletion of chromosome 2q37 and autism: A distinct subtype?' *Journal of Autism and Developmental Disorders, 29,* 3, 259–63.

Ghaziuddin, M. and Greden, J. (1998) 'Depression in children with autism/pervasive developmental disorders: A case-control family history study.' *Journal of Autism and Developmental Disorders, 28,* 2, 111–115.

Ghaziuddin, M., Zaccagnini, J., Tsai, L. and Elardo, S. (1999) 'Is megalencephaly specific to autism?' *Journal of Intellectual Disability Research, 43,* 279–82.

Gillberg, C. (1991) 'Autistic syndrome with onset at age 31 years: Herpes encephalitis as a possible model for childhood autism.' *Developmental Medicine and Child Neurology, 33,* 920–4.

Gordon, C.T., State, R.C., Nelson, J.E., Hamburger, S.D. and Rapoport, J.L. (1993) 'A double-blind comparison of clomipramine, desipramine, and placebo in the treatment of autistic disorder.' *Archives of General Psychiatry, 50,* 6, 441–7.

Hollander, E., Dolgoff-Kaspar, R., Cartwright, C., Rawitt, R. and Novotny, S. (2001) 'An open trial of divalproex sodium in autism spectrum disorders.' *Journal of Clinical Psychiatry, 62,* 7, 530–4.

Jaselskis, C.A., Cook, E.H. Jr., Fletcher, K.E. and Leventhal, B.L. (1992) 'Clonidine treatment of hyperactive and impulsive children with autistic disorder.' *Journal of Clinical Psychopharmacology, 12,* 5, 322–7.

Kanner, L. (1943) 'Autistic disturbances of affective contact.' *Nervous Child, 2,* 217–50.

Kerbeshian, J., Burd, L. and Fisher, W. (1987) 'Lithium carbonate in the treatment of two patients with infantile autism and atypical bipolar symptomatology.' *Journal of Clinical Psychopharmacology, 7,* 6, 401–405.

Krug, D.A., Arick, J. and Almond, P. (1980) 'Behavior checklist for identifying severely handicapped individuals with high levels of autistic behavior.' *Journal of Child Psychology and Psychiatry, 21,* 221–9.

Lord, C., Risi, S., Lambrecht, L., Cook, E.H. Jr., Leventhal, B.L., DiLavore, P.C., Pickles, A. and Rutter, M. (2000) 'The autism diagnostic observation schedule – generic: A standard measure of social and communication deficits associated with the spectrum of autism.' *Journal of Autism and Developmental Disorders, 30,* 205–23.

Lord, C., Rutter, M. and Le Couteur, A. (1994) 'Autism Diagnostic Interview – Revised: A revised version of a diagnostic interview for caregivers of individuals with possible pervasive developmental disorders.' *Journal of Autism and Developmental Disorders, 24,* 659–85.

Lovaas, O.I. (1987) 'Behavioral treatment and normal educational and intellectual functioning in young autistic children.' *Journal of Consulting and Clinical Psychology, 55,* 1, 3–9.

Martin, A., Scahill, L., Klin, A. and Volkmar, F.R. (1999) 'Higher-functioning pervasive developmental disorders: Rates and patterns of psychotropic drug use.' *Journal of the American Academy of Child and Adolescent Psychiatry, 38,* 923–31.

McCracken, J.T., McGough, J., Shah, B., Cronin, P., Hong, D., Aman, M.G., Arnold, L.E., Lindsay, R., Nash, P., Hollway, J., McDougle, C.J., Posey, D., Swiezy, N., Kohn, A., Scahill, L., Martin, A., Koenig, K., Volkmar, F., Carroll, D., Lancor, A., Tierney, E., Ghuman, J., Gonzalez, N.M., Grados, M., Vitiello, B., Ritz, L., Davies, M., Robinson, J. and McMahon, D. and Research Units on Pediatric Psychopharmacology Autism Network (2002) 'Risperidone in children with autism and serious behavioral problems.' *New England Journal of Medicine, 347,* 5, 314–21.

McDougle, C.J., Kem, D.L. and Posey, D.J. (2002) 'Case series: Use of ziprasidone for maladaptive symptoms in youths with autism.' *Journal of the American Academy of Child and Adolescent Psychiatry, 41,* 8, 921–7.

McDougle, C.J., Price, L.H., Volkmar, F.R., Goodman, W.K., Ward-O'Brien, D., Nielsen, J., Bregman, J. and Cohen, D.J. (1992) 'Clomipramine in autism: Preliminary evidence of efficacy.' *Journal of the American Academy of Child and Adolescent Psychiatry, 31,* 4, 746–50.

McEachin, J.J., Smith, T., and Lovaas, O.I. (1993) 'Long-term outcome for children with autism who received early behavioral treatment.' *American Journal on Mental Retardation, 97,* 4, 359–72.

Pichichero, M.E., Cernichiarim, E., Lopreiato, J. and Treanor, J. (2002) 'Mercury concentrations and metabolism in infants receiving vaccines containing thiomersal: A descriptive study.' *Lancet 360,* 1737–41.

Piven, J., Berthier, M.L., Starkstein, S.E., Nehme, E., Pearlson, G. and Folstein, S. (1990) 'Magnetic resonance imaging evidence for a defect of cerebral cortical development in autism.' *American Journal of Psychiatry, 147,* 734–9.

Piven, J., Chase, G.A., Landa, R., Wzorek, M., Gayle, J., Cloud, D. and Folstein, S. (1991) 'Psychiatric disorders in the parents of autistic individuals.' *Journal of the American Academy of Child and Adolescent Psychiatry, 30*, 471–8.

Prizant, B. and Rydell, P. (1984) 'Analysis of functions of delayed echolalia in autistic children.' *Journal of Speech and Hearing Disorders, 27*, 2, 183–92.

Rogers, S.J. (2000) 'Interventions that facilitate socialization in children with autism.' *Journal of Autism and Developmental Disorders, 30*, 5, 399–409.

Rogers, S.J., Hepburn, S. and Wehner, E. (2003) 'Parent reports of sensory symptoms in toddlers with autism and those with other developmental disorders.' *Journal of Autism and Developmental Disorders, 33*, 6, 631–42.

Rutter, M. (1970) 'Autistic children: Infancy to adulthood.' *Seminars in Psychiatry, 2*, 4, 435–50.

Rutter, M., Bailey, A., Berument, S.K., Lord, C. and Pickles, A. (2003) *Social Communication Questionnaire.* Los Angeles, CA: Western Psychological Services.

Schopler, E., Mesibov, G.B. and Hearsey, K. (1995) 'Structured teaching in the TEACCH system.' In E. Schopler and G.B. Mesibov (eds) *Learning and Cognition in Autism.* New York: Plenum.

Schopler, E., Reichler, R.J., DeVellis, R.F. and Daly, K. (1980) 'Toward objective classification of childhood autism: Childhood Autism Rating Scale (CARS).' *Journal of Autism and Developmental Disorders, 10*, 91–103.

Schultz, R.T., Gauthier, I., Klin, A., Fulbright, R.K., Anderson, A.W., Volkmar, F., Skudlarski, P., Lacadie, C., Cohen, D.J. and Gore, J.C. (2000) 'Abnormal ventral temporal cortical activity during face discrimination among individuals with autism and Asperger syndrome.' *Archives of General Psychiatry, 57*, 331–40.

Staller, J.A. (2003) 'Aripripazole in an adult with Asperger syndrome.' *Annals of Pharmacotherapy, 37*, 11, 1628–31.

Stromland, K., Nordin, V., Miller, M., Akerstrom, B. and Gillberg, C. (1994) 'Autism in thalidomide embryopathy: A population study.' *Developmental Medicine and Child Neurology, 36*, 351–6.

Watling, R., Deitz, J., Kanny, E.M. and McLaughlin, J.F. (1999) 'Current practice of occupational therapy for children with autism.' *American Journal of Occupational Therapy, 53*, 5, 498–505.

Weiss, M.J. and Harris, S.L. (2001) 'Teaching social skills to people with autism.' *Behavior Modification, 25*, 5, 785–802.

WHO (World Health Organization) (1993) *International Classification of Diseases, Tenth Revision, Criteria for Research* (ICD-10). Geneva: WHO.

Williams, G., King, J., Cunningham, M., Stephan, M., Kerr, B. and Hersh, J.H. (2001) 'Fetal valproate syndrome and autism: Additional evidence of an association.' *Developmental Medicine and Child Neurology, 43*, 202–206.

Wing, L., Leekam, S.R., Libby, S.J., Gould, J. and Larcombe, M. (2002) 'The Diagnostic Interview for Social and Communication Disorders: Background, inter-rater reliability and clinical use.' *Journal of Child Psychology and Psychiatry, 43*, 307–25.

CHAPTER 2

What is Asperger Syndrome?

Introduction

Asperger syndrome or AS (Asperger, 1944) is a pervasive developmental disorder (PDD) in which autistic social dysfunction and isolated obsessive interests occur in the presence of normal intelligence and a relatively intact language. The diagnosis requires that the full criteria of autism or of any other PDD are not met (APA, 1994). The term 'Asperger syndrome' is currently used in several ways: to describe persons with autism who have a normal IQ or those who are verbal; as a synonym for Pervasive Developmental Disorder Not Otherwise Specified (PDDNOS) and atypical autism; and to describe children who are obnoxious and oppositional and have some social deficits. It is also used, more narrowly, to describe a group of children and adults who show a mild but distinct type of social and communication deficit, with intense idiosyncratic interests.

Historical background

It has recently been claimed that the first person to describe this condition was a Russian psychiatrist, Ssucherewa. In a case-series of six boys with social dysfunction, she described the characteristics of 'schizoid personality' (Gillberg, 1998; Ssucharewa, 1926; Wolff, 1996). However, it is Hans Asperger whom the syndrome is named after. In the 1940s Asperger, a pediatrician in Vienna, described a group of four socially awkward boys under the title of 'autistic psychopathy' (Asperger, 1944). They had difficulties in understanding the emotions and feelings of others, and were also prone to behavioral problems. In addition, they were focused on narrow areas of interests, and were all of normal intelligence. In some respects, they resembled the children Leo Kanner had described a year earlier (Kanner, 1943). By coincidence, both Asperger and Kanner used the term 'autism' to refer to their cases – a term that described a state of withdrawn detachment and was derived from the literature on schizophrenia. While Kanner's contribution became widely known in the scientific community, Asperger's paper went largely unnoticed partly because it was published in German during the closing days of World War II. However, cases resembling Asperger syndrome continued to be published occasionally in the literature under various names. Mesulam described the so-called 'Right Brain syndrome' and Sula Wolff published a series of cases on schizoid personality disorder which bear marked resemblance to Asperger syndrome (Wolff and Chick, 1980).

Except for these occasional reports, not much was heard about Asperger syndrome until Lorna Wing described her case-series of 34 patients, both children and adults, seen in a variety of psychiatric settings. It was she who gave the condition its present name (Wing, 1981). Since Wing's paper there have been several publications on this topic, leading finally to its inclusion in the DSM (APA, 1994) and the ICD (WHO, 1993). Despite this, there is still ongoing confusion and debate about its existence as a distinct disorder, particularly its distinction from autism with normal intelligence, so-called 'high-functioning autism' (HFA). (As discussed in the previous chapter, at least 25 per cent of persons with autism do not suffer from mental retardation and are referred to as HFA.) Some researchers have suggested that Asperger syndrome and HFA are one and the same, and have cautioned against including AS as a distinct category; while others have pointed out that the current description of AS does not quite resemble the one that Asperger had in mind (Miller and Ozonoff, 1997). While strong arguments exist both for and against the validity of AS, what is clear is that a substantial number of children with relatively normal intelligence show problems with social relatedness. They have focused, idiosyncratic interests and do not seem to meet the traditional profile of autism. If not properly diagnosed, they are often mistakenly labeled as difficult or devious, and are often denied services. Clinical experience suggests that a number of such children fit the description of Asperger syndrome.

Prevalence

From the number of referrals and the internet sites that have cropped up in recent years, it would seem that Asperger syndrome has become a popular diagnosis, not only for children but also for adults. The last few years have also witnessed a sharp increase in the number of publications on this topic both in the scientific journals and in the popular press (see Attwood, 1998; Frith,

1991). Eminent people like Newton and Einstein, as well as several lesser-known figures, have been given the diagnosis of AS. However, little is known about the true prevalence of AS in the community. This is, in part, because of the confusion surrounding its diagnostic criteria (Ghaziuddin, Tsai and Ghaziuddin, 1992a).

One of the few population-based studies on this topic was done in Sweden by Gillberg and his colleagues (Ehlers and Gillberg, 1993). Children between 7 and 16 years of age, attending schools in the city of Göteborg, Sweden, were screened for the presence of Asperger syndrome using a two-stage process. In the first stage, screening instruments were used, and in the second stage, clinical interviews were conducted. The authors found that the minimum prevalence was 3.6 per 1000. If children with suspected and possible cases of AS were included, the prevalence rose to at least 7 per 1000. It is important to note that the authors used their own criteria (Gillberg and Gillberg, 1989) to define and diagnose Asperger syndrome. As these criteria differ from those given in the ICD/DSM systems of classification, the prevalence of this condition based on the ICD/DSM criteria is not known.

The disorder occurs more commonly in males than in females. In the Ehlers and Gillberg (1993) study, the ratio of males to females was 4:1. The disorder occurs more commonly in males than females. In the Ehlers and Gillberg (1993) study the ratio of males to females was 4:1. However, when doubtful cases were included, the ratio fell to 2.3:1. This suggests that many of the features of AS that attract attention in males are probably missed or ignored in females.

Clinical features

Onset/recognition

Although the exact *onset* of the disorder is difficult to define, most patients come to attention after 5 years of age. There is no history of language delay; some patients, in fact, give a history of having spoken early. A history of reading early may also be obtained. According to the diagnostic criteria, the first three years of life are usually normal. However, this history is not easy to obtain, especially in older patients, where informants may not be available. In any case, most patients who come for evaluation do not give a history typical of autism in the first few years of their life. Thus, the onset/recognition of the disorder is usually after the patient has reached 5 years of age; that is, later than that of traditional autism. At times, the disorder first comes to attention in the middle school (age range approximately 9–13 years) because this is the period when increasing social demands are placed on children. Children in middle school are often able to tell who among them is different and unusual. However, cases are sometimes missed, and other diagnoses are given instead, such as Attention Deficit Hyperactivity Disorder (ADHD) or conduct disorder. These additional disorders may then bring the child to professional attention. Occasionally, adults with a mistaken diagnosis of 'chronic schizo-phrenia' are referred for a diagnostic clarification to rule out Asperger syndrome. For example, the author is familiar with a middle-aged man who was referred with a diagnosis of schizophrenia. He was single and unemployed. His main area of interest was history, especially Jewish history of Eastern Europe, although he had never stepped out of Michigan! He often rambled about this interest with no regard to the social context. He had always been somewhat odd and isolated. He had never had hallucinations and delusions but was treated for schizophrenia, mainly because of his social awk-wardness, his tendency to fixate on history, and his deficits in the social use of language – features that strongly suggested a diagnosis of Asperger syndrome.

Social deficits

Patients with Asperger syndrome suffer from reciprocal social deficits of the same kind as those suffered by patients with autism. However, the symptoms are often milder than those typically seen in autistic patients. In fact, sometimes the symptoms are so mild as to go undetected. In addition, they seem to be qualitatively different. Clinical experience suggests that most patients with AS tend to be active but odd, compared to most patients with traditional autism who are either passive or aloof. Thus, it is not uncommon to find them approaching strangers and striking up a conversation. People with AS are often labeled as being odd and eccentric in their appearance and behavior. For example, some may insist on wearing sun glasses at night while others may go to undue lengths to make sure that they are breathing the right amount of oxygen in the air! Children and adolescents may adopt a 'Little Professor' appearance. Contrary to what is sometimes believed, people with AS are generally not mean or obnoxious. They are not aggressive or oppositional, even though some may fall into these categories. Although the four children described by Asperger had behavioral problems of varying degrees, there is no firm evidence that this applies to all cases of Asperger syndrome.

Communication

The conversation of people with AS lacks the to-and-fro quality of normal conversation; instead it tends to be one-sided, with little regard to the needs of the listener. In general, the speech tends to be rambling and pedantic (Ghaziuddin and Gerstein, 1996; Shriberg *et al.*, 2001). The tone of the voice may sound odd and stilted. In some cases, the individual seems as if he has a foreign accent! At other times, he may appear as if he is reading from a script. There is no history of language delay, at least not in the traditional sense. In fact, some families actually give a history of early and precocious language development. Phrase speech often develops by the time the child is 3 years of age. In practice, though, it is not often possible to determine this with certainty, since the child's history is usually based on parental recall. However, performance on tests of language function is often within the normal range. The eye contact is often inconsistent. Sometimes, there is an excess amount of eye contact, in the sense that the patient has a glaring, inappropriate look. This is sometimes perceived as threatening when given by an adolescent or young adult. The author is aware of at least one case of this, where a young man was fired from his job because his female colleagues complained of inappropriate staring which was interpreted as sexual harassment. When asked, he said that he was only trying to be friendly with his colleagues, and that he could not understand why he was asked to leave.

Single-minded pursuits

The presence of idiosyncratic pursuits and rigid ritualistic interests forms an important feature of Asperger syndrome. These interests are often of a more sophisticated nature than those of someone with traditional autism. For example, the patient may show an extreme interest in meteorology or astronomy. He may read about these topics, sometimes going to extraordinary lengths to sustain his interest. Surfing the internet is often a common way of doing this. In most cases, the special interests evolve over time. Thus, it is more likely to find an 18-year-old with an interest in algebra than a 7-year-old with similar interests. In clinical settings, especially in structured interviews, it may not be possible to see evidence of single-minded pursuits, especially if the patient is anxious or depressed. It is, therefore, important to do detailed and repeated interviews and gather data from as many sources as possible.

Cognitive functioning

People with Asperger syndrome do not have mental retardation, as opposed to those with autism who commonly do. Some researchers have contested this view, and suggested that Asperger syndrome can be diagnosed across the entire range of intelligence, and not just in those without mental retardation. While the DSM and the ICD systems of classification emphasize that there is no gross cognitive impairment, they do not comment on the range of IQ. Thus, it is not clear if the IQ is higher in patients with AS than in those with normal intelligence in the general population. Studies suggest, however, that most patients with Asperger syndrome seem to have a high verbal IQ (VIQ) in relation to the performance IQ (PIQ) (Ghaziuddin and Mountain-Kimchi, 2004; Klin et al., 1995). This VIQ>PIQ tendency is not often seen in patients with autism, where the trend is usually reversed. Also, deficits of executive functioning and Theory of Mind are often present in persons with AS. Unlike most patients with autism, those with AS are able to pass the lower-order Theory of Mind tests.

Clumsiness

While there is no generally accepted definition of clumsiness, this symptom often refers to deficits of physical coordination that are not due to cerebral palsy or other causes of physical handicap. Clumsiness was initially proposed as a distinguishing feature of Asperger syndrome. At one point, it was thought that people with AS were clumsier than those with autism. However, several studies have now shown that while clumsiness occurs in AS, it is not specific to this syndrome (Ghaziuddin et al., 1994; Ghaziuddin, Tsai and Ghaziuddin, 1992b). In fact, deficits of motor coordination and clumsiness occur across the entire range of PDD, including those with traditional autism. Many people with AS are clumsy; and some appear more physically clumsy than they usually are during formal tests of functioning. Problems with gait may also be present. Parents often give a history of the child having difficulties with such common activities as tying his shoe laces, kicking and catching a ball, and riding a bike. Abnormal movements, such as rocking and flapping of hands, are not usually present.

The above features are not found in every patient with Asperger syndrome. As in other disorders, it is the combination of symptoms that is more important in the diagnosis rather than the presence or absence of any one symptom.

Etiology

Genetic factors

Since AS is conceptualized as a form of pervasive developmental disorder related to autism, it is reasonable to assume that the same factors play a role in its causation. However, few studies have directly examined this issue. This is largely because of the confusion surrounding its diagnostic criteria and its distinction from high-functioning forms of autism. Few studies have investigated subjects with AS and examined to what extent their relatives show features of AS or autism or both. However, studies of families ascertained through subjects with autism have lent support to the assumption that the two conditions, autism and Asperger syndrome, are genetically related. Thus, in a family history study of autism, out of 137 siblings of autistic probands, one was diagnosed with Asperger syndrome (Bolton *et al.*, 1994). When compared to a control group of siblings with Down syndrome, it was found that 5.8 per cent in the autism group were diagnosed with autism, atypical autism or Asperger syndrome, compared to 0 per cent in the Down syndrome group (none out of 64 siblings with Down syndrome).

Many of the patients described by Asperger had similarly affected individuals in their families. Among the 200 children he saw over ten years, almost all had at least one parent with similar personality traits, and fathers were often highly intellectual (Asperger, 1944). Wing (1981) found that out of 34 cases, 5 of the 16 fathers and 2 of the 24 mothers showed behavioral traits resembling those of Asperger syndrome. In Gillberg's series of 23 patients with Asperger syndrome, several of the parents showed similar personality traits (Gillberg, 1989). In Wolff's series, out of 32 male patients, 7 fathers and 12 mothers had similar traits, compared to one mother and no father in the 32 males in the control group. Among 33 girls similarly examined, only one mother and four fathers were definitely affected compared to two mothers and two fathers in the control group (Wolff and McGuire, 1995). It has been claimed by some that AS is more strongly genetic than autism, though there is not much evidence at this stage to support this hypothesis.

Environmental factors

Compared to autism, fewer reports have investigated the role of biological factors in the etiology of AS (Rickarby, Carruthers and Mitchell, 1991). Although there is no direct evidence that environmental factors can cause AS, several associated medical conditions have been described. For example, cases of a muscle disorder, known as Steinart's muscular dystrophy, have been described in persons with Asperger syndrome (Blondis *et al.*, 1996). Reports have also described the association of thyroid dysfunction. Pregnancy and delivery complications have been identified, although there is no evidence of a direct cause and effect relationship (Ghaziuddin, Shakel and Tsai, 1995). Several other medical conditions have also been described but it is unclear if these are chance associations or causal factors.

Neurobiology

Although few studies have investigated the biological aspects of Asperger syndrome, the available evidence points to a biologic origin. For example, imaging studies have shown abnormalities of the frontal lobes. Volkmar and colleagues published an interesting case report in which a father and son pair, both with Asperger syndrome, had similar frontal lobe abnormalities (Volkmar *et al.*, 2000). Other reports have also suggested frontal lobe deficits. Functional imaging studies have revealed abnormalities in the nerve structure and function of the prefrontal region (Murphy *et al.*, 2002). Compared to normal controls, people with AS activate different areas of their brain when doing certain tasks that involve reading the minds and feelings of others. For example, on the Theory of Mind (TOM) tests, people with AS do not show task-related activity in the left medial prefrontal cortex (Brodmann's area 8/9); instead, activation occurs in adjacent areas of medial prefrontal cortex (Brodmann's area 9/10) (Happé *et al.*, 1996). Abnormalities of cortical migration have also been described. Therefore, as in autism, research has suggested an organic basis of the disorder, without pointing to a specific area or location of pathology.

Diagnosis

The diagnosis of Asperger syndrome is clinical. The current system of classification takes a hierarchical approach. The patient is first examined to see if he meets the criteria for autism and then for Asperger syndrome. If he does not meet the criteria for either of these disorders, then he is given a label of PDDNOS. Thus, according to the DSM-IV (APA, 1994), it is not possible to give two diagnoses at the same time to a patient, nor is it allowed to consider a diagnosis of Asperger syndrome if all the criteria for autism are satisfied. An important requirement is that the patient does not meet the criteria for schizophrenia or of any other pervasive developmental disorder. Although this diagnostic approach is not ideal, it is a start and will, no doubt, be revised in the future. While it is widely believed to be a variant of autism, Asperger syndrome is not likely to be a homogeneous entity, and some patients currently labeled as AS may fall outside the autistic spectrum. The diagnostic criteria do not capture the features of all the cases of AS. Revision of the criteria and long-term studies can clarify the overlap and differences between this group of patients and those with traditional autism.

Biological assessment

There is no biological test for Asperger syndrome. The diagnosis depends on a detailed history focusing on social development and behavior. History of language acquisition is difficult to obtain in older adolescents and adults, because parents are often not able to recall the details. Similarly, a detailed early history is almost impossible to obtain if the patient is referred for the first time in adulthood. Although there is no universally accepted definition of speech delay, this is usually defined as the lack of phrase speech by 3 years of age. Children in their preschool years do not often show the typical social deficits of Asperger syndrome. However, as the child grows older, especially in the middle school, these deficits become more apparent. This is often, therefore, the time when children with AS are referred for an evaluation. It is important also to remember that in structured one-on-one situations, these deficits are often not apparent.

Children with suspected Asperger syndrome should receive a detailed physical examination to rule out such conditions as thyroid dysfunction that can contribute to social problems by causing hyperactivity and impulsivity. Coordination deficits should be evaluated to plan interventions based on occupational and physical therapy. An EEG may help if seizures are suspected. However, only an abnormal EEG is useful for treatment planning, because a normal EEG can miss the seizures. A chromosome analysis should be done if there is a family history of developmental delay.

Psychological assessment

A neuropsychological assessment should be routinely performed along with a speech evaluation. The level of IQ should be ascertained and any discrepancy in the verbal and performance IQ noted. As discussed earlier in this chapter, many patients with AS have a high verbal IQ and a relatively lower performance IQ. Theory of Mind (TOM) tests such as the Eyes Test (Baron-Cohen *et al.*, 1997) and executive function tests also help in the diagnosis. AS patients' performance on these tests is often impaired, but less so than for patients with autism. While the diagnosis depends on clinical acumen and on a good history, a number of rating scales and interviews have been developed. These instruments can help obtain a comprehensive history, but are not, by themselves, diagnostic of Asperger syndrome. The Asperger Syndrome Diagnostic Scale (ASDS: Goldstein, 2002) gives an estimate of the current level of functioning and a description of problem behaviors. However, concerns have been expressed about its validity and utility (Goldstein, 2002). Another instrument is the CAST (Childhood Asperger Syndrome Test: Scott *et al.*, 2002), which attempts to pick out features of AS in children between the ages of 4 and 11 years. The Autism Spectrum Screening Questionnaire (ASSQ: Ehlers, Gillberg and Wing, 1999) is a 27-item checklist for completion by lay informants when assessing symptoms characteristic of Asperger syndrome and other high-functioning autism spectrum disorders in children and adolescents with normal intelligence or mild mental retardation. These instruments are useful to index high-risk cases of PDD, but do not necessarily help in the subtyping of the disorders, and are not very helpful in differentiating AS from autism.

Differential diagnosis

Several disorders, apart from high-functioning autism, need to be differentiated from Asperger syndrome.

Autism

The debate over the differentiation of Asperger syndrome from autism is not new. In 1971, Van Krevelen proposed a set of differences between the two conditions, which is summarized in Table 2.1 (p.52).

Building on the work of Van Krevelen and others, several studies have tried to investigate the differences between the two conditions using modern diagnostic criteria. Although the results are far from conclusive, what appears to be emerging is that there exists a group of persons with mild social deficits, a rather odd and pedantic way of communicating, and a tendency to marked idiosyncratic interests. They are often active but odd, and usually have a high verbal IQ compared to their performance IQ on formal tests of intelligence. These persons are often given a diagnosis of Asperger syndrome. At the risk of

Table 2.1 The differences between autism and Asperger syndrome according to Van Krevelen

	Autism	*Asperger syndrome*
Onset	Before third year	Third year or later
Speech	Delayed or absent	Speech earlier
Language	Does not attain the function of communication	Aims at communication but remains 'one-way.'
Walking	Walks earlier than he speaks	Walks later than he speaks
Eye contact	Other people do not exist	Other people are evaded
Prognosis	Poor	Relatively better

Source: After Van Krevelen 1971

Table 2.2 The differences between autism and Asperger syndrome

	Autism	*Asperger syndrome*
Onset/recognition	Before the age of 3 years	After the age of 5 years
Social deficits	Severe	Mild
Type of interaction	Aloof or passive	Active but odd
Speech	Usually not pedantic	Usually pedantic
Intellectual profile	Low verbal IQ	High verbal IQ
Focused interests	Intense	More intense and usually more sophisticated
Clumsiness	Present	Present but less severe

oversimplification, the differences between autism and Asperger syndrome are summarized in Table 2.2. It is to be noted that these are group differences and that many patients actually have overlapping features.

PDDNOS

Patients with Asperger syndrome need to be differentiated from those with PDDNOS. This is not always easy. The current system of classification assumes a hierarchical model, in that the patient is first examined for autism.

PDDNOS is a residual diagnosis with no clear diagnostic criteria. In clinical practice, the term is sometimes used interchangeably with Asperger syndrome. However, patients with AS have strong focused interests, whereas those with PDDNOS do not. In addition, the severity of symptoms is higher in AS than in PDDNOS.

Broader autistic phenotype

The term 'broader autistic phenotype' (BAP) applies to the presence of autistic-like traits in the first-degree relatives of patients with autism. These relatives, while possessing several traits of autism, do not meet the full criteria for that disorder. While no studies have systematically examined how BAP differs from AS, patients with AS are generally more impaired than those with BAP.

ADHD

Despite the obvious differences between ADHD and Asperger syndrome, patients with ADHD, especially those who are defiant and argumentative, are sometimes wrongly given the diagnosis of AS. The social deficits that result from hyperactivity and impulsivity may be mistaken for those of Asperger syndrome. Some patients with ADHD have the habit of saying things impulsively and inappropriately. The problem is further compounded by the fact that ADHD may occur with Asperger syndrome. However, patients with ADHD do not show the typical focused interests and fixations that are typical among those with Asperger syndrome.

Bipolar disorder

Another diagnosis that needs to be differentiated from Asperger syndrome is bipolar disorder, especially in its manic phase. Patients with bipolar disorder who are going through a hypomanic or manic phase talk fast in a pressured manner, appear socially disinhibited and awkward, and may be focused on a particular theme or activity. However, despite these superficial similarities, the two conditions can be separated by taking a careful history of the patient. The hallmark of the hypomanic phase of bipolar disorder is the presence of grandiosity. The patient's mood is elated, and sometimes irritable or hostile. The speech, though pressured, lacks the pedantic quality of the speech of someone with Asperger syndrome; instead, it tends to be tangential and sometimes disjointed. The focused interests that occur in bipolar disorder are usually fleeting and transitory, often occur in the context of grandiosity, and do not have the intensity of the interests that characterize Asperger syndrome. Above all, the onset and the course of bipolar disorder differ significantly from those of Asperger syndrome. However, bipolar disorder can sometimes occur with Asperger syndrome, as discussed in Chapter 7.

Obsessive-compulsive disorder

While the distinction between Obsessive-Compulsive Disorder (OCD) and Asperger syndrome appears straightforward, it is not always the case. This is particularly true in those cases when the patient with OCD has some social deficits. If the onset of OCD is before 4 years of age, the diagnosis of some form of autism spectrum disorder should be ruled out. In OCD, there is typically subjective distress, because the symptoms are regarded as being egodystonic. However, the interests of Asperger syndrome do not often cause distress to the individual.

Schizoid and schizotypal personality disorders

Asperger syndrome should be differentiated from schizoid and schizotypal personality disorders. In the DSM-IV (APA, 1994), AS is differentiated from schizoid personality disorder, whereas in the ICD-10 (WHO, 1993), it is not. Also, the ICD classifies schizotypal personality disorder with schizophrenia, whereas the DSM-IV classifies it with the personality disorders. To make matters more confusing, different authors have used different diagnostic criteria to describe their samples. Wolff (1996) has suggested that the patients described by Wing (1981) and Tantam (1988) were lower-functioning (and resembling more patients in the autistic spectrum) than those described by herself and Asperger. Relatively little is known about the occurrence of schizotypal personality disorder in children and adolescents; therefore, it is unclear to what extent it overlaps with Asperger syndrome. In one of the few reports on this topic, Nagy and Szatmari (1986) examined 20 children, 18 boys and 2 girls, who met the DSM-III criteria of schizotypal personality disorder. They suggested that schizotypal personality disorder may be a mild form of autism or related to schizophrenia.

Giftedness

Some recent reports have claimed that many famous and gifted people 'suffered' from Asperger syndrome. The list is long and growing, and includes such people as Einstein, Mozart, and Newton (see Fitzgerald, 2000). However, giftedness is a difficult concept to define. It includes people who are highly intelligent, with IQ scores that go 'off the chart,' and also those who are experts in their fields, such as famous scientists and musicians. Highly gifted people have personality traits that may have an overlap with some of the features seen in people with high-functioning autism and Asperger syndrome. However, it is important to emphasize that the diagnosis of Asperger syndrome should be reserved only for those who meet the criteria of social deficits, communication impairment, and rigid ritualistic interests, *and* who suffer from a significant amount of distress and impairment.

Normality

Asperger believed that autistic psychopathy was an extreme variant of normal personality. Adults who are referred for an evaluation generally fall under the following categories. The first category consists of those who have never been diagnosed with any autistic spectrum disorder and who request an evaluation because of ongoing personal problems or difficulties at work. For example, a 30-year-old bank clerk presented to the clinic with the complaint that he had no girlfriend and was wondering if he had Asperger syndrome! The second category consists of those who are referred to adult psychiatric services. These individuals have had a variety of psychiatric diagnoses in the past, such as schizophrenia, psychotic depression, and borderline personality disorder. The third category consists of those with forensic problems and legal troubles. One young man, in his early twenties, was brought to the clinic by his parents, for a diagnostic evaluation. It emerged later that the main reason of the referral was an imminent court appearance for substance abuse. In all such cases, it is critical to obtain a detailed history of deficits in the areas of socialization, communication, and rigid ritualistic interests, and consider the diagnosis only in the presence of significant distress either to the self, or to the community.

Nonverbal Learning Disability

Similarities have also been proposed between Asperger syndrome and Nonverbal Learning Disability or NLD (Klin *et al.*, 1995; Rourke, 1988). The latter is a neuropsychological disability characterized by a combination of assets and deficits, and a discrepancy between VIQ (Verbal IQ) and PIQ (Performance IQ) scores on tests of intelligence. The main asset in NLD consists of the capacity to deal with information delivered through the auditory modality, and the basic deficits lie in visual-spatial, organizational, and psychomotor skills. It is said to involve dysfunction of the white-matter and affects the right side of the brain more than the left. Because of the right hemisphere's greater functional dependence on the white matter, the NLD syndrome is likely to develop under any conditions that affect adversely the functioning of the right hemisphere, and the amount and timing of white matter dysfunction determine the severity of the symptoms. Persons with NLD have better-preserved verbal skills but remain concrete in their thought processes, and have difficulty in coping with novel situations, which leads to their lower ability on 'performance' skills. An important characteristic of the NLD syndrome is the discrepancy between VIQ and PIQ on the Wechsler scales (Rourke, 1988). Children with NLD are able to store a large amount of verbal material and verbal information that accounts for their higher scores on the verbal subtests of the Wechsler scales. However, people with NLD do not typically show the same sort of early developmental history as those with AS; also, they do not have the subtle communication impairment nor do they have the rigid idiosyncratic interests characteristic of Asperger syndrome.

Treatment

The principles of treating AS are the same as those of mild or high-functioning autism, as discussed in the preceding chapter. In many cases, the diagnosis itself serves a therapeutic purpose. Parents are often relieved that the behaviors are part of a disability and not the result of malice. Teachers and other professionals are then able to understand the deficits, and devise suitable treatments. In many cases, categorizing of the child as 'autistic impaired' is helpful. This allows the child to access special services meant for children with high-functioning autism. In the absence of a suitable diagnosis, children with AS often grow up being labeled as difficult, oppositional, or obnoxious.

As in the case of autism, treatment consists of providing structure and support. The purpose of therapy is to focus on the here-and-now and on problems of daily living. In higher-functioning individuals, cognitive behavioral approaches are sometimes used. Insight-oriented psychotherapy often does not work. Help with transitions, such as moving schools, and with unpleasant events such as bereavement, is essential. Social skills training forms a critical component of the treatment plan. Speech therapy is also indicated even though the child does not have a formal speech abnormality. The purpose of therapy is to help increase the social use of language by modulating both the form and content of the communication. Psychotropic medications are often used for the control of superimposed behavioral and psychiatric problems, such as ADHD and depression. These are discussed further in Chapters 6 and 7.

Outcome

While several studies have investigated the outcome of autism, relatively little is known about the outcome of Asperger syndrome (Szatmari *et al.*, 1989). Drawing on outcome studies of autism, some researchers have proposed a better outcome in AS than in traditional autism. These suggestions are based on the good verbal skills and the normal level of intelligence that are charac-teristic of the disorder. However, others have found no differences in the outcome between AS and high-functioning autism (Howlin, 2003). It is important to note, though, that the presence of additional psychiatric disorders is often not taken into account when predicting the outcome. To what extent these disorders cast a modifying effect on the long-term outcome of Asperger syndrome is not clear. Despite their problems, many people with Asperger syndrome live independently. Many marry and hold on to jobs, and some never come to the attention of mental health professionals.

Conclusion

Despite the dramatic increase in its prevalence, Asperger syndrome remains a controversial category whose boundaries with autism are not yet defined clearly. In a general way, the term AS is being used to describe all those children and adolescents who are either odd and eccentric or difficult and obnoxious. However, it is important to underscore that an indiscriminate broadening of its criteria will render it meaningless. An approach that strictly adheres to the diagnostic criteria, however difficult they may be to apply, is necessary to clarify the many questions that surround this interesting condition.

References

APA (American Psychiatric Association) (1994) *Diagnostic and Statistical Manual of Mental Disorders, Fourth Edition* (DSM-IV). Washington, DC: APA.

Asperger, H. (1944) 'Die "autistischen Psychopathen" im Kindersalter.' *Archiv für Psychiatrie und Nervenkrankheiten, 117*, 76–136.

Attwood, T. (1998) *Asperger's Syndrome: A Guide for Parents and Professionals.* London: Jessica Kingley Publishers.

Baron-Cohen, S., Jolliffe, T., Mortimore, C. and Robertson, M. (1997) 'Another advanced test of theory of mind: Evidence from very high functioning adults with Autism or Asperger syndrome.' *Journal of Child Psychology and Psychiatry, 38*, 813–22.

Blondis, T.A., Cook, E., Jr., Koza-Taylor, P. and Finn, T. (1996) 'Asperger syndrome associated with Steinert's myotonic dystrophy.' *Developmental Medicine and Child Neurology, 38*, 840–7.

Bolton, P., Macdonald, H., Pickles, A., Rios, P., Goode, S., Crowson, M., Bailey, A. and Rutter, M. (1994) 'A case-control family history study of autism.' *Journal of Child Psychology and Psychiatry, 35*, 5, 877–900.

Ehlers, S. and Gillberg, C. (1993) 'The epidemiology of Asperger syndrome. A total population study.' *Journal of Child Psychology and Psychiatry, 34*, 8, 1327–50.

Ehlers, S., Gillberg, C. and Wing, L. (1999) 'A screening questionnaire for Asperger syndrome and other high-functioning autism spectrum disorders in school age children.' *Journal of Autism and Developmental Disorders, 29*, 2, 129–41.

Fitzgerald, M. (2000) 'Einstein: Brain and behavior.' *Journal of Autism and Developmental Disorders, 30*, 6, 620–1.

Frith, U. (1991) *Autism and Asperger Syndrome.* Cambridge: Cambridge University Press.

Ghaziuddin, M., Butler, E., Tsai, L. and Ghaziudddin, N. (1994) 'Is clumsiness a marker for Asperger syndrome?' *Journal of Intellectual Disability Research, 38*, 519–27.

Ghaziuddin, M. and Gerstein, L. (1996) 'Pedantic speaking style differentiates autism from Asperger syndrome.' *Journal of Autism and Developmental Disorders, 26*, 6, 585–95.

Ghaziuddin, M. and Mountain-Kimchi, K. (2004) 'Defining the intellectual profile of Asperger syndrome: Comparison with high-functioning autism.' *Journal of Autism and Developmental Disorders, 34*, 3, 279–84.

Ghaziuddin, M., Shakal, J. and Tsai, L. (1995) 'Obstetric factors in Asperger syndrome: Comparison with high-functioning autism.' *Journal of Intellectual Disability Research, 39*, 538–43.

Ghaziuddin, M., Tsai, L. and Ghaziuddin, N. (1992a) 'A comparison of the diagnostic criteria for Asperger syndrome.' *Journal of Autism and Developmental Disorders, 22*, 4, 643–9.

Ghaziuddin, M., Tsai, L. and Ghaziuddin, N. (1992b) 'A reappraisal of clumsiness as a diagnostic feature of Asperger syndrome.' *Journal of Autism and Developmental Disorders, 22*, 4, 651–6.

Gillberg, C. (1989) 'Asperger syndrome in 23 Swedish children.' *Developmental Medicine and Child Neurology, 31*, 520–31.

Gillberg, C. (1998) 'Asperger syndrome and high-functioning autism.' *British Journal of Psychiatry, 172*, 200–209.

Gillberg, I.C. and Gillberg, C. (1989) 'Asperger syndrome – some epidemialogical considerations: A research note.' *Journal of Child Psychology and Psychiatry, 30*, 4, 631–8.

Goldstein, S. (2002) 'Review of the Asperger Syndrome Diagnostic Scale.' *Journal of Autism and Developmental Disorders, 32*, 6, 611–14.

Happe, F., Ehlers, S., Fletcher, P., Frith, U., Johansson, M., Gillberg, C., Dolan, R., Frackowiak, R. and Frith, C. (1996) '"Theory of mind" in the brain. Evidence from a PET scan study of Asperger syndrome.' *Neuroreport, 8*, 1, 197–201.

Howlin, P. (2003) 'Outcome in high-functioning adults with autism with and without early language delays: Implications for the differentiation between autism and Asperger syndrome.' *Journal of Autism and Developmental Disorders, 33*, 1, 3–13.

Kanner, L. (1943) 'Autistic disturbances of affective contact.' *Nervous Child, 2*, 217–50.

Klin, A., Volkmar, F.R., Sparrow, S.S., Cichetti, D.V. and Rourke, B.P. (1995) 'Validity and neuropsychological characterization of Asperger syndrome: Convergence with nonverbal learning disabilities syndrome.' *Journal of Child Psychology and Psychiatry, 36*, 7, 1127–40.

Miller, J.N. and Ozonoff, S. (1997) 'Did Asperger's cases have Asperger disorder? A research note.' *Journal of Child Psychology and Psychiatry, 38*, 247–51.

Murphy, D.G., Critchley, H.D., Schmitz, N., McAlonan, G., Van Amelsvoort, T., Robertson, D., Daly, E., Rowe, A., Russell, A., Simmons, A., Murphy, K.C. and Howlin, P. (2002) 'Asperger syndrome: A proton magnetic resonance spectroscopy study of brain.' *Archives of General Psychiatry, 59*, 885–91.

Nagy, P. and Szatmari, P. (1986) 'A chart review of schizotypal personality disorders in children.' *Journal of Autism and Developmental Disorders, 16*, 3, 351–67.

Rickarby, G., Carruthers, A. and Mitchell, M. (1991) 'Brief report: Biological factors associated with Asperger syndrome.' *Journal of Autism and Developmental Disorders, 21*, 3, 341–8.

Rourke, B.P. (1988) 'The syndrome of nonverbal learning disabled children: Developmental manifestations of neurological disease.' *Clinical Neuropsychologist, 2*, 293–330.

Scott, F.G., Baron-Cohen, S., Bolton, P. and Brayne, C. (2002) 'The CAST (Childhood Asperger Syndrome Test): Preliminary development of a UK screen for mainstream primary school children.' *Autism, 6*, 9–13.

Shriberg, L.D., Paul, R., McSeeny, J.L., Klin, A., Cohen, D.J. and Volkmar, F.R. (2001) 'Speech and prosody characteristics of adolescents and adults with high-functioning autism and Asperger syndrome.' *Journal of Speech, Language, and Hearing Research, 44*, 1097–1115.

Ssucharewa, G.E. (1926) 'Die schizoiden Psychopathien in Kindesalter.' *Monatsschrift für Psychiatrie und Neurologie, 60*, 235–61.

Szatmari, P., Tuff, L., Finlayson, A.J. and Bartolucci, G. (1989) 'Asperger's syndrome and autism: Neurocognitive aspects.' *Journal of the American Academy of Child and Adolescent Psychiatry, 29*, 1, 130–6.

Tantam, D. (1988) 'Lifelong eccentricity and social isolation. II: Asperger syndrome or schizoid personality disorder?' *British Journal of Psychiatry, 153*, 783–91.

Van Krevelen, D.A. (1971) 'Early infantile autism and autistic psychopathy.' *Journal of Autism and Childhood Schizophrenia, 1*, 82–6.

Volkmar, F.R., Klin, A., Schultz, R.T., Rubin, E. and Bronen, R. (2000) 'Asperger's Disorder.' *American Journal of Psychiatry, 157*, 262–7.

WHO (World Health Organization) (1993) *International Classification of Diseases, Tenth Revision, Criteria for Research* (ICD-10). Geneva: WHO.

Wing, L. (1981) 'Asperger's syndrome: A clinical account.' *Psychological Medicine, 11*, 115–29.

Wolff, S. (1996) 'The first account of the syndrome Asperger described?' *European Child and Adolescent Psychiatry, 5*, 119–32.

Wolff, S. and Chick, J. (1980) 'Schizoid personality in childhood: A controlled follow-up study.' *Psychological Medicine, 10*, 85–100.

Wolff, S. and McGuire, R.J. (1995) 'Schizoid personality in girls: A follow-up study – What are the links with Asperger syndrome?' *Journal of Child Psychology and Psychiatry, 36*, 5, 793–817.

CHAPTER 3

Other Pervasive Developmental Disorders

PDDNOS

Introduction

As discussed in Chapters 1 and 2, according to the DSM-IV classification pervasive developmental disorder (PDD) is an overarching term that includes autism and Asperger syndrome (AS), along with Rett's syndrome and disintegrative disorder. Those patients who do not meet the full criteria for any of these disorders are given the label of Pervasive Developmental Disorder Not Otherwise Specified (PDDNOS). In addition, the term PDDNOS is also applied to those patients who have autistic social deficits plus either communication problems or rigid ritualistic behaviors. Although PDDNOS is defined slightly differently in the ICD system of classification, the two systems resemble each other closely.

The boundaries of PDDNOS from other psychiatric disorders remain unclear (Buitelaar *et al.*, 1999). Although the condition is vague in nature and does not have clear diagnostic criteria, it is a useful category for the following reasons. First, it captures those patients who are difficult to diagnose and who can not be easily placed under any of the existing categories. Second, it is a 'parking space' for conditions that are not fully understood at present. In that sense, it is an evolving diagnostic category. For example, DSM-III had only two categories of PDDs: autism and PDDNOS. Based on subsequent research, however, the PDDNOS of DSM-III was split into the DSM-IV subtypes of Asperger syndrome, Rett's syndrome and disintegrative disorder. Third, a variety of socially impaired children seen in psychiatric settings may otherwise be denied services if they are not given this diagnosis. These include those with severe aggression and poor social skills, and children with 'multiplex disorders' or 'childhood personality disorders' (Towbin *et al.*, 1993).

Prevalence

Few studies have focused specifically on PDDNOS. A recent computerized search (using the keyword 'PDDNOS') returned only about 25 publications. Although there has been a steady increase in the number of children being diagnosed with PDDNOS, exact figures about its prevalence are not known. Clinic figures, especially for psychiatric departments and inpatient units, suggest high rates. It is likely that PDDNOS forms a substantial part of the autistic spectrum and contributes significantly to the recent increase in the number of patients with autism.

Clinical features

The diagnosis of PDDNOS is often missed when the patient is first assessed. The symptoms are often mild and non-specific. In some cases, usually those involving mood swings and aggressive outbursts, the initial presentation may resemble a combination of a mood disorder and a disruptive disorder. The onset of the condition is not typically like that seen in autism. In most cases the symptoms come to attention only after the child starts school. Social deficits are always present. These are not as severe as those of children with autism and Asperger syndrome, and not usually apparent when assessed in a formal medical/psychiatric interview. These deficits are often characterized by temper tantrums and, in some cases, by aggression. Parents and care-givers are often struck by the patients' lack of empathy. A history of previous psychiatric referral, mainly for aggression and impulsivity, is not uncommon. Patients often have a past history of admission to psychiatric units and carry several diagnoses. A past diagnosis of Attention Deficit Hyperactivity Disorder (ADHD) or impulsive control disorder is usual.

Communication deficits are so mild that they often go unnoticed. In fact, most of the patients perform well on tests of language functioning. Yet, on repeated examination, subtle problems become apparent. These often consist of deficits in nonverbal communication, such as an inconsistency of eye contact, or an awkwardness of body posture. Typical features of autism, such as language delay and echolalia, are usually absent. A history of pronoun reversal or of verbal rituals is uncommon. Features suggestive of Asperger syndrome, such as pedantic speech, are not present either. However, articulation problems without formal language delay are often found.

Rigidity in thinking or in interests is commonly present. The patient often has problems with transitions. Also usual is an intense interest in certain activities, such as movies, video games etc. Yet, these interests are often not as overwhelming as they are in Asperger syndrome, nor are they as ritualistic as in autism. They are usually of a brief duration, lasting fewer than three months. However, when present, this area of deficits gives a clue to the diagnosis.

The level of intelligence is variable. The IQ is often in the borderline range. There is usually no split seen between the verbal IQ and the performance IQ. Other features, such as sensory deficits, are uncommon. Interestingly, many patients show chromosomal abnormalities (Weidmer-Mikhail, Sheldon and Ghaziuddin, 1998). Theory of Mind (TOM) deficits, which interfere with the ability to empathize and read the thoughts and feelings of others, are also present in PDDNOS, but to a lesser extent than in autism (Sicotte and Stemberger, 1999). Problems with coordination and soft neurological signs are also seen. The following case study is typical of PDDNOS.

Case Study: Graham F

Graham F is a 14-year-old Caucasian male. He was admitted to a psychiatric unit with the complaints of severe aggression, hyperactivity, and impulsivity. He carried several diagnoses – ADHD, Oppositional Defiant Disorder, and dysthymia. He had become increasingly disruptive both at home and at school. At the time of admission, he was taking Ritalin for the control of his symptoms.

His family history was positive for psychiatric illness. He was the youngest of three boys. His eldest brother had a history of major depression with suicide attempts; the other brother had been diagnosed with Asperger syndrome and was doing well. His father, now deceased, had a history of ADHD as a child, and later suffered from major depression.

His birth and early developmental history were unremarkable. At the age of 8 years, he was diagnosed with ADHD and placed on medications. However, the symptoms were never totally brought under control. As well as taking Ritalin, Graham F had been on Trazodone and Risperdal. His medical history was negative. There was no history of seizure disorder. However, a few days after admission to hospital, other details of his behavior came to light.

His mother reported that Graham F was in the habit of collecting unusual articles. At around 4 years of age, he began carrying screwdrivers in his pocket. He would never use them for any purpose; instead, he would take them out of his pocket and keep staring at them. In addition to screwdrivers, he had a history of collecting objects such as knives, tools, and razor blades. Recently, he had begun collecting lighters and would carry them with him. However, the interests were not overwhelming. Also, he had a habit of sticking gum wrappers on items of furniture in his bedroom and would get very upset if these were removed. He had some difficulty with transitions and was hypersensitive to sounds.

At interview, Graham F said that he had two friends, but his mother disagreed. When asked, he said: 'I just call them friends.' He was unable to explain what particular activities they enjoyed together. He admitted that he preferred to do things alone, and his fantasy was to live on an island with many turtles and very few people (he was fond of collecting turtles as well, and had eight of them!). Nurses observed that his interactions with the other patients on the unit were minimal and sporadic. He had a blank look, and appeared to have 'staring spells.' (There was, however, no evidence of seizures.) He spoke when spoken to, but showed no abnormalities of speech. His eye contact was inconsistent. His physical appearance was unremarkable, except for his closely cropped hair which was colored green.

Based on the above history and the examination, it was clear that Graham had problems in areas of social interaction with a restricted range of interests. His communication was within the normal range except some impairment of eye contact. Because these problems were not marked, he did not meet the DSM-IV criteria for autism or Asperger syndrome. Nor did he meet the cut-off on the Autism Behavior Checklist and the Autism Diagnostic Interview. His symptoms could not be explained on the basis of ADHD or any of the other diagnoses that he carried. He was, therefore, given a diagnosis of PDDNOS.

Etiology

The cause of PDDNOS is not known. However, since the condition is regarded as part of the autistic spectrum, probably the same factors which cause autism play a role in the etiology of PDDNOS. However, the nature of the relationship is not clear. While some studies have shown that persons with autism have first-degree relatives with PDDNOS, it is not known if the reverse is also true. No systematic family genetic studies have explored this issue. For example, it is not known if PDDNOS is more (or less) strongly affected by genetic factors than autism. Likewise, it is not clear if PDDNOS is more commonly associated with medical conditions such as seizure disorder.

Diagnosis

The diagnosis depends on a high level of suspicion. Any child with a history of impulsivity and hyperactivity displaying evidence of rigid interests should be carefully evaluated. Although the diagnosis is made on clinical grounds, valuable information can be obtained from rating scales and interviews. For example, the total score on the Autism Behavior Checklist (ABC: Krug, Arick and Almond, 1980) can be helpful in supporting the diagnosis. Also, while the patient does not meet the cut-off for autism on such structured instruments as the Autism Diagnostic Interview (ADI: Lord, Rutter and Le Couteur, 1994) and the Autism Diagnostic Observation Schedule (ADOS: Lord *et al.*, 2000), systematic data collected with these instruments can assist in the diagnosis and treatment planning.

Differential diagnosis

ATTENTION DEFICIT HYPERACTIVITY DISORDER (ADHD)

ADHD is probably the most common diagnosis that is not only mistaken for PDDNOS but also co-occurs with it. Patients with ADHD do not have the fixations and preoccupations that characterize those with PDDNOS. Besides, the impulsivity that occurs in ADHD is more often the result of unbridled hyperactivity, and not of deficits in relatedness and reciprocity. Also, the typical communication abnormalities of the autistic spectrum, such as difficulties with eye contact, or echolalia, etc. do not occur in ADHD.

OPPOSITIONAL DEFIANT DISORDER (ODD)

ODD often occurs with ADHD. The usual symptoms are hyperactivity, impulsivity, and varying degrees of aggressive behavior. Patients do not have the features of autistic spectrum disorders, especially in areas of social interaction and imagination. Ritualistic behaviors of the autistic kind are also absent. However, a hallmark of this condition is a tendency to indulge in frequent arguments with care-givers and to refuse to follow directions. When these symptoms increase in intensity, and are accompanied by frequent aggressive outbursts and attempts to violate the rights of others, the diagnosis of conduct disorder is considered. Again, the social deficits that occur in oppositional and conduct disorders are different from those that occur in autism spectrum disorders. More important, there is no history of intense focused interests or other forms of autistic routines and rituals. Sensory abnormalities are not seen in these conditions. In some cases, patients may present with a mixture of ODD and PDD.

BROADER AUTISTIC PHENOTYPE (BAP)

Another condition that should be considered in the differential diagnosis of PDDNOS is the BAP. 'BAP' refers to the concept that close relatives of patients with autism show features resembling autism without meeting the full criteria for that disorder. At the time of writing, BAP is not an official category. In clinical practice, it is difficult to draw the line between PDDNOS and BAP. For the sake of convenience, BAP may be considered a milder version which does not involve significant distress or disability. By contrast, in PDDNOS, there is always some degree of accompanying impairment and handicap.

SPECIFIC LANGUAGE IMPAIRMENT (SLI)

In SLI, isolated language impairment occurs in the context of otherwise normal development. Thus, features such as rigid ritualistic interests are not present. In addition, patients with SLI do not show deficits in the pragmatic (social) use of language, which is typical of PDD. However, some children show features of both SLI and PDD, and the distinction may be difficult to make.

Psychiatric conditions

Since associated psychiatric conditions are almost always present in those with PDDNOS, these must be carefully investigated. Indeed, associated psychiatric conditions seem to be more common in PDDNOS than in traditional autism, although this issue has not been investigated systematically. There are enough preliminary data to suggest that patients are sometimes initially referred for an assessment of ADHD. Many carry a diagnosis of disruptive behavior disorders, such as ADHD, impulsive control disorder, and ODD. Tics are sometimes present. Mood symptoms consist of irritability, and sometimes of frank depression. Sometimes, in inpatient samples, patients with PDDNOS present with psychotic symptoms. These are often transitory in nature. Brief psychotic episodes and delusional disorders also occur (Kurita, 1999), although frank schizophrenic illnesses are not common. Suicidal behavior and other destructive acts can also occur. Thus, a wide range of psychiatric symptoms are seen. These are discussed more fully in later chapters.

Treatment

The treatment of PDDNOS is multimodal. The principles of treatment are the same as those for autism. These consist of increasing access to social skills training, providing structure and support, and giving speech therapy, if indicated. However, almost all children are referred for behavioral problems, such as temper tantrums and aggression. Therefore, in addition to following a strict and consistent behavioral plan, these children often require the use of psychotropic medications. Stimulants are probably the most commonly used medications, followed by antipsychotics and mood stabilizers. Recurrent aggression and defiant behavior are the main reasons for referral, and form the main focus of treatment. Sometimes, a brief period of stay in an acute psychiatric hospital may be necessary for the purpose of monitoring the behavior, clarifying the diagnosis, and starting medications if necessary.

Outcome

A change in symptoms is common. Many patients with PDDNOS continue to have problems, mostly in the areas of impulsivity and hyperactivity. However, systematic data are not available about the long-term outcome of the condition. It is not known for example, if PDDNOS is associated with a worse prognosis compared to autism or Asperger syndrome. In clinical practice, these patients present with major treatment challenges. This is because most patients come late to medical attention, usually in their late school years, and therefore lose the advantage of an early diagnosis and intervention.

Conclusion

Persons with PDDNOS show features suggestive of autism without meeting the full criteria of that disorder. They either have mild symptoms in the three areas of functioning (social interaction, communication, and imagination), or show social deficits and impairment in either communication or imagination. Despite the lack of clarity about its boundaries, PDDNOS remains a useful diagnosis. Since children with PDDNOS are often mislabeled as being obnoxious and incorrigible, at the very least, the diagnosis helps care-givers to understand the nature of the disability and plan appropriate interventions. While treatment of the core deficits remains the same as for autism, patients with PDDNOS appear to suffer from a wide array of psychiatric abnormalities, in particular disruptive behavior disorders, which need to be diagnosed and treated.

Rett's syndrome

Introduction

In 1966, Rett described 22 females with a distinct pattern of neurological and social deficits and a specific developmental course, accompanied by a variety of unusual behaviors (see Hagberg *et al.*, 1983). It was introduced as a subtype of pervasive developmental disorders in DSM-IV (APA, 1994). Some authorities have objected to its designation as a PDD because of its overt neurological symptoms, while others have contended that its categorization as a PDD is justified because it is accompanied by autistic-like features in one of its stages (see below).

Prevalence

The prevalence of Rett's syndrome (RS) is about 1 in 15,000 according to studies done in Sweden and Scotland. In a community sample of children and adolescents aged between 6 and 17 years, 13 girls with RS were found, out of a total of about 300,000 (Hagberg, 1985). Kerr and Stephenson identified 19 cases in Scotland out of 5400 referrals to a pediatric neurology center in Scotland (Kerr and Stephenson, 1986). RS almost always occurs in females, although some cases in males have also been reported.

Clinical features

Patients with RS develop normally for the first year of life; then, usually between the ages of 6 and 12 months, they regress in all areas of functioning. They lose their cognitive, motor, and language skills, and compared to age and sex matched controls, show a progressive decrease in their head circumference. In addition, many patients suffer from seizures. Gradually, as the disorder progresses, autistic symptoms develop.

Autistic symptoms typically consist of regression of verbal skills, loss of eye contact, and a characteristic pattern of repetitive hand movements. These hand movements typically consist of midline 'handwashing' movements, which are characteristic of the disorder. In addition, the stereotyped movements may consist of squeezing, clapping or patting. These are sometimes seen as early as the first year of life, but become more prominent around 2 years of age. Recognition of the hand movements is often an early diagnostic feature. The clinical presentation is variable; some patients develop the full-blown syndrome, while others remain asymptomatic (Naidu *et al.*, 2003).

STAGES

The clinical course of RS can be divided into the following stages:

1. *Early onset stagnation stage* – 6 months to 18 months.

2. *Rapid developmental regression stage* – Starts around 18 months. It is in this stage that autistic features occur.

3. *Pseudostationary stage* – 3–4 years of age. This stage can be delayed or may persist for several years.

4. *Late motor deterioration stage* – Often occurs during school age or adolescence.

Etiology

A great deal of excitement was generated by the discovery of the MECP2 gene in a group of patients with RS (Amir *et al.*, 1999). Mutation of the gene causes a specific defect in presynaptic development, the effects of which become apparent by 2 years of age. In addition to classic RS, MECP2 mutations have been associated with a milder variant of RS in which speech and motor skills are better preserved. MECP2 mutations were believed to be lethal to male fetuses, explaining the exclusive occurrence of RS in females. However, we now know that some male patients can also show MECP2 mutations. In general, female patients with the MECP2 mutation exhibit the typical features of RS, whereas most male patients with the same mutation exhibit moderate to severe forms of mental retardation. The discovery of the MECP2 mutations in patients with RS raised the question of whether the same mutations occurred in patients with traditional autism. So far, this has not been borne out by research (Lobo-Menedez *et al.*, 2003).

Diagnosis

The diagnosis of Rett's syndrome rests on three types of criteria: necessary, supportive, and exclusion criteria (those that rule out a particular diagnosis).

NECESSARY DIAGNOSTIC CRITERIA

1. Apparent normal prenatal and perinatal development through the first 6 to 18 months of age.

2. Normal head circumference at birth.

3. Deceleration of head circumference between 5 months and 4 years of age.

4. Loss of acquired hand skills occurring between 6 and 30 months.

5. Development of stereotypic hand movements, such as wringing, squeezing, clapping, and rubbing.

6. Gait and truncal apraxia (difficulty performing a given movement)/ataxia (unsteadiness of gait) between 1 and 4 years of age.

SUPPORTIVE DIAGNOSTIC CRITERIA

1. Breathing dysfunction such as periodic apnea (breath holding), and hyperventilation.

2. EEG abnormalities.

3. Seizures.

4. Scoliosis (lateral curvature of the spine).

EXCLUSION DIAGNOSTIC CRITERIA

1. Storage diseases (a group of disorders characterised by the storage of certain substances e.g. glycogen).

2. Acquired neurological disorders.

3. Head trauma.

Differential diagnosis

Rett's syndrome should be differentiated from neurological and storage disorders. This requires a good history and thorough investigations. It is differentiated from autism by the presence of the typical handwashing movements, marked motor impairment, breathing abnormalities, and scoliosis. The latter condition is rarely present at birth, but appears in the majority of cases by early adulthood. It is severe in nature and often leads to secondary complications. Its cause is probably linked to the underlying genetic mutation.

Psychiatric disorders

Information is limited about the co-occurrence of formal psychiatric disorders. Anecdotal reports have described hyperactivity and impulsivity. Sleep disorders have also been described (Yamashita *et al.*, 1999), as well as nonspecific behavioral problems such as aggression and temper tantrums.

Treatment

Treatment of Rett's syndrome is symptomatic. It consists of occupational therapy, nursing care, and the judicious use of medications. Surgical intervention to correct the scoliosis may also be necessary. The long-term outcome is not good. The needs of parents and siblings should not be overlooked.

Disintegrative disorder

Introduction

Disintegrative disorder has been described under various names, such as 'Heller's dementia' and 'dementia infantilis.' The condition was first described by Theodore Heller, a Viennese educator, observing a group of six children (Heller, 1908), and was initially termed as 'Heller's dementia.' It is currently classified as a pervasive developmental disorder in the DSM/ICD systems of classification. According to the criteria, a child with disintegrative disorder has a history of normal development until about 3–4 years of age and then shows signs of regression in his social, adaptive, communicative, and motor skills. Abnormalities occur in the areas of social interaction, communication, and play, resembling those occurring in autism.

Prevalence

Disintegrative disorder is extremely rare with a pooled estimate in studies of 0.2 per 10,000 (Fombonne, 2003). Only about 100 cases have been reported worldwide. Some authorities believe that this condition should not be placed in the PDD group of disorders; others have argued that it is the same as autism with regression. Although disintegrative disorder is classified as a PDD, its genetic overlap with traditional autism is not clear. Some reports have described both the conditions occurring in the same family (Zwaigenbaum *et al.*, 2000).

Clinical features

The critical diagnostic feature is that there is a sustained period of normal development before regression occurs. This period of normal development can be relatively prolonged. The onset is often between the ages of 3 and 5 years of age. In a review of 77 cases, the mean age of onset was 3.4 years (Volkmar, 1992). However, some authorities have suggested that early development is not always totally normal (Kurita, 1988).

Diagnosis

As the name indicates, the key to the diagnosis lies in the fact that the child disintegrates after a period of normal development. There may or may not be an environmental stressor to account for this regression (Evans-Jones and Rosenbloom, 1978). The history of normal development serves to differentiate it from cases of late-onset autism, in which the symptoms are not apparent till 3–4 years of age. The distinction is not always easy; some studies have suggested that cases of late-onset autism tend to be higher-functioning, while those with disintegrative disorder tend to be mute and lower-functioning.

Psychiatric complications

Since the condition is rare, little information is available about its psychiatric comorbidity. However, affective symptoms and general behavioral problems are common.

Treatment

Treatment is the same as that of low-functioning autism and consists of behavioral interventions, structure and support. Medications are used to treat superimposed behavioral problems. Systematic data are not available about the frequency and efficacy of the use of psychotropic medications in this population.

References

Amir, R.E., Van Den Veyver, I.B., Wan, M., Tran, C.Q., Franke, U. and Zoghby, H. (1999) 'Rett syndrome is caused by mutations in X-linked MECP2, encoding methyl CpG binding protein 2.' *Nature Genetics, 23*, 18–188.

APA (American Psychiatric Association) (1994) *Diagnostic and Statistical Manual of Mental Disorders, Fourth Edition* (DSM-IV). Washington, DC: APA.

Buitelaar, J.K., Van der Gaag, R., Klin, A. and Volkmar, F. (1999) 'Exploring the boundaries of pervasive developmental disorder not otherwise specified: Analyses of data from the DSM-IV Autistic Disorder Field Trial.' *Journal of Autism and Developmental Disorders, 29,* 1, 33–43.

Evans-Jones, L.G. and Rosenbloom, L. (1978) 'Disintegrative psychosis of childhood.' *Developmental Medicine and Child Neurology, 20,* 4, 462–70.

Fombonne, E. (2003) 'Epidemiological surveys of autism and other pervasive developmental disorders: An update.' *Journal of Autism and Developmental Disorders, 33,* 4, 365–82.

Hagberg, B. (1985) 'Rett Syndrome: Swedish approach to analysis of prevalence and cause.' *Brain and Development, 7,* 277–80.

Hagberg, B., Aicardi, I., Dias, K. and Ramos, O. (1983) 'A progressive syndrome of autism, dementia, ataxia, and loss of purposeful hand use in girls: Rett's syndrome: Report of 35 cases.' *Annals of Neurology, 14,* 4, 471–9.

Heller, T. (1908) 'Dementia infantilis.' *Zeitschrift für die Erforschung and Behandlung de Jugenlichen Schwachsinns, 2,* 141–65.

Kerr, A.M. and Stephenson, J.B.P. (1986) 'A study of the natural history of Rett syndrome in 23 girls.' *American Journal of Medical Genetics, 24,* 77–83.

Krug, D.A., Arick, J. and Almond, P. (1980) 'Behavior checklist for identifying severely handicapped individuals with high levels of autistic behaviour.' *Journal of Child Psychology and Psychiatry, 21,* 3, 22–9.

Kurita, H. (1988) 'The concept and nosology of Heller's Syndrome: Review of articles and report of two cases.' *Japanese Journal of Psychiatry and Neurology, 42,* 785–93.

Kurita, H. (1999) 'Brief report: Delusional disorder in a male adolescent with high-functioning PDDNOS.' *Journal of Autism and Developmental Disorders, 29,* 5, 419–23.

Lobo-Menendez, F., Sossey-Alaoui, K., Bell, J.M., Copeland-Yates, S.A., Plank, S.M., Sanford, S.O., Skinner, C., Simensen, R.J., Schroer, R.J. and Michaelis, R.C. (2003) 'Absence of MeCP2 mutations in patients from the South Carolina autism project.' *American Journal of Medical Genetics, 117,* 1, 97–101.

Lord, C., Risi, S., Lambrecht, L., Cook, E.H.Jr., Leventhal, B.L., DiLavone, P.C., Pickles, A. and Rutter, M. (2000) 'The autism diagnostic observation schedule – generic: A standard measure of social and communication deficits associated with the spectrum of autism.' *Journal of Autism and Developmental Disorders, 30,* 3, 205–23.

Lord, C., Rutter, M. and Le Couteur, A. (1994) 'Autism Diagnostic Interview – Revised: A revised version of a diagnostic interview for caregivers of individuals with possible pervasive developmental disorders.' *Journal of Autism and Deveopmental Disorders, 24,* 5, 659–85.

Naidu, S., Bibat, G., Kratz, L., Kelley, R.I., Pevsner, J., Hoffman, E., Cuffari, C., Rohde, C., Blue, M.E. and Johnston, M.V. (2003) 'Clinical variability in Rett syndrome.' *Journal of Child Neurology, 18,* 662–8.

Sicotte, C. and Stemberger, R.M. (1999) 'Do children with PDDNOS have a theory of mind?' *Journal of Autism and Developmental Disorders, 29,* 3, 225–33.

Towbin, K.E., Dykens, E.M., Pearson, G.S. and Cohen, D.J. (1993) 'Conceptualizing "borderline syndrome of childhood" and "childhood schizophrenia" as a developmental disorder.' *Journal of the American Academy of Child and Adolescent Psychiatry, 32*, 775–82.

Volkmar, F.R. (1992) 'Childhood Disintegrative Disorder: Issues for DSM-IV.' *Journal of Autism and Developmental Disorders, 22*, 4, 625–42.

Weidmer-Mikhail, E., Sheldon, S. and Ghaziuddin, M. (1998) 'Chromosomes in autism and related pervasive developmental disorders: A cytogenetic study.' *Journal of Intellectual Disabilility Research, 42*, 8–12.

Yamashita, Y., Matsuishi, T., Murakami, Y. and Kato, H. (1999) 'Sleep disorder in Rett syndrome and melatonin treatment.' *Brain Development, 21*, 8, 570.

Zwaigenbaum, L., Szatmari, P., Mahoney, W., Bryson, S., Bartolucci, G. and MacLean, J. (2000) 'High functioning autism and Childhood Disintegrative Disorder in half brothers.' *Journal of Autism and Developmental Disorders, 30*, 2, 121–6.

CHAPTER 4

Medical Conditions in Autism

Introduction

This chapter gives an overview of some of the medical conditions that occur in pervasive developmental disorders (PDDs) Most cases of autism do not have a known cause; however, in a substantial number of cases, autism occurs with other known medical conditions. Although the purpose of this book is to describe the presentation and treatment of psychiatric disorders in persons with PDDs, it is important to recognize that medical and psychiatric conditions often occur together. Also, medical disorders frequently increase the risk of psychiatric complications. Most of the discussion applies to traditional autism because relatively little is known about the association of medical conditions with Asperger syndrome and Pervasive Developmental Disorder Not Otherwise Specified (PDDNOS). Also, only those conditions are discussed here which have important research and treatment implications. Conditions that seem to occur by chance are excluded.

Prevalence

The prevalence rate of these conditions has been a matter of ongoing debate. It is likely that the rate is at least 10 per cent (Rutter *et al.*, 1994) and may be as high as 25 per cent (Gillberg and Coleman, 1996). Apart from the diagnostic criteria used and the type of investigations performed, the prevalence rate depends on several factors, especially the characteristics of the sample. For example, patients referred to pediatric neurology clinics show higher rates of associated medical conditions; the same is also true of cases with severe degrees of mental retardation referred to specialists working in the areas of learning/intellectual disability and mental handicap. In general, the lower the IQ of the sample, the higher the likelihood of finding associated medical conditions. Although data on Asperger syndrome are limited, patients with this disorder seem to suffer from fewer medical conditions than those with autism. This is not surprising because, according to the diagnostic criteria, patients with AS do not have cognitive delay and mental retardation. Also, patients with PDDNOS may show higher rates of medical conditions, as indicated by an increased risk of chromosome abnormalities than those with traditional autism (Weidmer-Mikhail, Sheldon and Ghaziuddin, 1998). This is probably because the group PDDNOS consists of a collection of disorders of disparate etiologies. However, few systematic studies have focused specifically on PDDNOS, and data are, therefore, limited.

Presentation of symptoms

Irrespective of the type and nature of the associated medical condition, it is important to emphasize that there is no difference in the core symptoms of autism. Thus, whether or not autism is complicated by the presence of an additional medical disorder, the core symptoms of deficits in the areas of socialization, communication, and imagination are unchanged. Studies have also tried to investigate if autistic patients with known medical conditions differ in the pattern of their neurochemical abnormalities from those who do not have such conditions. No significant differences have been found (Garreau et al., 1984).

Autism and associated conditions: A classification

Medical conditions in autism can be divided into two broad categories: general and specific medical conditions. The former category consists of those disorders that are heterogeneous in nature, such as mental retardation and seizure disorder, while the latter consists of distinct conditions such as Fragile X syndrome, tuberous sclerosis, and Down syndrome (see Box 4.1).

Autism and general medical conditions

Mental retardation in autism

DEFINITION

Mental retardation is characterized by a sub-average level of intellectual functioning indicated by an IQ of 70 or below on a test of intelligence; deficits in adaptive functioning as shown by problems in at least two of such areas as self-care, home living, interpersonal skills, work and leisure; and an onset before 18 years of age. On the basis of the IQ and general level of functioning,

Box 4.1 Classification of medical conditions in autism

General conditions:

- mental retardation
- seizure disorder

Specific conditions:

- chromosomal/single gene disorders
  - Fragile X syndrome
  - Down syndrome
- disorders caused by infectious agents (e.g. viruses)
  - herpes
  - cytomegalovirus
  - other
- disorders of the nervous system
  - neurocutaneous syndromes e.g. tuberous sclerosis
  - encephalopathies e.g. cerebral palsy
- miscellaneous
  - skeleton and collagen disorders (e.g. Marfan syndrome)
  - disorders of the endocrine system (e.g. XXY syndrome; Noonan syndrome)
  - disorders of eye movement and alignment (e.g. Moebius syndrome)

it is classified into the following types: mild, moderate, severe, and profound (APA, 1994). It is a heterogeneous condition with a variety of causes, ranging from environmental to genetic, all of which are characterized by a low level of adaptive functioning and a sub-average IQ. It is important to note that the onset is before 18 years of age; this differentiates it from loss of function resulting from brain injury or disease.

PREVALENCE

In his classic paper of 1943, Kanner did not propose a direct association between autism and mental retardation. Indeed, it was assumed that autism often occurred in people with high intelligence. However, subsequent research established the close and specific relationship between the two conditions. At least 70 per cent of persons with traditional autism (excluding those with Asperger syndrome and PDDNOS) suffer from mental retardation. In a recent review, Fombonne (1999) noted that intellectual functioning was within the normal range in only about 20 per cent of persons with autism. However, if the variants of autism are included, the prevalence rate tends to be lower. Nordin and Gillberg (1996) found that the prevalence rates for autism and autistic-like conditions approximated 20 per cent in children with severe mental retardation and 5 per cent in those with mild mental retardation. In a study of children aged 5 to 19 years, Deb and Prasad (1994) found that the prevalence of autistic disorder, diagnosed according to the DSM-III-R (APA, 1987) criteria, was 14.3 per cent in children with a learning disability (mental retardation). Although autism and mental retardation are closely related, there is no known association between mental retardation and the broader phenotype of autism. Thus, first-degree relatives of individuals with autism do not have an excess of mental retardation as discussed in Chapter 1.

PRESENTATION OF SYMPTOMS

Symptoms of autism are modified when mental retardation complicates the disorder. An early study by Bartak and Rutter (1976) compared autistic persons with and without mental retardation on the basis of a full-scale IQ of 70, and noted that the two groups differed in the pattern of symptoms and in the outcome. The lower-functioning group showed a high rate of stereotypic behaviors and had a worse outcome. However, the core symptoms were similar across the two groups. Some researchers have suggested that different genetic factors may account for the higher- and lower-functioning forms of autism spectrum disorder (Szatmari et al., 1998).

AUTISM, MENTAL RETARDATION, AND PSYCHIATRIC DISORDERS

It is well known that the incidence of psychiatric disorder is increased in the presence of mental retardation. Therefore, it is reasonable to assume that persons with autism who suffer from mental retardation are more vulnerable to superimposed psychiatric disorders than those who are of normal intelligence, although few systematic studies have focused on this topic. On the other hand, it has been suggested that higher-functioning autistic persons are more prone to psychiatric disorders, such as depression, in part because of their greater insight into their deficits. However, this may not necessarily be true because of the greater difficulties involved in the assessment of psychiatric disorders in people with mental retardation in general.

Seizure disorder in autism

Seizures are common in children with autism, occurring in at least 30 per cent. The fact that patients with autism are vulnerable to seizures was one of the earliest pointers to the biologic underpinnings of this disorder. The prevalence is higher in those with severe mental retardation. In one of the early studies, DeMyer and colleagues (White, DeMyer and DeMyer, 1964) found that out of a series of 58 autistic children, 19 per cent showed epilepsy; 58 per cent had EEG abnormalities and the incidence of these abnormalities was higher in those with mental retardation. Findings from two early longitudinal studies showed incidence rates between 25 per cent (Lockyer and Rutter, 1970) and 33 per cent (Gillberg and Steffenburg, 1987).

While all types of seizures can occur, complex partial seizures are particularly common and pose special problems in diagnosis, because they are often mistaken for behavioral outbursts and temper tantrums. It is worth noting that while autism *per se* is associated with epilepsy, the broader phenotype of autism, that is, the occurrence of mild autistic features in the relatives without meeting the full syndrome of the disorder, is not.

The age of onset of seizure disorder in autism is bimodal. While the majority of seizures occur around puberty, a substantial number have their onset in the preschool years. Thus, although a patient with autism can have seizures any time during his life span, his risk is relatively low between the ages of 5 and 13 years. Possible reasons for the increased risk at puberty include changes in the level of hormones. Several mechanisms have also been proposed for the association of autism with epilepsy. Epilepsy may disrupt brain functions that are necessary for language development either by its associated intellectual disabilities or directly as a consequence of the seizures. Impairment of language function has long-term consequences for social and academic functions, including causing deficits in memory and learning. The relationship between epilepsy and language function is complicated by the fact that neuroanatomic circuits are common to both. The diagnosis of seizure disorder is of critical importance to the outcome of autism. Apart from exposing the patient to physical dangers, epilepsy also increases the risk of psychiatric complications. Some epilepsy syndromes which are particularly related to autism are discussed below.

INFANTILE SPASMS (WEST SYNDROME)

This is an epileptic syndrome of infants and young children. The typical seizure is described as a jack-knife attack in which the child suddenly bends forward at the waist. It is often associated with tuberous sclerosis. When present, infantile spasms may directly contribute to the emergence of autistic symptoms (Taft and Cohen, 1971). However, autism is not the only disorder that occurs in this condition. In a long-term follow-up study of 192 children with infantile spasms, psychiatric symptoms, in particular hyperactivity, were found in 53 of the children. Twenty-four subjects had autism, and a further 14 had 'transient' symptoms of autism, while 16 of the autistic children were also hyperactive. In the entire group, 29 cases were hyperactive (Riikonen, 2001). Children identified as autistic in this sample often had psychomotor epilepsy and temporal lobe abnormalities; this suggests that organic lesions that selectively occur in these areas of the brain are associated with an increased risk of autism (Riikonen, 2001), possibly through mutations of the AXR gene on the X chromosome (Stromme et al., 2002). While adrenocorticotrophic hormone (ACTH) is the mainstay of treatment of infantile spasms, glucocorticoids, pyridoxine, and ketogenic diet therapy are also sometimes used.

LANDAU-KLEFFNER SYNDROME

In this condition, the child loses speech with the onset of seizures. This typically occurs around 2 years of age, and is sometimes referred to as 'acquired epileptiform aphasia'. There is evidence that the language disorder is directly caused by epileptic discharges in the critical language areas. Since about a quarter of autistic children also show signs of language regression around 2 years of age, it is important to rule out if this is because of Landau-Kleffner syndrome. Treatment with steroids is helpful: some reports have described improvement in speech and behavior following high doses of steroids (Tsuru et al., 2000).

Autism and specific medical conditions

Specific conditions can be divided into two broad categories: conditions that are commonly associated with autism (such as Fragile X syndrome and tuberous sclerosis) and conditions that are uncommonly associated with autism (such as Down syndrome and cerebral palsy). These are briefly described below.

Fragile X syndrome

Fragile X syndrome is the most common cause of familial mental retardation. It accounts for about 10 per cent of individuals with mental retardation and about 50 per cent cases of X-linked mental retardation (Turk, 1992). A smaller percentage of females are affected because females have two X chromosomes and males have only one. Since females have a normally functioning gene to compensate for the abnormal gene, the impact of the disorder is diminished. Besides mental retardation, the clinical features of Fragile X syndrome as expressed in males include an elongated face and chin, prominent ears, large testicles, and sensory abnormalities. Hyperactivity and perseveration of speech are also present. The risk of developing the disease increases in successive generations through maternal transmission.

The expansion of a trinucleotide repeat (CGG) located in the FMRP X-linked gene is the main cause of Fragile X syndrome. FMRP is an RNA-binding protein, and loss of this protein results in the clinical features associated with the disease. Two main types of mutation are observed in affected families. A full mutation is found in patients with mental retardation and corresponds to large expansions of the repeat. Premutations are moderate expansions and are found in normal transmitting males and in the majority of clinically normal carrier females. About 15 per cent of patients show a mosaic pattern consisting of both full mutations and premutations.

Initial reports of its association with autism suggested high prevalence rates. For example, in a Swedish multicenter study of 122 cases of autism, 16 boys (13%) were found to test positive for autism (Wahlstrom et al., 1986). However, later reports suggested lower rates, partly because of methodological differences. In a study of 75 children with autism aged 5 years, only 2 subjects were found who expressed the Fragile X abnormality in 40 per cent of cells; an additional 2 subjects expressed the abnormality at lower rates (Piven et al., 1991). Another large study of autistic individuals whose diagnosis was confirmed using a standardized diagnostic instrument found the anomaly in 1.6 per cent of cases, and the prevalence was similar among autistic individuals of both sexes (Bailey et al., 1993).

Patients with the Fragile X anomaly often show a different kind of social and communicative deficit compared to that of autism, and, in some cases, a distinct pattern of social anxiety; although executive function deficits of the type seen in autism are often present (Garner, Callias and Turk, 1999). In a small study of nine subjects with Fragile X syndrome and nine controls with mental retardation but without this syndrome, Kerby and Dawson (1994) found that the subjects with Fragile X syndrome were more likely to be shy, socially withdrawn, and anxious than those with mental retardation alone. Also, tangential language is said to be more prevalent among those with Fragile X syndrome compared to those with autism (Sudhalter and Belser, 2001). In another study, 31 boys with Fragile X syndrome who did not have autism, matched on chronological age, gender, and race, were compared with 31 boys with autism but no Fragile X syndrome. Children with autism showed a greater degree of social and communication deficits, a lower level of physical activity, and a more variable profile of development compared with the Fragile X group (Bailey *et al.*, 2000).

The association of autism with Fragile X syndrome suggests the possible role of the X chromosome in child neuropsychiatric disorders such as autism. However, molecular genetic studies have not shown a major gene effect causing autism on the X chromosome (Hallmayer *et al.*, 1996).

Tuberous sclerosis

Another condition closely associated with autism is tuberous sclerosis (TS). Sometimes referred to as 'tuberous sclerosis complex' (TSC), it is a genetic disorder that results in benign tumors in several organs of the body such as the skin, kidneys, heart, and the brain. Both males and females are affected. Its incidence in the US is given as one in 6000 live births. Those affected often present with mental retardation and epilepsy. Other features emerge later. These consist of cardiac tumors, cortical tubers (small areas on the outer layer of the brain, the cortex, which do not develop normally), small nodules on the walls of the cerebral ventricles, depigmented macules or areas of skin with light patches, and tumors in the lungs and eyes. The severity of the disorder is variable. Mutations in one of two genes, TSC1 and TSC2, have been identified as the underlying cause of tuberous sclerosis.

Several behavioral and psychiatric symptoms have been described in persons with TSC. These include aggression, hyperactivity, seizure episodes, and obsessive-compulsive behaviors. Psychiatric disorders such as schizophrenia and depression have also been described. Autistic features occur in about 60 per cent of patients with the tuberous sclerosis complex (Bolton *et al.*, 2002). Epidemiologic studies (Fombonne *et al.*, 1997) suggest a strong association between the two disorders. The degree of impairment and the risk of autism are positively correlated with the number and location of cortical tubers. The risk is substantially increased when tubers are located in the area of the temporal lobes (Bolton *et al.*, 2002). However, this finding has not been replicated in all studies (Walz *et al.*, 2002).

Down syndrome

Described in 1867 by Langdon Down, an English physician, Down syndrome is the most common cause of mental retardation, occurring in about 1 in 800 live births. About 95 per cent of cases are caused by an extra copy of chromosome 21 (trisomy 21) and the rest by an inherited genetic abnormality called 'translocation' (transfer of one part of the chromosome to another). Older women are at an increased risk to having a baby with trisomy 21. It is characterized by a distinct facial appearance and a collection of signs and symptoms. Other organs of the body that are affected include the heart and the thyroid gland. Medical complications of Down syndrome include hypothyroidism, cardiac abnormalities, and an increased risk of certain types of blood cancers.

Patients with Down syndrome are also vulnerable to a host of psychiatric complications. Among these, the most prominent is Alzheimer's disease. Memory changes and other behavioral abnormalities typical of this disorder start appearing in most patients with Down syndrome after the age of 40 years. These changes are accompanied by pathological deposits of abnormal proteins in certain parts of the brain. Depressive symptoms are also common in persons with Down syndrome and are sometimes misdiagnosed as dementia. Therefore, any patient who shows signs of cognitive and social decline should first be evaluated for depression. Sometimes, depression heralds the onset of dementia.

Despite their various physical difficulties, patients with Down syndrome are often pleasant and friendly. Over the years, a so-called 'Down syndrome personality' has emerged which is characterized by friendliness, flexibility, and good-natured humor. However, research suggests that while an over-whelming majority of patients with Down syndrome may fall under this category, a small minority exists that is prone to behavioral problems. These problems consist of temper tantrums, aggressive outbursts, oppositional and disruptive behavior, rigidity and aloofness, and, in some cases, by tics and abnormal movements. While the proportion of these patients is probably around 10 per cent, they cause a significant degree of distress to parents and care-givers. Emerging evidence suggests that several of these patients with behavioral problems show features of autism.

The prevalence of autism in Down syndrome is probably higher than usually assumed. Several case reports have described the co-occurrence of autism and Down syndrome. At least one population-based study has shown high rates. For example, in an epidemiologic study, Kent and colleagues (1999) estimated that about 7 per cent of children with Down syndrome suffered from an autistic spectrum disorder.

It is not known why some persons with Down syndrome show additional autism. While the two conditions can occur together by chance, it has been suggested that those who have both Down syndrome and autism have an increased family history of the BAP compared with those who have Down syndrome without autism (Ghaziuddin, 2000). This raises the possibility that, even when autism occurs with known medical conditions such as Down syndrome, autism-specific genetic factors may play a role.

The presentation of autistic symptoms in Down syndrome consists of the usual deficits in the areas of socialization, communication, and imagination. However, case reports suggest that most of the patients are diagnosed in their adolescence or adulthood. Rigid ritualistic behaviors are often the referring problems. Many have tics and abnormal body movements and some present with depression. It is not known if the risk of dementia is increased in those patients with Down syndrome who also suffer from autism.

The diagnosis of autism in Down syndrome is often missed. Clinicians often fail to go beyond the visible physical features and consider additional diagnoses in persons with mental retardation, a process referred to as 'diagnostic shadowing.' Therefore, any patient with Down syndrome who shows behavioral problems should be screened for autism, especially if there is a strong evidence of rigid ritualistic behaviors. The diagnosis rests on eliciting a detailed history showing a combination of the three types of deficits of autism.

An early diagnosis is important because of the treatment implications. Children who have Down syndrome and autism should receive services for *both* the disorders. Otherwise, these children run the risk of being labeled as 'behaviorally challenged,' without receiving the specific help for their deficits of autism.

Cerebral palsy

Cerebral palsy is a heterogeneous group of disorders characterized by motor deficits and gait disturbances. It was thought that autism rarely occurred in patients with cerebral palsy. However, there is increasing evidence that this assumption is inaccurate. Gillberg and colleagues investigated the prevalence of autism in patients with mental and/or physical disabilities in a Scandinavian sample. Autism spectrum disorders were found in 19.8 per cent of children with mental retardation, including strictly defined autistic disorder (DSM-III-R criteria) in 8.9 per cent; the two-year follow-up yielded a higher prevalence of 11.7 per cent with autistic disorder. Among children with cerebral palsy, 10.5 per cent had an autism spectrum disorder. A close association was found between mental retardation, epilepsy, and autism spectrum disorders in this sample of children with neurodevelopmental disorders (Gillberg and Coleman, 1996). Fombonne *et al.* (1997) found that the rate of cerebral palsy in a sample of autistic children in France was higher than the rate in the general population. Patients with cerebral palsy who present with autistic behaviors are probably misdiagnosed and labeled as being 'behaviorally disordered.' Recognition of autistic features in cerebral palsy is important because of the treatment implications.

Miscellaneous conditions

In addition to Fragile X syndrome, several chromosome abnormalities have been described in association with autism (Gillberg, 1998). Reports have speculated on the possibility that certain chromosome abnormalities with autism may represent distinct behavioral phenotypes. For example, MacLean *et al.* (2000) suggested that ring abnormalities of chromosome 22 present with subtle but identifiable physical stigmata. These include mental retardation, autistic disorder, dolichocephaly (a disproportionately long and narrow face), low-set and large ears, mid-face hypoplasia (incomplete development of an organ), and syndactyly (fingers joined together). Similar associations have been suggested between abnormalities of chromosome 2 (deletion 2 syndrome) and autistic disorder. Ghaziuddin and Burmeister (1998) described two patients with deletion of chromosome 2 q37 and physical features consisting of frontal bossing (broadening of the forehead), deep-set eyes with dark circles underneath, depressed nasal bridge, and long eyelashes. Patients with tetrasomy 15 often show autism, mental retardation, a high arched palate, and seizure disorder. Attempts have been made to identify the putative autistic disorder gene on the basis of studies implicating the chromosome 15 q11–q13 region (Maddox, Menold and Bass, 1999; Salmon *et al.*, 1999). Several other chromosome regions have also been studied (Barrett *et al.*, 1999).

Autism and XYY syndrome

The XYY syndrome has an incidence of approximately 1 in 1000 male births (Forssman *et al.*, 1975). Initial interest in this condition was generated by the reported association between this disorder and aggressive behavior as suggested by its relatively high concentration in special hospitals for offenders. Besides its association with antisocial and aggressive behavior, links have been proposed with other psychiatric disorders such as schizophrenia. Some case reports have described the association of 47XYY in patients with schizophrenia or having a psychotic-type disorder (Kumra *et al.*, 1998; Rajagopalan, MacBeth and Varma, 1998). Approximately 50 per cent of XYY children have learning difficulties (Ratcliffe, Murray and Teague, 1986). Although the problems in learning vary, the most common are deficits in speech and language development. Some reports have also described the association of autism with XYY syndrome (Abrams and Pergament, 1971; Gillberg, Winnergard and Wahlstrom, 1984; Nielsen *et al.*, 1973). In addition, many of the cases described in the literature had behavioral symptoms (such as social withdrawal, odd ways of interacting with others, a tendency to indulge in fantasy, deficits in abstract reasoning, communication deficits) suggestive of autism. Gillberg and colleagues proposed that the XYY genotype combined with organic brain damage or severe seizure disorder increased the risk of autism, as did the Y chromosome itself (see Gillberg *et al.*, 1984).

Autism and XXY syndrome

The XXY syndrome, also called 'Klinefelter's syndrome,' consists of infertility, hypogonadism (underfunctioning of the gonads, testes and the ovaries), and gynecomastia (enlargement of the breasts). There is increased secretion of the follicle-stimulating hormone. While 47XXY is the most common type, several other variants have been described with additional X and Y chromosomes (such as 48XXYY, 48XXXY, 49XXXXY). Generally, the higher the number of chromosomes, the more severe the phenotype. The XXY syndrome is estimated to be the most common disorder of sex chromosomes in humans, with a frequency of one in 600 males. Despite this relatively high incidence, little is known about its psychiatric aspects. A consistent finding is that boys with Klinefelter's syndrome have impairment in school, and as adults, they attain lower occupational ranks than controls. This, however, is not due to low IQ, since most affected males have a variable range of general cognitive abilities, with many showing above average to superior intelligence. In boys, there is a significant difference between performance IQ and verbal IQ, with a ten or greater point lag in the verbal IQ. Neurocognitive deficits found in individuals with Klinefelter's syndrome include impairments in language and arithmetic, deficits in frontal-executive domains, and abnormalities in gross and fine motor coordination. Patients are often described as introverted, unassertive, anxious, and socially withdrawn, with some showing autistic tendencies (Collacott *et al.*, 1990; Geschwind *et al.*, 2000; Temple and Sanfilippo, 2003; Visootsak, Aylstock and Graham, 2001).

Autism and Moebius syndrome

There have been increasing reports of the association of Moebius syndrome with autism. In this disorder, which is also known as 'congenital facial diplegia,' muscles of the face are affected on both sides. Usually it is associated with weakness of cranial nerves supplying the muscles of the eyes. The face has an expressionless mask-like appearance. Mental retardation is present in some cases. Skeletal abnormalities may also be present. Severe cases often die in infancy because of complications of the nervous system. Cases of co-existing autism have been described (Gillberg and Steffenburg, 1987). The association of Moebius syndrome and autism is of interest because exposure in the first trimester of pregnancy to certain chemicals results in the clinical picture of Moebius syndrome (Bandim *et al.*, 2003). Therefore, if autistic symptoms occur in such cases, it implies that the cause of autism lies in the first trimester. A few cases of familial Moebius syndrome have also been reported. The treatment of Moebius syndrome is nonspecific and aimed at reducing the negative impact of the muscular paralysis. When a child presents with Moebius syndrome co-existing with autism, he should receive additional specialized services for autism.

Assessment and treatment

There is no consensus about the range of investigations that should be done when autism is associated with a medical condition. As discussed in Chapter 1, all autistic children should have a systematic physical examination. Skin patches and spots of depigmentation typical of tuberous sclerosis should be looked for, preferably with a UV lamp. More extensive examination is justified on clinical grounds (see Box 4.2 below). Since the symptoms of autism with or without associated medical conditions is the same, treatment is based on the standard principles of treating autism – providing structure, social skills

Box 4.2 Assessment of a child with an autism spectrum disorder

- Physical examination:
  - facial appearance
  - head circumference
  - height and weight
  - skin
  - brief neurological survey
- Psychiatric examination:
  - level of activity
  - abnormal movements
  - degree of relatedness
  - evidence of aggression/self-abuse
  - mood
  - abnormal ideas or beliefs
  - cognition
- Psychological examination:
  - IQ tests
  - executive function tests
  - tests for motor coordination
  - Theory of Mind tests
- Speech and language evaluation:
  - receptive/expressive language
  - pragmatics
- Laboratory examination:
  - complete blood picture
  - DNA for karyotype and Fragile X syndrome
  - thyroid function tests
  - liver function tests
  - ECG (if indicated)
  - EEG (if indicated)
  - imaging studies (if indicated)

training, and appropriate education placement. In addition, attention should be paid to the specific medical condition. Appropriate medications should be used for additional target symptoms, such as seizures, hyperactivity, and aggression. Where necessary, family therapy and genetic counseling should also be provided.

Conclusion

In as many as 10–25 per cent of cases, autism is associated with medical disorders. The range of conditions is varied and includes neurological and infective conditions. Asperger syndrome can also occur with medical conditions, although the degree of association is not as high as that in autism. The exact meaning of these associations is not clear. In some cases, these may be incidental findings; in others, such as some chromosome disorders and tuberous sclerosis, the reasons may suggest common etiological factors. In several cases, associated medical conditions are also associated with psychiatric symptoms such as hyperactivity and aggressive behavior. A greater understanding of the occurrence of medical conditions in autism is necessary for planning treatment. It is not known why some patients with a medical condition present with autism and others with the same condition do not. Since autism has a strong genetic basis, it is possible that autism-specific genetic factors may be important even when autism occurs with known medical conditions. In some cases, this may explain why patients with certain medical conditions present with comorbid autism while others with the same conditions do not. Studies of this nature have not been performed systematically. Studies of the comorbidity of autism with medical conditions can shed light on the disorder itself and also help in treatment strategies.

References

Abrams, N. and Pergament, E. (1971) 'Childhood psychosis combined with XYY abnormalities.' *Journal of Genetic Psychology, 118*, 13–16.

APA (American Psychiatric Association) (1987) *Diagnostic and Statistical Manual of Mental Disorders, Third Edition, revised* (DSM-III-R). Washington, DC: APA.

APA (American Psychiatric Association) (1994) *Diagnostic and Statistical Manual of Mental Disorders, Fourth Edition* (DSM-IV). Washington, DC: APA.

Bailey, A., Bolton, P., Butler, L., Le Couteur, A., Murphy, M., Scott, S., Webb, T. and Rutter, M. (1993) 'Prevalence of the fragile X anomaly amongst autistic twins and singletons.' *Journal of Child Psychology and Psychiatry, 34*, 5, 673–88.

Bailey, D.B Jr., Hatton, D.D., Mesibov, G., Ament, N. and Skinner, M. (2000) 'Early development, temperament, and functional impairment in autism and fragile X syndrome.' *Journal of Autism and Developmental Disorders, 30*, 1, 49–59.

Bandim, J.M., Ventura, L.O., Miller, M.T., Almeida, H.C. and Costa, A.E. (2003) 'Autism and Mobius sequence: An exploratory study of children in northeastern Brazil.' *Arq Neuropsiquiatry, 61*, 181–5.

Bartak, L. and Rutter, M. (1976) 'Differences between mentally retarded and normally intelligent autistic children.' *Journal of Autism and Childhood Schizophrenia, 6*, 109–120.

Barrett, S., Beck, J.C., Bernier, R., Bisson, E., Braun, T.A., Casavant, T.L. *et al.* (1999) 'An autosomal genomic screen for autism. Collaborative linkage study of autism.' *American Journal of Medical Genetics, 15*, 609–615.

Bolton, P.F., Park, R.J., Higgins, J.N., Griffiths, P.D. and Pickles, A. (2002) 'Neuro-epileptic determinants of autism spectrum disorders in tuberous sclerosis complex.' *Brain, 125*, 1247–55.

Collacott, R.A., Mitchell, C., Dawes-Gamble, L., Young, I.D. and Duckett, D. (1990) 'Brief report: A 48XXXY/49XXXXY male with expressive speech defect.' *Journal of Autism and Developmental Disorders, 20*, 4, 577–80.

Deb, S. and Prasad, K.B.G. (1994) 'The prevalence of autistic disorder among children with a learning disability.' *British Journal of Psychiatry, 164*, 395–9.

Fombonne, E. (1999) 'The epidemiology of autism: A review.' *Psychological Medicine, 29*, 769–86.

Fombonne, E., Mazaubrun, C.D., Cans, C. and Grandjean, H. (1997) 'Autism and associated medical disorders in a French epidemiological survey.' *Journal of the American Academy of Child and Adolescent Psychiatry, 36*, 1561–9.

Forssman., H., Wahlstrom, J., Wallin, L. and Akesson, H.O. (1975) *Males with Double Y-Chromosomes.* Göteborg: Scandinavian University Books.

Garner, C., Callias, M. and Turk, J.J. (1999) 'Executive function and theory of mind performance of boys with fragile-X syndrome.' *Journal of Intellectual Disability Research, 43*, 466–74.

Garreau, B., Barthelemy, C., Sauvage, D., Leddet, I. and LeLord, G. (1984) 'A comparison of autistic syndromes with and without associated neurological problems.' *Journal of Autism and Developmental Disorders, 14*, 1, 105–111.

Geschwind, D.H., Boone, K.B., Miller, B.L. and Swerdloff, R.S. (2000) 'Neurobehavioral phenotype of Klinefelter Syndrome.' *Mental Retardation and Developmental Disabilities Research Reviews, 6*, 107–116.

Ghaziuddin, M. (2000) 'Autism in Down syndrome: A family history study.' *Journal of Intellectual Disability Research, 44*, 562–6.

Ghaziuddin, M. and Burmeister, M. (1998) 'Deletion of chromosome 2 q37 and autism: A distinct subtype?' *Journal of Autism and Developmental Disorders, 29*, 3, 259–63.

Gillberg, C. (1998) 'Chromosomal disorders in autism.' *Journal of Autism and Developmental Disorders, 28*, 5, 415–25.

Gillberg, C. and Coleman, M. (1996) 'Autism and medical disorders: A review of the literature.' *Developmental Medicine and Child Neurology, 38*, 191–202.

Gillberg, C. and Steffenburg, S. (1987) 'Outcome and prognostic factors in infantile autism and similar conditions: a population-based study of 46 cases followed through puberty.' *Journal of Autism and Developmental Disorders, 17,* 2, 273–87.

Gillberg, C., Winnergard, I. and Wahlstrom, J. (1984) 'The sex chromosomes – one key to autism? An XYY case of infantile autism.' *Applied Research in Mental Retardation, 5,* 353–60.

Hallmayer, J., Hebert, J.M., Spiker, D., Lotspeich, L. McMahon, W.M., Peterson, P.B. *et al.* (1996) 'Autism and the X chromosome: Multipoint sib-pair analysis.' *Archives of General Psychiatry, 53,* 980–3.

Kanner, L. (1943) 'Autistic disturbance of affective contact.' *Nervous Child, 2,* 217–50.

Kent, L., Evans, J., Paul, M. and Sharp, M. (1999) 'Comorbidity of autistic spectrum disorders in children with Down syndrome.' *Developmental Medicine and Child Neurology, 41,* 153–8.

Kerby, D.S. and Dawson, B.L. (1994) 'Autistic features, personality, and adaptive behavior in males with the fragile X syndrome and no autism.' *American Journal on Mental Retardation, 98,* 4, 455–62.

Kurma, S., Wiggs, E., Krasnewich, D., Meck, J., Smith, A.C., Bedwell, J. *et al.* (1998) 'Brief report: Association of sex chromosome anomalies with child-onset psychotic disorders.' *Journal of the American Academy of Child and Adolescent Psychiatry, 37,* 3, 292–6.

Lockyer, L. and Rutter, M. (1970) 'A five- to fifteen-year follow-up study of infantile psychosis. IV: Patterns of cognitive ability.' *British Journal of Social and Clinical Psychology, 9,* 152–63.

MacLean, J.E., Teshima, I.E., Szatmari, P. and Nowaczyk, M.J. (2000) 'Ring chromosome 22 and autism: Report and review.' *American Journal of Medical Genetics, 28,* 382–5.

Maddox, L.O., Menold, M.M. and Bass, M.P. (1999) 'Autistic disorder and chromosome 15q11–q13: Construction and analysis of a BAC/PAC contig.' *Genomics, 15,* 325–31.

Nielsen, J., Christensen, K.R., Friedrich, V., Zeuthen, E. and Ostergaard, O. (1973) 'Childhood of males with the XYY syndrome.' *Journal of Autism and Childhood Schizophrenia, 3,* 5–26.

Nordin, V. and Gillberg, C. (1996) 'Autism spectrum disorders in children with physical or mental disability or both. I: Clinical and epidemiological aspects.' *Developmental Medicine and Child Neurology, 38,* 297–313.

Piven, J., Gayle, J., Landa, R., Wzorek, M. and Folstein, S. (1991) 'The prevalence of fragile X in a sample of autistic individuals diagnosed using a standardized interview.' *Journal of the American Academy of Child and Adolescent Psychiatry, 30,* 5, 825–30.

Rajagoalan, M., MacBeth, R. and Varma, S.L. (1998) 'XYY chromosome anomaly and schizophrenia.' *American Journal of Medical Genetics, 81,* 64–5.

Ratcliffe, S.G., Murray, L. and Teague, P. (1986) 'Edinburgh study of growth and development of children with sex chromosome abnormalities III. BD: OAS XXII (3)' New York: March of Dimes Birth Defects Foundation, 73–118.

Riikonen, R. (2001) 'Long-term outcome of patients with West syndrome.' *Brain Development, 23*, 7, 683–7.

Rutter, M., Bailey, A., Bolton, P. and Le Couteur, A. (1994) 'Autism and known medical conditions: Myth and substance.' *Journal of Child Psychology and Psychiatry, 35*, 311–22.

Salmon, B., Hallmayer, J., Rogers, T., Kalaydjievae, L., Peterson, P.B., Nicholas, P., *et al.* (1999) 'Absence of linkage and linkage disequilibrium to chromosome 15q11±q13 markers in 139 multiplex families with autism.' *American Journal of Medical Genetics, 15*, 551–6.

Stromme, P., Mangelsdorf, M.E., Scheffer, I.E. and Gecz, J. (2002) 'Infantile spasms, dystonia, and other X-linked phenotypes caused by mutations in Aristaless related homeobox gene, ARX.' *Brain Development, 24*, 5, 266–8.

Sudhalter, V. and Belser, R.C. (2001) 'Conversational characteristics of children with fragile X syndrome: Tangential language.' *American Journal on Mental Retardation, 106*, 5, 389–400.

Szatmari, P., Jones, M.B., Zwaigenbaum, L. and MacLean, J.E. (1998) 'Genetics of autism: Overview and new directions.' *Journal of Autism and Developmental Disorders, 28*, 5, 351–69.

Taft, L.T. and Cohen, H.J. (1971) 'Hypsarrhythmia and childhood autism: A clinical report.' *Journal of Autism and Childhood Schizophrenia, 1*, 327–36.

Temple, C.M. and Sanfilippo, P.M. (2003) 'Executive skills in Klinefelter's syndrome.' *Neuropsychologia, 41*, 1547–59.

Tsuru, T., Mori, M., Mizuguchi, M. and Momoi, M.Y. (2000) 'Effects of high-dose intravenous corticosteriod therapy in Landau-Kleffner syndrome.' *Pediatric Neurology, 22*, 2, 145–7.

Turk, J. (1992) 'The fragile-X syndrome. On the way to a behavioural phenotype.' *British Journal of Psychiatry, 160*, 24–35.

Visootsak, J., Aylstock, M. and Graham, J.M. (2001) 'Klinefelter syndrome and its variants: An update and review for the primary pediatrician.' *Clinical Pediatrics, 40*, 639–51.

Wahlstrom, J., Gillberg, C., Gustavson, K.H. and Holmgren, G. (1986) 'Infantile autism and the fragile X. A Swedish multicenter study.' *American Journal of Medical Genetics, 23*, 1–2, 403–408.

Walz, N.C., Byars, A.W., Egelhoff, J.C. and Franz, D.N. (2002) 'Supratentorial tuber location and autism in tuberous sclerosis complex.' *Child Neurology, 17*, 11, 830–2.

Weidmer-Mikhail, E., Sheldon, S. and Ghaziuddin, M. (1998) 'Chromosomes in autism and related pervasive developmental disorders: A cytogenetic study.' *Journal of Intellectual Disability Research, 42*, 8–12.

White, P.T., DeMyer, W. and DeMyer, M. (1964) 'EEG abnormalities in early childhood schizophrenia: A double-blind study of psychiatrically disturbed and normal children during promazine sedation.' *American Journal of Psychiatry, 120*, 950–58.

CHAPTER 5

Psychiatric Comorbidity: An Introduction

Introduction

This chapter gives an overview of psychiatric disorders with particular reference to those occurring in persons with autism and Asperger syndrome. It deals with the definition of mental disorder, the principles of psychiatric classification, the concept of comorbidity, and the association of psychological and behavioral problems with autism spectrum disorders. Recent years have witnessed a steady increase in the prevalence of psychiatric disorders all over the world. In most industrialized countries, the rate is about 20 per cent of the population. Apart from an increasing awareness of psychiatric disorders, especially in developing countries, factors that have contributed to this increase include crime, substance abuse, and the breakdown of the family. Also, any factor that causes a medical illness also increases the risk of psychiatric disorder. This is particularly true if the medical illness affects brain function, as is the case in autism.

Definition of psychiatric disorder

There is no universally accepted definition of 'psychiatric disorder' because of the lack of a clear demarcation between normality and pathology. Some researchers have suggested that any problem that is referred to a psychiatrist constitutes a psychiatric disorder! Such an over-inclusive approach has obvious drawbacks. However, in general, a psychiatric or mental disorder may be defined as a clinically significant behavioral or psychological syndrome or pattern that occurs in an individual and that is associated with present distress or disability (APA, 1994). Moreover, this syndrome or pattern of behavior must not be an expected and culturally sanctioned response to an external event, such as bereavement. Irrespective of its cause, psychiatric disorder is accompanied by behavioral, psychological, or biological dysfunction in the individual.

Most psychiatric disorders arise from a combination of factors; some are unique to the person, while others are rooted in the environment. The age of onset is variable; some disorders, such as autism, start early while others, such as dementia, begin in late life. The course is also variable: some disorders, such as some kinds of Attention Deficit Hyperactivity Disorder (ADHD) and depression, end in adult life; while others, such as autism, persist throughout life, albeit in a modified form. By definition, all psychiatric disorders cause distress, and affect the life of the individual in a negative way. Although they range from mild to severe, even mild disorders can cause serious problems over time, and should, therefore, be treated. An example is mild depression which, if untreated, can have negative effects. While episodes of many psychiatric disorders tend to be self-limited, they should not be left untreated. The purpose of treatment is to minimize distress, shorten the course of the disorder, and prevent complications such as suicide.

Although the symptoms of psychiatric disorders are mainly behavioral, almost all areas of functioning are affected, including bodily functions. Persons who have psychiatric disorders report more physical complaints, such as fatigue and headache, and experience more problems in their employment and interpersonal relationships than those who do not. They are also more likely to suffer from such problems as substance and alcohol abuse.

There is a mistaken belief that psychological distress caused by environmental factors should not be treated. Sometimes psychiatric disorders are wrongly classified as those that are stress-induced and those that are not precipitated by stress. This argument is flawed, because there are no differences between the features of psychiatric disorders that are provoked by environmental factors and those that are not. The distinction between biologic and psychological mental disorder is not supported by data. Eventually, all psychiatric disorders are biologic in nature, in the sense that all of them result from dysfunction of the brain at some level, even if this is not always apparent.

Another mistaken belief, still prevalent in some circles, is that the treatment of psychiatric symptoms with medications is harmful and counterproductive. Based on outdated theories, some people believe that if the patient does not work through his conflicts and 'masks' his symptoms with the use of medications, his symptoms will emerge in some other form, and eventually harm him. There is no evidence to support this belief. While the role of environmental stressors should always be investigated, and psychological causes always looked for, it is not necessary to prolong the distress of the patient or of his family in the interest of 'working through conflicts.' Although the rush to prescribe medications should be avoided, it is equally unethical to avoid medications on ideological grounds alone.

Multiaxial classification

Classification deals with the grouping of psychiatric disorders into different categories. This is done in several ways, such as the age of onset or the type of symptoms. For example, conditions such as autism, ADHD, and mental retardation are placed under conditions beginning in childhood. Likewise, patients who suffer from a persistently depressed mood lasting for a specific period of time, accompanied by certain types of signs and symptoms, are given a diagnosis of major depression.

Classification serves at least two important functions. One purpose is to provide a language to clinicians to enable them to communicate with each other and to make predictions about the course, treatment, and outcome of the disorder. Another purpose is to facilitate research. The two important systems of classification are the World Health Organization's ICD (WHO, 1994) and the American Psychiatric Association's DSM (APA, 1994). These classifications are revised and updated regularly, based on new advances and discoveries. Over the years, these two systems of classification have grown closer and the gap between them has narrowed substantially. For example, the criteria for autism and Asperger syndrome are almost identical in the ICD-10 and the DSM-IV systems of classification. It is important to underscore that the aim of classification is to categorize *diseases*, not the individuals affected by them. In this context, it should be noted both the DSM and the ICD systems of classification adopt a categorical approach, which relies on different sets of predetermined diagnostic criteria. This is not a perfect approach because mental disorders are not discrete categories that can be easily demarcated from normal variants of functioning. As opposed to this, the dimensional approach classifies clinical features based on quantification of attributes rather than on assignment of categories and is most suited for describing phenomena that are normally distributed, such as height, weight, or blood pressure. However, a dimensional approach suffers from its own weaknesses, such as lack of clarity in the choice of dimensions, and is less useful in clinical practice and research (APA, 1994).

An important aspect of the DSM (and the ICD) system of classification is that it is multiaxial in nature. This means that a patient can be diagnosed as having more than one disorder at a time. The first axis deals with the presenting condition; the second relates to the level of intellectual functioning or type of personality; the third axis describes any medical condition that may be present; the fourth records the level of social and environmental stressors; and the fifth gives an estimate of the level of functional impairment. For example, a patient with autism, mental retardation, and epilepsy is diagnosed as follows: Axis I – autistic disorder; Axis II – mental retardation; Axis III – seizure disorder; Axis IV – level of psychosocial stressors: mild, moderate or severe depending on the situation; and Axis V – level of functioning, given by a score on a scale. The introduction of the multiaxial system of classification marked a major step forward in the conceptualization of mental disorders. It enabled clinicians and researchers to take all relevant biological and social factors into consideration while making a psychiatric diagnosis, and also helped them in making predictions about the course and outcome of a disorder. In addition, it increased awareness of the co-occurrence of psychiatric disorders and stressed the importance of comorbidity.

What is comorbidity?

The term 'comorbidity' refers to the occurrence of two or more disorders together. Although some authorities believe that comorbid conditions should be causally related to each other, this is not always the case. In a broad sense, comorbidity simply documents the co-existence of more than one condition in the same patient, which is the approach taken in this book. (An example is the occurrence of depression in a child with autism.) This approach is somewhat broader than that advocated by some researchers, and does not take into account the issue of spurious or artificial comorbidity, in which patients with a particular disorder may show increased rates of another disorder due to referral patterns or ascertainment bias. However, since relatively little is known about the comorbidity of persons with autism spectrum disorders, the broader definition of comorbidity is used here in order to review as many studies as possible. Comorbidity can also be divided into psychiatric and medical subtypes. While it may be argued that all disorders are basically biological (that is, medical) in nature, separation between medical and psychiatric types helps with both research and with the planning of services. For example, depression occurs not only with certain psychiatric disorders, such as anxiety disorders, but also with known medical conditions, as shown in Table 5.1.

Table 5.1 Medical comorbidity of depression

	Prevalence (%)	Comments
General population	10–15	12-month prevalence
Coronary artery disease	18	Current episode of depression
Myocardial infarction	16	6 months post-MI
Cancer	20–25	At some time during illness
Diabetes	25	Meta-analysis of 42 studies
HIV	36	12-month prevalence
Alzheimer's disease	17–31	Current episode of depression
Migraine	22–32	Lifetime prevalence in young adults
Multiple sclerosis	Up to 50	Lifetime prevalence

In child psychiatry, the association of a disorder with other conditions is often the rule, not the exception. Therefore, to study the factors which contribute to the causes and consequences of a particular disorder, it is critical to examine the conditions that accompany it (Angold, Costello and Erkanli, 1999; Caron and Rutter, 1991). The study of psychiatric comorbidity is important for two main reasons. First, identification and treatment of co-occurring conditions affects the long-term outcome of the patient: for example, a patient with ADHD has a worse outcome if he has accompanying conduct disorder than a patient with ADHD alone. Second, an examination of the factors underlying the comorbidity can help understand the etiology of the individual disorders: investigating why depression often occurs in Alzheimer's disease can help understand the factors that cause the two disorders separately. The impact of psychiatric comorbidity can be summarized as being:

- excess functional disability
- increased morbidity and mortality
- increased health-care utilization and costs
- decreased adherence to treatment regimens
- higher potential for drug interactions due to the use of multiple drugs
- increased likelihood of medical complications.

Psychiatric comorbidity of autism and Asperger syndrome

Although clinicians have only recently started paying attention to the prevalence of psychiatric disorders in persons with autism and Asperger syndrome, the overlap between the disorders can be traced back to the first publications by Kanner and Asperger. Some of the patients described by Leo Kanner in his classic paper seem to have co-existing psychiatric conditions, such as anxiety disorders. For example, Case 1 (Donald) 'was fearful of tricycles and seems to have almost a horror of them...' (Kanner, 1943, p.218). The same applies to the case descriptions of Asperger syndrome provided in the literature. Many of the patients described by Hans Asperger were oppositional and defiant, and seemed to have frequent temper tantrums. They would probably be diagnosed as meeting the current DSM criteria for disruptive behavior disorders today. Thus, the patient Fritz V 'never did what he was told. He did just what he wanted to, or the opposite of what he was told. He was always restless and fidgety, and tended to grab everything within his reach' (Frith, 1991, p.39). The second patient, Harro L, was also referred because he was 'unmanageable.' He was defiant and disrespectful, and 'rarely did what he was told.' 'One of the principal reasons for his being referred by the school was his savage tendency to fight' (p.50). Ernst K, the third patient, was also referred 'because of severe conduct and learning problems.' He was extremely aggressive and would 'instantly get embroiled in fighting.' The fourth patient, Hellmuth L, 'also showed spiteful behavior' and 'enjoyed hiding or destroying objects... He did a lot of malicious things to the people he lived with and to other children' (p.65). Thus, the main reason for referral for all the patients was a range of externalizing behaviors such as defiance, disrespect of authority, difficulty in following directions, and additionally in one case, restless and fidgety behavior.

The key question is whether these psychiatric symptoms are part of autism (and Asperger syndrome) or whether they are distinct conditions. It has been proposed by some authorities that these symptoms are epiphenomena, that is, chance findings that do not rise to the level of being given separate diagnoses. In some cases, this may well be true. For example, an occasional mood swing or aggressive outburst is not sufficient to justify an additional diagnosis of bipolar disorder. However, in other cases these symptoms may be severe enough to form the main reason of referral and, therefore, the main focus of clinical intervention. An example might be when a teenager with autism, with no prior psychiatric history, starts having crying spells, becomes withdrawn and talks about killing himself after the death of his pet. He appears unhappy and depressed, and appears to have lost interest in his usual activities. His sleep and appetite are also impaired. In cases of this nature, it is justified to give an additional diagnosis of a psychiatric disorder.

Prevalence rates

Clinical experience suggests that a wide variety of psychiatric disorders occur in patients with autism and Asperger syndrome. These range from common conditions, such as depression and anxiety disorders, to uncommon conditions, such as selective mutism and gender identity disorder. While no systematic epidemiological studies have been performed, reports from evaluation clinics suggest high rates of prevalence. At least 10 per cent of children and adolescents referred to special clinics and diagnostic centers seem to suffer from superimposed psychiatric disorders. In an outpatient sample of subjects with autism we found that, out of 68 children and adolescents, 9 per cent suffered from other psychiatric disorders (Ghaziuddin, Tsai and Ghaziuddin, 1992). This sample consisted mostly of persons with mental retardation and did not rely on standardized instruments of assessment, suggesting that the true prevalence is probably higher. In persons with Asperger syndrome/high-functioning autism, clinic samples suggest higher rates. It is worth noting that all of Wing's 34 patients were recruited from psychiatric settings (Wing, 1981). Out of the 18 patients aged over 16 years at the time of evaluation, 4 had an affective illness and 4 had become increasingly odd and withdrawn. 'One patient had a psychosis with delusions and hallucinations that could not be classified, one had had an episode of catatonic stupor, one had bizarre behavior and an unconfirmed diagnosis of schizophrenia, and 2 had bizarre behavior, but no diagnosable psychiatric illness' (Wing, 1981, p.118).

In another clinic study of the comorbidity of Asperger syndrome, 23 out of 35 subjects (66%) were rated positive for a comorbid psychiatric disorder at the time of the evaluation or at follow-up two years after the initial evaluation (Ghaziuddin, Weidmer-Mikhail and Ghaziuddin, 1998). The two most common diagnoses were ADHD and depression (including major depression, dysthymia (chronic depression), and bipolar disorder). Ten patients were diagnosed with ADHD, 13 with depression (8 with major depression, 4 with dysthymia, and 1 with bipolar disorder) one with Tourette syndrome, one with Obsessive-Compulsive Disorder (OCD) and one with tic disorder. Three patients had two diagnoses each (one had ADHD with major depression, one had OCD with major depression, and another had tic disorder with dysthymia). None of the patients was given a diagnosis of schizophrenia. Since autism and mental retardation often occur together, some studies have examined to what extent mental retardation contributes to the psychiatric comorbidity. In a more recent study, Bradley and colleagues (2004) compared 12 subjects with autism and severe mental retardation, with age- and sex-matched controls who only had severe mental retardation (and no autism), and found that the autistic group showed a significantly greater level of psychopathology as measured by scores on the Diagnostic Assessment for the Severely Handicapped–II. The autistic group scored higher on scales for depression, anxiety, and several other disorders (Bradley *et al.*, 2004).

It is not known if patients with Asperger syndrome are more vulnerable to developing psychiatric disorders than those with autism. This is partly because of the confusion surrounding the diagnostic criteria of Asperger syndrome. However, it is possible that patients with Asperger syndrome may *report* more psychiatric symptoms because they are more verbal than those with autism, and, therefore, more able to offer a reliable account of their symptoms. At the same time, there is increasing clinical experience that the prevalence of psychiatric disorders is particularly increased in persons with atypical autism or those who are labeled as having Pervasive Developmental Disorder Not Otherwise Specified (PDDNOS).

Because of the significant association of autism and Asperger syndrome with psychiatric disorders, it is important to investigate their impact on their long-term adjustment. What is the role of psychiatric comorbidity on the outcome of autism and Asperger syndrome? This question has not been systematically addressed in the literature. While it is often stated that the two main criteria that define the outcome of autism (and presumably also of Asperger syndrome) are the level of intelligence and communication, it is unclear to what extent the presence of psychiatric disorders, such as depression and ADHD, affect the symptoms of autism and the overall life of the individual.

Barriers to psychiatric care

Although persons with pervasive developmental disorders (PDDs) often present with psychiatric disorders, they do not receive the psychiatric care they deserve. This is evident from the pattern of referral of these individuals to educational and non-psychiatric settings. A substantial number of referrals to these centers are made for what are commonly called 'behavioral problems' when, in fact, the real reason for the referral is the presence of psychiatric disorders.

There are several reasons why access to psychiatric services is difficult for persons with autism spectrum disorders. First, there are few skilled professionals working in this field. There is an acute shortage of psychiatrists who are experienced in the psychiatric care of persons with PDD both in the US and elsewhere. Also, psychiatrists who take care of these patients often do not have a background in child psychiatry. This issue is important because autism is a childhood-onset disorder. In order to avoid diagnostic mistakes, such as confusing autism with schizophrenia, a background in child psychiatry is essential.

Second, some people wrongly believe that people with autism cannot develop psychiatric disorders. According to them, autistic persons lack the cognitive and emotional maturity to experience such states as depression and anxiety. Clinical experience suggests otherwise. In addition, having autism does not make one resistant to disorders and diseases which affect those without autism. Some people express the fear that diagnosing mental illness in people with autism is stigmatizing and should be avoided. This view, though well-intentioned, is not helpful because of the treatment implications. It is unethical to deny treatment solely because of a fear of labeling. Besides, most parents and care-givers appear relieved when informed that the maladaptive behavior is the result of a psychiatric disorder and not of any other reason.

Third, some countries have an unfortunate division of services that makes access to psychiatric services extremely difficult. For example, in the US, people with mental retardation, who form a sizeable number of people with autism, are placed under the category of 'developmentally disabled.' Those who are mentally ill belong to the MI (mentally ill) services. Thus, someone who is both developmentally disabled and mentally ill is placed at a disadvantage. Moreover, centers for the 'developmentally disabled,' which often means mentally retarded, are often managed by professionals with little or no background in psychiatry. A similar situation exists in other western countries such as the UK where services for the intellectually disabled (mentally retarded) do not often involve psychiatric care. In developing countries, pediatricians and teachers, and not psychiatrists, often take the lead in coordinating services for people with autism and other developmental disabilities.

Fourth, the current systems of classification do not make it easy to give additional psychiatric diagnoses to persons with autism and other developmental disorders. The DSM and the ICD systems are not meant for people with mental retardation and developmental disabilities. For example, the DSM system specifically advises that ADHD should not be diagnosed in children with autism. According to it, ADHD cannot be diagnosed during the course of a pervasive developmental disorder. This is clearly not borne out by clinical experience because many children with autism do show symptoms of hyperactivity or impulsivity severe enough to be regarded as the main focus of clinical intervention.

Fifth, relatively few standardized instruments exist for the diagnosis of psychiatric disorders in persons with mental retardation. This is relevant to the study of psychiatric comorbidity of autism spectrum disorders because a substantial number of subjects have additional mental retardation. The Reiss Scale is a care-giver-based scale that gives information about the occurrence of various behavioral and psychiatric symptoms in persons with mental retardation (Reiss and Valenti-Hein, 1994). The Diagnostic Assessment for the Severely Handicapped or DASH (Matson *et al.*, 1991) provides data on the occurrence of major psychiatric disorders. In general, though, the study of psychopathology in persons with mental retardation has not received enough attention. For this reason, even common psychiatric conditions, such as depression, are missed in those autistic persons who also suffer from mental retardation. However, the usual rating scales and instruments can be used with those without mental retardation, that is, those with Asperger syndrome and high-functioning autism. Even when diagnosing those with mental retardation, existing instruments can be modified.

Finally, in countries such as the US, where treatment is funded by insurance, insurance companies are often unwilling to pay for psychiatric services for persons with developmental disorders and mental retardation. This is because some argue that autism is a 'medical' condition while others refuse to accept that psychiatric disorders can occur in this population. Also, many adults with autism, especially those with mental retardation, survive on state support, and are not able to afford private psychiatric care.

Types of psychiatric disorders

All types of psychiatric disorders occur in persons with autism and Asperger syndrome, as illustrated in Figure 5.1. The most common are disruptive behavior disorders, such as ADHD, and mood disorders, such as depression. There is some evidence that in higher-functioning individuals, such as those with Asperger syndrome and high-functioning autism, the most common disorders are ADHD (before puberty) and depression (during adolescence). In addition, other disorders that can occur in this population include anxiety disorders, such as phobias and OCD. Movement disorders can also occur. Psychotic disorders are not common. However, some patients do develop schizophrenia and other types of psychotic illnesses. The most common cause of psychosis in autism is not schizophrenia but depression. Other disorders that sometimes occur in this population include gender identity disorder, Post-Traumatic Stress Disorder, and dissociative disorders.

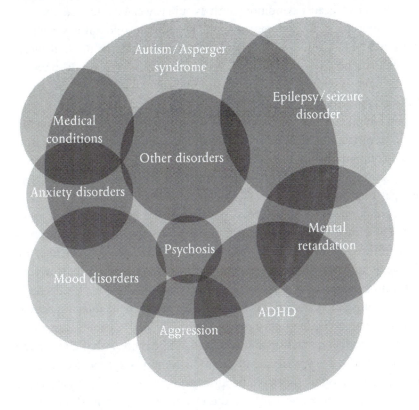

Figure 5.1 Comorbidity of autism and Asperger syndrome

Assessment

Despite the strides made in the field of diagnosis and detection of mental illness, there is no biologic test that can be done for diagnostic purposes. Psychiatric diagnosis continues to be clinical and is based on the traditional methods of obtaining a detailed history from a variety of sources, and doing a systematic mental status examination. Any individual who shows a decline in his level of functioning or anyone who shows a qualitative change in long-standing symptoms should be evaluated for the presence of additional psychiatric disorders. For example, if an adolescent starts crying frequently, loses interest in his usual hobbies, and becomes aggressive or disruptive he should be evaluated for a mood disorder. This is especially relevant if there is family history of a mood disorder, and a history of exposure to a negative life event such as bereavement.

A detailed physical examination should be performed not only because the presence of medical disorders increases the risk of psychiatric disorders in general, but also because conditions such as epilepsy can complicate the psychiatric symptoms. Care should, therefore, be taken to rule out any complicating physical factor that may account for or contribute to the behavioral symptoms. In people with marked verbal deficits, even minor physical problems, such as constipation, can result in behavioral symptoms and occasionally in aggressive outbursts. In rare cases, a serious underlying cause, such as a brain tumor, may be the reason for the disturbed behavior. In addition to a physical examination, laboratory investigations should be performed to rule out such common disorders as thyroid dysfunction, which can cause psychiatric symptoms. While intrusive laboratory tests are usually not indicated, investigations such as an EEG (electroencephalogram) or an ECG (electrocardiogram) may be helpful depending on the history and the examination. These investigations provide a baseline and also help in monitoring the side-effects of medications. Where clinically indicated, brain imaging studies (e.g. an MRI) should be performed (for example, in a patient with autism who becomes catatonic and who has a history of severe headaches).

Performing a mental status examination in a person with autism spectrum disorder can be a challenging exercise, especially if the patient (usually a child) is extremely hyperactive or aggressive; or if he is nonverbal. Even in the case of those who are verbal and higher-functioning, assessment of psychiatric symptoms is usually difficult, because of the tendency of the patients to give literal and concrete answers to the examiner's questions. Since some verbal patients may come across as higher-functioning than their actual level of functioning, their answers should be interpreted with caution. When examining those who have severe mental retardation and verbal deficits, attention should be paid to the presence of observed signs, such as weight loss and sleep disturbance.

Rating scales and structured instruments can be modified for use in this population. It is helpful to use a screening scale such as the Aberrant Behavior Checklist or the Reiss Scale (Reiss and Valenti-Hein, 1994), for persons with

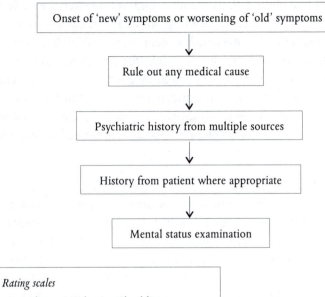

Rating scales
- Aberrant Behavior Checklist
- Reiss scales
- DASH–II
- Scales for specific symptoms
    - Hamilton for depression
    - Connors for ADHD
    - YMRS for bipolar disorder
    - YB-OCD Checklist
    - Other

Structured interviews
- SADS or K-SADS
- Other

DASH = Diagnostic Assessment for the Severely Handicapped–II
Hamilton = Hamilton Rating Scale for Depression
Connors = Connors Parent Teacher Rating Scale for ADHD
YMRS = Young Mania Rating Scale
YB-OCD = Yale Brown Obsessive Compulsive Disorder Checklist
SADS = Structured Assessment Depression and Schizophrenia (K=Kiddie)

Figure 5.2 An algorithm for assessment of psychiatric symptoms in persons with autism / Asperger syndrome

limited levels of functioning. Parents and care-givers are interviewed directly for the presence of symptoms. Depending on the initial clinical impression, rating scales for specific disorders, such as depression or ADHD, can be used. Structured interviews, such as the Schedule for Affective Disorders and Schizophrenia (Kaufman *et al.*, 1997), can be used with the help of parents or care-givers. Even though these instruments are not validated for use with persons with autism and Asperger syndrome, they assist in obtaining information and help the clinician in reaching a diagnosis, as illustrated in Figure 5.2.

Treatment

The treatment of psychiatric disorders in persons with autism and Asperger syndrome follows the principles of treatment of psychiatric disorders in general. The goal is to lessen distress and improve the quality of life, because people with autism have the same rights to treatment of psychiatric disorders as those without autism. There is no single treatment that works for all the patients. As a rule, multiple approaches are used, employing a wide range of services. These include psychological and social interventions, along with medications. These are discussed in Chapters 6 to 12 which deal with specific disorders.

Conclusion

Persons with autism are not immune from developing psychiatric disorders. Although epidemiological data are not available, clinical experience suggests that psychiatric disorders occur more commonly in autistic persons than in the rest of the population. While patients falling across the entire range of the autistic spectrum are affected, the disorders seem to be particularly common in those with PDDNOS. Patients with Asperger syndrome are also referred more commonly to psychiatric clinics; however, this might be because they are more verbal than those with traditional autism. Both children and adults are affected. A wide variety of psychiatric abnormalities can occur. The diagnosis and assessment of psychiatric disorders is difficult because most of these patients have problems with communication and many also have cognitive deficits such as mental retardation. Assessment depends to a large degree on demonstrating an onset of new symptoms and/or a qualitative change in the type and degree of existing symptoms. Treatment is symptomatic and is based on a multimodal approach employing both therapy and medications. Any contributory physical conditions, such as hypothyroidism, should be investigated. Untreated, these disorders complicate the course of the autism and Asperger syndrome and may even result in serious problems such as aggression towards self and others. Chapters 6 to 12 provide an overview of the presentation and the treatment of common psychiatric conditions in persons with autism spectrum disorders.

References

Angold, A., Costello, E. and Erkanli, A. (1999) 'Comorbidity.' *Journal of Child Psychology and Psychiatry, 40,* 1, 57–87.

APA (American Psychiatric Association) (1994) *Diagnostic and Statistical Manual of Mental Disorders, Fourth Edition* (DSM-IV). Washington, DC: APA.

Asperger, H. (1944) 'Die "autistischen Psychopathen" im Kindersalter.' *Archiv für Psychiatrie und Nervenkrankheiten, 117,* 76–136.

Bradley, E.A., Summers, J.A., Wood, H.L. and Bryson, S.E. (2004) 'Comparing rates of psychiatric and behavior disorders in adolescents and young adults with severe intellectual disability with and without autism.' *Journal of Autism and Developmental Disorders, 34,* 151–61.

Caron, C. and Rutter, M. (1991) 'Comorbidity in child psychopathology: Concepts, issues and research strategies.' *Journal of Child Psychology and Psychiatry, 32,* 7, 1063–80.

Frith, U. (1991) *Autism and Asperger Syndrome.* Cambridge, UK: Cambridge University Press.

Ghaziuddin, M., Tsai, L. and Ghaziuddin, N. (1992) 'Comorbidity of autistic disorder in children and adolescents.' *European Child and Adolescent Psychiatry, 1,* 209–213.

Ghaziuddin, M., Weidmer-Mikhail, E. and Ghaziuddin, N. (1998) 'Comorbidity of Asperger syndrome: A preliminary report.' *Journal of Intellectual Disability Research, 42,* 279–83.

Kanner, L. (1943) 'Autistic disturbances of affective contact.' *Nervous Child, 2,* 217–50.

Kaufman, J., Birmaher, B., Brent, D., Rao, U., Flynn, C., Moreci, P., Williamson, D. and Ryan, N. (1997) 'Schedule for Affective Disorders and Schizophrenia for School-Age Children – Present and Lifetime Version (K-SADS-PL): Initial reliability and validity data.' *Journal of the American Academy of Child and Adolescent Psychiatry, 36,* 980–8.

Matson, J.L., Gardner, W.I., Coe, D.A. and Sovner, R. (1991) 'A scale for evaluating emotional disorders in severely and profoundly mentally retarded persons. Development of the Diagnostic Assessment for the Severely Handicapped (DASH) scale.' *British Journal of Psychiatry, 159,* 404–409.

Reiss, S. and Valenti-Hein, D. (1994) 'Development of a psychopathology rating scale for children with mental retardation.' *Journal of Clinical and Consulting Psychology, 62,* 1, 28–33.

WHO (World Health Association) (1994) *International Classification of Disease, Tenth Edition* (ICD-10). Geneva: WHO.

Wing, L. (1981) 'Asperger's syndrome: A clinical account.' *Psychological Medicine, 11*, 115–29.

CHAPTER 6

Attention Deficit Hyperactivity Disorder

Introduction

Few psychiatric conditions have received as much attention in recent times as Attention Deficit Hyperactivity Disorder (ADHD). Sometimes referred to as 'ADD' (Attention Deficit Disorder) and 'hyperkinetic syndrome,' the central features of this condition are inattention, lack of concentration, impulsivity, and hyperactivity. The last symptom may not be present in all cases. Although primarily a disorder of children, it can occur in adolescents and adults. Since its early description in the late nineteenth century by Heinrich Hoffman, a German physician (see Thome and Jacobs, 2004), the disorder and its diagnostic criteria have undergone various revisions and refinements. The DSM-IV classifies it as a childhood-onset disorder with three main subtypes: hyperactive, inattentive, and the mixed types. In most cases patients have a combination of inattention and hyperactivity.

There has been a dramatic increase in the number of cases of ADHD in the US over the last few years. About 5 per cent of school-age children in the US meet the diagnosis of ADHD, making it by far the most common psychiatric condition in children. Even if allowance is made for local diagnostic practices, it is difficult to minimize the implications for treatment and provision of services. The extent of the problem is underscored by the growing number of prescriptions for stimulants, which are the most commonly used medications for this condition.

ADHD occurs in both sexes, although much more commonly in males. Gender differences exist in the pattern of symptoms. Girls with ADHD often present with the inattentive type of the disorder, and are less likely to be hyperactive and impulsive than boys. They are also at increased risk of social problems. In contrast, boys often present with more behavioral problems and associated conditions such as oppositional and conduct disorders (Biederman et al., 2002a, 2002b). Some children as young as 4 years old are referred for symptoms of hyperactivity and impulsivity, and the disorder is often diagnosed before the age of 7 years. It occurs in all cultures and countries, although the diagnosis is more frequently made in the west than in the developing world. Even among industrialized countries, there are important differences in the prevalence rates of the disorder. For example, the diagnosis is more commonly made in the US than in the UK (Thorley 1984). This may be due to differences in which diagnostic criteria are applied across countries.

As in other psychiatric disorders, the precise cause of ADHD is not known although a combination of genetic and environmental factors is involved. Family studies have shown a significant genetic contribution to the illness. The risk of ADHD is increased in first-degree relatives of patients with ADHD. Twin studies have also confirmed the role of genetic factors. Although preliminary, molecular genetic studies have implicated at least three genes: the D4 dopamine receptor gene, the dopamine transporter gene, and the D2 dopamine receptor gene (Faraone and Biederman, 1998). Environmental factors that may contribute to the symptoms of ADHD include pregnancy and delivery complications, marital distress, family dysfunction, and low social class. Toxins, such as alcohol, tobacco, and lead, have also been implicated. Studies have shown that children with fetal alcohol syndrome – many of whom have features of Pervasive Developmental Disorder Not Otherwise Specified (PDDNOS) – are at an increased risk for ADHD. In this condition, ADHD is more likely to be of the earlier-onset, inattention subtype, with comorbid developmental, psychiatric, and medical conditions (O'Malley and Nanson, 2002). Maternal smoking is probably an independent environmental risk factor to the development of hyperactivity in persons with an underlying genetic predisposition to ADHD. In a large population-based study, an association was found between maternal smoking during pregnancy and hyperactivity in childhood even after allowance was made for sex, family structure, socioeconomic status, maternal age, and maternal alcohol use (Kotimaa et al., 2003). Smokers are over-represented among both child and adult patients with ADHD. Despite their limitations, most of the studies suggest that maternal smoking is associated with ADHD in their offspring (Linnet et al., 2003). In addition to toxins, environmental and family adversity is also associated with an increased risk for ADHD. Psychosocial adversity in general and low social class, maternal psychopathology, and family conflict in particular, increase the risk for ADHD, especially in boys (Biederman et al., 2002a; 2002b). Other social factors that have been linked to the etiology of

ADHD include low birth weight, large family size, marital discord, low socioeconomic status, and paternal criminality.

Brain imaging studies have shown abnormalities in the frontal lobes, especially in the frontosubcortical pathways. Interestingly, these pathways are rich in catecholamines (chemicals produced by the brain and the adrenal glands), which have been implicated in ADHD by the mechanism of the action of stimulants. Neuropsychological studies have found deficits in executive functioning and in working memory. Of note, these kinds of deficits are not specific to ADHD and are found in a wide range of psychiatric disorders including autism.

The mainstay of treatment is psychopharmacological, although behavioral therapy is often used successfully in mild cases. Stimulants such as Ritalin are the most commonly used and are among the most researched medications. However, medications alone seldom help. Almost all patients need a combination of behavioral therapy and counseling.

The course of the disorder is variable. While many patients improve over time, a significant number continue to have problems even as adults. Undiagnosed ADHD in adults may contribute to maladaptive ways of functioning and to other forms of psychiatric comorbidity. Of the main symptoms of ADHD, hyperactivity is not often seen in adults, although problems with attention and concentration may persist. ADHD is associated with a wide range of psychiatric disorders, in particular, mood and disruptive behavioral disorders. These disorders influence the course of ADHD and also affect its long-term outcome. A significant number of patients with untreated ADHD go on to develop antisocial personality disorder. Academic failure and the breakdown of relationships are other important complications. Many people in the juvenile justice system suffer from this condition, although their exact numbers are not known.

ADHD and developmental disabilities

All those conditions that are associated with mental retardation and developmental disabilities increase the risk of ADHD. Indeed, any condition that affects the brain, and causes some degree of impairment, raises the risk for ADHD. In some cases, it is not possible to decide whether the behavior is the result of mental retardation or of superimposed ADHD. A significant number of persons with mental retardation are referred for psychiatric help because of their problems with hyperactivity and impulsivity. ADHD forms part of the behavioral phenotype of several chromosomal disorders. For example, patients with abnormalities of chromosome 15 (interstitial duplication of 15q11–q13) are often characterized by hyperactivity and impulsivity (Thomas *et al.*, 2003). Also, ADHD occurs more frequently in persons with epilepsy. For example, a recent population-based case-control study in Iceland found a twofold increase of ADHD in children with epilepsy (Hesdorffer *et al.*, 2004).

ADHD and pervasive developmental disorder (PDD)

Problems with attention and concentration are commonly seen in persons with autism, especially during childhood. Autistic children have difficulty in processing information. These deficits affect other areas of functioning and contribute substantially to the social and communication deficits seen in autism (Burack, Ennis and Johannes, 1997). However, attentional problems are not specific to ADHD, and can occur in a variety of conditions. Thus, a child who lacks motivation due to any reason may appear inattentive. Since other psychiatric disorders, such as depression and anxiety disorders, may also be accompanied by inattention, it is important to rule these out before arriving at a diagnosis of ADHD.

Similarly, problems with the level of activity are also frequently seen in persons with autism. Some autistic children are slow and passive in their movements, while others are active. Some appear overactive and intrusive. Most children who are overactive tend to slow down as they grow older and reach adulthood. In most cases, the intensity of symptoms is not severe enough to cause distress and impairment. However, in some cases, the symptoms are so severe that they cause significant impairment and meet the criteria for the diagnosis of ADHD.

It is not known why only some patients with autism and PDDs suffer from superimposed hyperactivity. Some patients may be genetically vulnerable and form a distinct subtype. Thus, the presence of ADHD in close relatives of subjects with autism increases the risk of that disorder. Some studies have implicated common chromosome regions in ADHD and autism. For example, there is evidence that genes on chromosomes 5p13, 16p13, and 17p11 are involved in the causes of both ADHD and autism (Ogdie *et al.*, 2003). Research has also shown that autism has a tendency to cluster with symptoms of hyperactivity and motor coordination. The clustering of these symptoms is sometimes referred to as the DAMP syndrome (deficits in motor coordination, attention and perception: Hellgren *et al.*, 1993). Many patients present with this pattern. In their epidemiologic study ofAsperger Syndrome (AS), Ehlers and Gillberg (1993) found that of the five definite cases of AS (ages 7–16 years), four met the criteria for DAMP (ADHD and motor performance dysfunction).

Prevalence

Exact estimates of the prevalence of ADHD in autism and Asperger syndrome are not available because of the lack of systematic community surveys and epidemiological studies. Indirect evidence for the increasing prevalence of hyperactivity and impulsivity in children with autism comes from autism clinics and from reports about the increasing use of medications in children with autism spectrum disorders. Surveys suggest that about 12 per cent of children with autism are prescribed stimulant medications (Aman *et al.*, 1995), despite the mistaken belief among some clinicians that stimulants do not work in patients with these disorders. Clinic reports suggest high rates of ADHD across the entire spectrum of pervasive developmental disorders. Both males and females are affected, although males are more often diagnosed. The presence of accompanying mental retardation also affects the diagnosis of ADHD. Those who have severe mental retardation are less likely to be diagnosed as having ADHD even in the presence of extreme hyperactivity and impulsivity, because of the assumption that these symptoms cannot reliably be distinguished from cognitive impairment. For example, in a consecutive series of 69 subjects with DSM-III-R autistic disorder, 57 of whom had mental retardation, 6 subjects were given a diagnosis of a comorbid psychiatric disorder. Three patients were diagnosed as suffering from a mood disorder; one from an Obsessive-Compulsive Disorder (OCD) and one from a tic disorder. None was given a diagnosis of ADHD. This was because the diagnosis of ADHD could not be made confidently because of the presence of mental retardation (Ghaziuddin, Tsai and Ghaziuddin, 1992).

The diagnosis of ADHD can be made with a reasonable degree of confidence in those who are higher-functioning and in those with Asperger syndrome, however. Thus, in a consecutive series of 35 patients with Asperger syndrome, aged 8–51 years, diagnosed according to the official criteria, 23 out of 35 subjects (66%) were rated positive for a comorbid psychiatric disorder. The two most common diagnoses were ADHD and depression (including major depression, dysthymia, and bipolar disorder). Ten patients were diagnosed with ADHD, 13 with depression (8 with major depression, 4 with dysthymia, and 1 with bipolar disorder), 1 with Tourette syndrome, 1 with OCD and 1 with tic disorder. Three patients had two diagnoses each (one had ADHD with major depression, 1 had OCD with major depression and another had tic disorder with dysthymia). The findings were further analyzed based on two age groups: pre-adolescents (6–12 years) and adolescents and adults (over 13 years of age). In the younger group (n = 20), 10 patients (50%) had a diagnosis of ADHD; 4 of depression and 1 patient was diagnosed with both ADHD and depression. In the older age group (n = 15), 8 had a diagnosis of depression and 1 each of ADHD, OCD, Tourette syndrome and tic disorder. In 2 patients, the diagnosis of an additional psychiatric disorder was unclear. Thus, ADHD was a common diagnosis in persons with Asperger syndrome, especially before the age of puberty (Ghaziuddin, Weidmer-Mikhail and Ghaziuddin, 1998).

In those with PDDNOS, especially in those who are referred for psychiatric attention, ADHD is almost always diagnosed as a comorbid condition. It is important to note that the few studies that have investigated the comorbidity of autism have tended to exclude subjects with PDDNOS. For example, in the study by Ghaziuddin *et al.* (1992), subjects with PDDNOS (n = 19) were excluded. Thus, if patients with PDDNOS are included, the rates of hyperactivity and impulsivity rise even further among those with autism spectrum disorders.

Presentation of ADHD in PDD

Despite DSM-IV's caveat that ADHD should not be diagnosed concurrently with autism (APA, 1994), children with autism often present with hyperactivity and impulsivity. In fact, these symptoms are probably the most common reason for short-term admission to psychiatric units. Usually, the symptoms of ADHD are mixed with those of other disorders, such as depression and anxiety. This is illustrated by the following case studies.

Case study: Daniel

Daniel is an 11-year-old Caucasian youngster with autism and mild mental retardation. He was referred to the emergency room of the hospital because of severe aggressive behavior. He had severely assaulted a peer after losing a race in the 'special' Olympics for children with disabilities. He was angry and disruptive, and could not be contained at home. In the hospital, he was constantly 'on the go.' He needed close and continuous supervision because he refused to follow directions.

In the hospital-school, he would constantly fidget in his seat, interrupt others, and walk around the classroom aimlessly. He had been diagnosed with autism when he was about 4 years old. Apart from his social and communication deficits, he was always in trouble for his intrusive, hyperactive, and aggressive behavior. His family history was positive for ADHD; one of his siblings had been diagnosed with ADHD and was on stimulant medications. His medical history was otherwise unremarkable. There was no history of seizure disorder.

On examination, he was found to be hyperactive and disruptive with marked problems in remaining focused. His overall symptoms were beyond what would be expected for an autistic child of his age and his level of functioning. Therefore, in addition to autistic disorder, he was given a diagnosis of ADHD because symptoms of the latter disorder were the main focus of clinical attention. He was placed on a combination of behavioral therapy and medications. A week after admission to hospital, his symptoms of hyperactivity and impulsivity were much improved, along with the level of aggression.

Presentation of PDD as ADHD

Patients with autism spectrum disorders are sometimes misdiagnosed as suffering from ADHD. This is likely to occur when the patients are relatively high-functioning and do not suffer from mental retardation. Patients with Asperger syndrome are included in this category. Based on his experience with five patients, Perry (1998) described the characteristics of PDD patients who are mislabeled as ADHD. None of the patients in the series was retarded, and, although some had a history of delay or deviance in early language, verbal skills were reported to be grossly intact by the end of their preschool years. The symptoms appeared to become more prominent with age. The most important signs that suggested underlying PDD were unusual interests and extreme preoccupations. All met the criteria of Asperger syndrome at the time of the examination and two may have met the criteria for autism in the past (Perry, 1998).

It is possible that Asperger syndrome is more likely to be misdiagnosed as ADHD than is traditional autism. As discussed earlier, persons with Asperger syndrome are more likely to be active but odd, rather than aloof and passive. The clinical implication of this is clear. Children with ADHD who do not respond to the usual interventions, and who suffer from social deficits, should be screened for the presence of Asperger syndrome. Also, since an increasing number of adults are now being diagnosed with ADHD, symptoms of

Asperger syndrome should be looked for in patients presenting to adult ADHD clinics. The same applies for patients with PDDNOS.

Case study: John

John is a 13-year-old Caucasian youngster who was referred for a psychiatric evaluation for his hyperactivity, impulsivity, and his difficulty in making friends. He had never been diagnosed with autism, although he was known for being somewhat 'different' from others.

The first symptoms to arouse concern were hyperactivity and impulsivity. He was diagnosed with ADHD at the age of 4 years and was placed on Ritalin. After this, he apparently became 'mute in school' and also developed motor tics (repeatedly blinking and stroking his hair). His medication was changed to Adderall, another stimulant related to Ritalin. Also, an additional diagnosis of tic disorder was given. A small dose of an antipsychotic medication (Risperdal) was also added. Although the medications slowed him down, he continued to have problems in the classroom.

Around the same time, it emerged that he was extremely afraid of certain social situations, such as crowds, and heights. The psychiatrist thought he had a phobic disorder and gave an additional diagnosis of an anxiety disorder. Another medication, Zoloft (sertraline) was added to the Adderall and Risperdal. John, however, continued to have problems in the classroom with attention and concentration. In addition, as he grew older, he seemed to stand out from others. He was somewhat shy and avoidant, and did not enjoy interacting with others. He had no close friends. He was known as a loner. Subsequently, with the onset of puberty, he seemed to become increasingly depressed. He was having frequent crying spells, and talking about being different from others, feeling sad and distressed, and sometimes wishing that he was never born. Subsequently, another diagnosis, depression, was added. By the time John was 12 years of age, he had a string of diagnoses – ADHD, tic disorder, anxiety disorder, and depression. At this time, his parents read an article on autism and decided that he should be evaluated for it.

During the course of the evaluation it emerged that John had always had problems with social interaction. He was isolative and seemed not to understand social cues. His other diagnoses, ADHD and anxiety disorder, appeared to mask his social deficits. In addition, his eye contact was inconsistent, which was attributed to his being 'shy' and 'anxious.' Also, he had a restricted range of interests; for example, he was on the computer playing games for extended periods of time. While these interests were not intrusive, in the sense that he would leave the computer albeit with some difficulty, they did distract him from other meaningful activities. Based on the combination of social and communication deficits, along with restricted interests, a diagnosis of autism was considered. However, since the interests were not overwhelming, and since John's general level of functioning was not substantially impaired, it was felt that he met only the partial criteria for autism. He was, therefore, given a diagnosis of PDDNOS (in addition to his other diagnoses).

The two case studies describing Daniel and John illustrate different aspects of the comorbidity of autism with ADHD. In the first case, the diagnosis of autism was already known. Many younger patients with autism present with hyperactivity and impulsivity that do not respond to traditional behavioral methods, and that make other aspects of treatment difficult if not impossible. No amount of social skills training can work if the child is bouncing off the walls! The second case illustrates how the diagnosis of PDD is missed in some children whose main symptoms are hyperactivity and impulsivity. Additionally, this case highlights the fact that multiple conditions are not uncommon in children with autism spectrum disorders.

So far as the presentation of ADHD in lower-functioning persons with PDD is concerned, the clinical presentation here is often dominated by aggression and temper tantrums. These behaviors consist of pushing, kicking, and biting, and are often exacerbated by changes in the environment and other significant life events. Quite often, other physical complications, such as seizure disorder, are also present.

Case study: Shawna

Shawna is a 15-year-old African-American female with a diagnosis of autism and mental retardation. She was admitted to the child psychiatry inpatient unit because of her increasing aggression directed against caregivers both at home and at school. She was nonverbal and her level of retardation was severe. She had a history of past seizure disorder. Her behaviors appeared to have escalated in the three months prior to her admission; there was no history of any significant life events, except for the onset of menarche about six months prior to admission. The family history was positive for learning disabilities and ADHD, which some of her siblings had.

On examination, Shawna was extremely hyperactive and impulsive, repeatedly moving and sometimes attacking staff if she was restrained. On examination, she constantly moved her head from side to side, as if it soothe herself. There was no evidence of akathisia (restlessness resulting from med- ications), tics, or any other types of abnormal movements. She was fidgety, impulsive, and overactive. She walked constantly round the ward. Her mood was irritable but only when she was crossed. Although Shawna did not carry a formal diagnosis of ADHD, it was the hyperactivity that was the main presenting symptom along with aggression.

Diagnosis

One of the qualifiers for the diagnosis of ADHD in the DSM-IV system of classification is that the symptoms 'do not occur exclusively during the course of a Pervasive Developmental Disorder' (APA, 1994, p.85). This assumes that if the symptoms of ADHD occur 'during the course' of PDD, then the diagnosis of ADHD should not be given; that the course of PDD is time-limited; and that there is an inherent overlap between the symptoms of ADHD and those of PDD. These assumptions are not supported by clinical evidence because of the following reasons.

First, the symptoms of ADHD may form the focus of clinical intervention, and may be more important than the symptoms of PDD. Both the disorders occur across a wide range of severity, thus, even in the case of a child with autism, hyperactivity, and impulsivity may be the presenting problems that need more immediate attention than any problems with socialization and communication. Therefore, to deny the diagnosis of ADHD in a child with autism, especially if there is evidence of a recent worsening in the symptoms of hyperactivity and impulsivity, is not helpful from a clinical standpoint. The co-occurrence of ADHD and PDD calls for a different set of treatment inter- ventions.

Second, the course of PDD is life-long. The symptoms persist, even in those who are high-functioning or very mildly impaired. Although the severity of symptoms decreases over time, the patient is often left with residual symptoms. Complete resolution of symptoms occurs rarely, if at all. Therefore, to deny that there may be a diagnosis of ADHD simply because the symptoms appear 'during the course' of PDD is not accurate.

Third, the symptoms of ADHD do not form part of PDD. Some children with autism and Asperger syndrome are not hyperactive or impulsive, nor do they show problems with attention and concentration. Only a subset of patients with these conditions suffer from additional symptoms that meet the criteria for ADHD (Ghaziuddin and Tsai, 1995). Therefore, when the symptoms of ADHD and PDD occur together, they should be diagnosed separately.

Symptoms of hyperactivity and inattention can, of course, occur in a variety of psychiatric conditions, and these should be ruled out systematically. For example, it is common for a child with depression to appear inattentive and distractible. The child is so preoccupied with his depressive thoughts and feelings that he does not pay attention to what is being taught in the class. This is particularly true of patients who are higher-functioning. Inattention can also occur in other conditions, such as anxiety disorder. Similarly, hyperactivity can occur in other conditions as well, such as psychotic disorders. Sometimes, side-effects caused by such medications as haloperidol may present as hyperactivity. It is important, therefore, that any child with autism/Asperger syndrome who presents with the symptoms of hyperactivity and inattention is carefully evaluated for the presence of other psychiatric disorders such as depression.

The diagnosis of ADHD, as in the presence of other types of psychiatric disorders in PDD, rests on the onset of the symptoms and a history of recent worsening. Rating scales should be completed with the help of the parents and the care-givers to provide a baseline before intervention and also to monitor progress over time. Scales that are commonly used are the Aberrant Behavior Checklist (Aman et al., 1985) and the Conners Parent–Teacher Scale (Conners et al., 1988). Instruments such as the Reiss scales (1990) may be used with patients with mental retardation. Structured interviews can also be used, an example being the SADS-PL (Kaufman et al., 2000). These scales and interviews help in the systematic collection of data so that a diagnosis may be reached, and also help in monitoring the effects of treatments.

Medical factors that may account for the hyperactivity should be ruled out. As discussed elsewhere, some children with thyroid dysfunction can present with hyperactivity. This includes both hyper- and hypothyroidism. Accordingly, any child with suspected ADHD should have a thyroid function test. An EEG is indicated if seizures are suspected. Seizures are not always full-blown in nature with loss of consciousness and fits. Although a negative EEG is not helpful, a positive EEG (that is, one with abnormal findings) is diagnostic. Apart from select biological tests, the patient should undergo a complete neuropsychological assessment. The purpose is to assess the patient's level of intelligence and to observe how he performs tests specifically suited for the detection of the symptoms of ADHD. These include tests of attention and concentration such as the Continuous Performance Test

(Conners, 1985). Finally, a comprehensive family assessment should also be performed to investigate the possible contribution of family stressors to the symptoms of ADHD. Thus, the assessment of ADHD in persons with autism and Asperger syndrome requires input from several sources, including teachers, parents, social agencies, and others who may be involved in the care of the child, and should not be based on a brief interview in the doctor's office.

Complications

If untreated, symptoms of hyperactivity and impulsivity almost always interfere with learning and with the acquisition of social skills. It is difficult, if at all possible, to try behavioral interventions and other treatments if a child is so overwhelmed with his symptoms that he cannot even remain still. Impulsivity and distractibility lead to aggressive outbursts and tantrums especially if the demands are not satisfied immediately. Additional disorders, such as substance abuse, can also occur in those individuals who are labeled as PDDNOS or those who have normal levels of functioning. Finally, the symptoms result in marked distress to the care-givers.

Treatment

As in any other neuropsychiatric condition, the treatment of persons with autism and Asperger syndrome who suffer from additional symptoms of ADHD combines both behavioral and medication approaches. While milder symptoms of hyperactivity and impulsivity may respond to behavioral intervention alone, in most cases psychopharmacological methods play an important role.

Medications

A variety of medications is currently used for the treatment of ADHD. This applies to both persons without autism, and those with autism, although information in the latter category is much more limited. Medications can be divided into two broad categories: stimulants and non-stimulants.

Stimulants are the oldest type of drugs used in the treatment of ADHD. They are also the most widely researched and the most commonly used. These include such commonly used medications as Ritalin, Adderall, and Concerta.

Non-stimulant medications are of several types. These include the newly released atomoxetine (Strattera), and more traditional antidepressants, such as Tofranil. Other types of medications that are sometimes used either on their own or in combination with stimulants include selective serotonin reuptake inhibitors, such as fluoxetine (Prozac) and sertraline (Zoloft), and atypical antidepressants, such as trazodone (Desyrel). In addition, antipsychotic medications, such as haloperidol (Haldol) and risperidone (Risperdal), are also sometimes used to help organize the child and decrease impulsivity. This is particularly the case in those autistic persons who also suffer from severe mental retardation or those who are aggressive and disruptive. Anticonvulsants are also sometimes used for the treatment of hyperactivity in autistic persons and to stabilize their mood; they include drugs such as carbamazepine (Tegretol) and valproic acid (Depakote). Other types of medications that are sometimes used include Clonidine, a drug used for the control of blood pressure.

It is important to note that the medications may themselves cause hyperactivity, and have other kinds of side-effects, such as sleep and appetite disturbance, weight disturbance, onset of tics, excessive drowsiness, and falls in blood pressure. In addition, medications may also cause adverse interactions when used together. Thus, it is advisable to decrease the dose and monitor the patients closely so they can be maintained on the lowest effective dose. Some authorities suggest the need for brief periods when such medications as Ritalin are discontinued. Sometimes referred to as 'drug holidays,' these periods often occur during vacations or weekends. The assumption is that taking the child off the medications at least during some periods of time is better than not discontinuing the medications at all. However, drug holidays are not always effective. In fact, the fluctuating drug levels can sometimes cause chaos and disruption, especially during times, such as vacations, when family members are more likely to spend time together. In addition to the core symptoms of ADHD, medical conditions, such as thyroid dysfunction and seizure disorder, should be treated. Finally, since other psychiatric symptoms such as depression and anxiety often coexist with those of ADHD, these should be carefully looked for and aggressively treated.

Recent surveys have shown that stimulants are widely prescribed for persons with autism and related conditions. For example, Martin and colleagues found that stimulants were the second most frequently used drugs by persons with higher-functioning forms of autism, including Asperger syndrome (1999). Earlier reports had suggested that stimulants are not effective in these conditions. In fact, there have been some reports claiming that stimulants do more harm than good in the setting of autism. This is not necessarily true (Birmaher, Quintana and Greenhill, 1988; Handen, Johnson and Lubetsky, 2000). The adverse response to Ritalin and other stimulants seen in some children with ADHD and autism may be linked more to the presence of seizure disorder and other medical complications than to the diagnosis of autism. For example, a child with severe mental retardation, extreme hyperactivity, and a difficult-to-treat seizure disorder, may respond adversely to Ritalin, compared to another who is of normal intelligence, has no complicating medical factors, and whose main symptoms are hyperactivity and inattention. Sometimes, stimulants and the other medications mentioned above may not be sufficient to calm a child with extreme hyperactivity and impulsivity. It is not uncommon to hear statements describing such children as being 'driven like an engine.' When this occurs, stronger medications, such as antipsychotic drugs, are sometimes used. Medications used in this category include Risperdal (risperidone) and Geodon (ziprasidone), as discussed in Chapter 1.

Behavioral therapy

Along with medications, psychosocial interventions should also be considered. Although there are several types of psychotherapy, it is important to emphasize the role of consistency, structure, supervision, and support. The mainstay of the treatment of ADHD is behavioral therapy. For children with both ADHD and autism/Asperger syndrome, insight-oriented psychotherapy is rarely employed, if at all. The focus of the treatment is on the 'here and now,' and on the immediate antecedents and consequences of behavior. The objective is to minimize the chances of maladaptive behavior by making use of structure, redirection, and support. This is particularly true in patients with concomitant mental retardation. In fact, many of the same principles of behavioral intervention used with persons with mental retardation are also effective when autism occurs with mental retardation. Finally, family factors that may contribute to the symptoms, such as discord and abuse, should be identified and addressed.

Outcome

In general, the outcome of untreated ADHD is poor. Despite the fact that some patients 'grow out of it,' untreated ADHD results in significant distress both to the child and to the family. Academic failure is common, and so is a tendency to antisocial behavior. Studies have shown a strong association between ADHD and antisocial disorder.

The outcome of ADHD in autism and Asperger syndrome is not known, beyond the general assumption that untreated hyperactivity and impulsivity in children with autism interferes with their schooling and subsequent adjustment in the community. It is not clear if high-functioning people with autism, or those with Asperger syndrome, who have additional ADHD, are liable to criminal behavior and antisocial disorder as adults. However, clinical experience suggests that adults with autism and Asperger syndrome who present with problems in living independently often have histories of ADHD-like symptoms in childhood.

Conclusion

Children with autism spectrum disorders often present with symptoms of inattention, hyperactivity, and impulsivity. Individually, these symptoms can occur in a variety of psychiatric disorders, such as depression and anxiety disorders. Some medical conditions also present with these behaviors. However, in ADHD, the symptoms cluster together often without any discernable underlying cause. Disruptive behavior, which often includes hyperactivity, constitutes the most common reason for psychiatric referral of autistic youngsters. In some cases, the symptoms are severe enough to justify an additional diagnosis of ADHD, even though the diagnostic manuals, such as the DSM, recommend against giving this in the context of autism.

The diagnosis of ADHD is difficult, especially in the case of those autistic children who fall in the severe range of mental retardation, and of those who suffer from other medical and psychiatric conditions, such as epilepsy. The condition is often missed in some patients with milder symptoms of autism, and in those who do not meet the full criteria for that syndrome (PDDNOS). At times, persons with high-functioning autism and Asperger syndrome are misdiagnosed as suffering from ADHD. Assessment of ADHD should include a systematic attempt to rule out both medical and psychiatric conditions; in particular, seizure disorder, hypothyroidism, and depression. Treatment consists of a combination of medications and psychotherapy, particularly behavioral intervention. A variety of medications is used, particularly stimulants. There is no hard evidence that stimulants such as Ritalin do not work in children with autism. Side-effects are more likely to occur in those who have complicating medical conditions such as epilepsy. The principles of behavior therapy consist of providing structure and support. In higher-functioning individuals, other forms of brief therapy may also be helpful. While no systematic studies have specifically focused on the outcome of children with joint ADHD and PDD, clinical experience suggests that those autistic children who are hyperactive and disruptive, and those who are left untreated, often do worse over the long term, which underscores the need for early diagnosis and treatment.

References

Aman, M.G., Singh, N.N., Stewart, A.W. and Field, C.J. (1985) 'Psychometric characteristics of the aberrant behaviour checklist.' *American Journal of Mental Deficiency, 89*, 5, 492–502.

Aman, M.G., Van Bourondier, M.E., Wolford, P.L., and Sarphare, G. (1995) 'Psychotropic and anticonvulsant drugs in subjects with autism: Prevalence and patterns of use.' *Journal of the American Academy of Child and Adolescent Psychiatry, 34*, 12, 1672–81.

APA (American Psychiatric Association) (1994) *Diagnostic and Statistical Manual of Mental Disorders, Fourth Edition* (DSM-IV). Washington, DC: APA.

Biederman, J., Faraone, S.V. and Monuteaux, M.C. (2002a) 'Differential effect of environmental adversity by gender: Rutter's index of adversity in a group of boys and girls with and without ADHD.' *American Journal of Psychiatry, 159*, 1556–62.

Biederman, J., Mick, E., Faraone, S.V., Braaten, E., Doyle, A., Spencer, T., Wilens, T.E., Frazier, E. and Johnson, M.A. (2002b) 'Influence of gender on attention deficit hyperactivity disorder in children referred to a psychiatric clinic.' *American Journal of Psychiatry, 159*, 1, 36–42.

Birmaher, B., Quintana, H. and Greenhill, H.L. (1988) 'Methylphenidate treatment of hyperactive autistic children.' *Journal of the American Academy of Child and Adolescent Psychiatry, 27*, 241–51.

Burack, J.A., Ennis, J.T. and Johannes, E.A. (1997) 'Attention and autism: behavioral and electrophysiological evidence.' In D.J. Cohen and F.R. Volkmar (eds) *Handbook of Autism and Pervasive Developmental Disorders.* New Jersey: John Wiley and Sons.

Conners, C.K. (1985) 'The computerized continuous performance test.' *Psychopharmacology Bulletin, 21*, 4, 891–2.

Conners, C.K., Sitarenios, G., Parker, J.D. and Epstein, J.N. (1988) 'The revised Conners' Parent Rating Scale (CPRS-R): Factor structure, reliability, and criterion validity.' *Journal of Abnormal Child Psychology, 26*, 4, 257–68.

Ehlers, S. and Gillberg, C. (1993) 'The epidemiology of Asperger syndrome. A total population study.' *Journal of Child Psychology and Psychiatry, 34*, 8, 1327–50.

Faraone, S.V. and Biederman, J. (1998) 'Neurobiology of attention deficit hyperactivity disorder.' *Biological Psychiatry, 44*, 10, 951–8.

Ghaziuddin, M. and Tsai, L. (1995) 'PDD changes in DSM-IV.' *Journal of the American Academy of Child and Adolescent Psychiatry, 34*, 3, 264–5.

Ghaziuddin, M. Tsai, L. and Ghaziuddin, N. (1992) 'Comorbidity of autistic disorder.' *European Child and Adolescent Psychiatry, 1*, 4, 209–213.

Ghaziuddin, M., Weidmer-Mikhail, E. and Ghaziuddin, N. (1998) 'Comorbidity of Asperger syndrome: A preliminary report.' *Journal of Intellectual Disability Research, 42*, 4, 279–83.

Handen, B.L., Johnson, C.R. and Lubetsky, M. (2000) 'Efficacy of methylphenidate among children with autism and symptoms of Attention Deficit Hyperactivity Disorder.' *Journal of Autism and Developmental Disorders, 30*, 3, 245–55.

Hellgren, L., Gillberg, C., Gillberg, I.C. and Enerskog, I. (1993) 'Children with deficits in attention, motor control and perception (DAMP) almost grown up: General health at 16 years.' *Developmental Medicine and Child Neurology, 35*, 881–92.

Hesdorffer, D.C., Ludvigsson, P., Olafsson, E., Gudmundsson, G., Kjartansson, O. and Hauser, W.A. (2004) 'ADHD as a risk factor for incident unprovoked seizures and epilepsy in children.' *Archives of General Psychiatry, 61*, 7, 731–6.

Kaufman, J., Birmaher, B., Brent, D., Ryan, N.D. and Rao, U. (2000) 'K-SADS-PL.' *Journal of the American Academy of Child and Adolescent Psychiatry, 39*, 10, 1208.

Kotimaa, A.R., Moilanen, I., Taanila, A., Ebeling, H., Smalley, S., McGough, J.J., Hartikainen, A. and Jarvelin, M. (2003) 'Maternal smoking and hyperactivity in 8-year-old children.' *Journal of the American Academy of Child and Adolescent Psychiatry, 42*, 7, 826–33.

Linnet, K.M., Dalsgaard, S., Obel, C., Wisborg, K., Henriksen, T.B., Rodriguez, A., Kotimaa, A., Moilanen, I., Thomsen, P.H., Olsen, J. and Jarvelin, M.R. (2003) 'Maternal lifestyle factors in pregnancy risk of attention deficit hyperactivity disorder and associated behaviors: Review of the current evidence.' *American Journal of Psychiatry, 160*, 1028–40.

Martin, A., Scahill, L., Klin, A. and Volkmar, F. (1999) 'Higher-functioning pervasive developmental disorders: Rates and patterns of psychotropic drug abuse.' *Journal of the American Academy of Child and Adolescent Psychiatry, 38*, 923–31.

Ogdie, M.N., Macphie, I.L., Minassian, S.L., Yang, M., Fisher, S.E., Francks, C., Cantor, R.M., McCracken, J.T., McGough, J.J., Nelson, S.F., Monaco, A.P. and Smalley, S.L. (2003) 'A genomewide scan for attention-deficit/hyperactivity disorder in an extended sample: Suggestive linkage on 17p11.' *American Journal of Human Genetics, 72*, 5, 1268–79.

O'Malley, K.D. and Nanson, J. (2002) 'Clinical implications of a link between fetal alcohol spectrum disorder and attention-deficit hyperactivity disorder.' *Canadian Journal of Psychiatry, 47*, 349–54.

Perry, R. (1998) 'Misdiagnosed ADD/ADHD: Rediagnosed PDD.' *Journal of the American Academy of Child and Adolescent Psychiatry, 37*, 1, 113–14.

Reiss, S. (1990) *Reiss Scales for Children's Dual Diagnosis (Mental Retardation and Psychopathology)*. Worthington, OH: International Diagnostic Systems.

Thomas, J.A., Johnson, J., Peterson Kraai, T.L., Wilson, R., Tartaglia, N., LeRoux, J., Beischel, L., McGavran, L. and Hagerman, R.J. (2003) 'Genetic and clinical characterization of patients with an interstitial duplication 15q11–q13, emphasizing behavioral phenotype and response to treatment.' *American Journal of Medical Genetics, 1*, 119A, 111–20.

Thome, J. and Jacobs, K.A. (2004) 'Attention deficit hyperactivity disorder in a 19th century children's book.' *European Psychiatry, 19*, 5, 303–306.

Thorley, G. (1984) 'Hyperkinetic syndrome of childhood: clinical characteristics.' *British Journal of Psychiatry, 144*, 16–24.

CHAPTER 7

Depression and Other Mood Disorders

Introduction

Mood disorders are the most common psychiatric disorders that occur in the general population. They form a group of disorders characterized by a disturbance of mood (inappropriate depression or elation), and by a range of physical and psychological symptoms. These disorders occur across all countries and cultures, although with some differences in the pattern and frequency of their symptoms. (For instance, depressed patients in Asian and African countries more often report physical symptoms and health concerns than those in the west.) Historically, mood disorders have been classified in several ways: endogenous versus exogenous, neurotic versus psychotic, primary versus secondary, etc. In addition to several minor subtypes, the present revision of the DSM/ICD systems of classification divides mood disorders into two broad categories: 'major depression' and 'bipolar disorder.' Major depression (or 'depression' as it is more commonly called) is characterized by a depressed mood which is qualitatively different from normal sadness. Bipolar disorder (sometimes referred to as 'manic depression') is defined by its cyclical nature characterized by alternating periods of excessive sadness and happiness.

According to the National Institute of Mental Health, depression affects about 10 per cent of adults in the US in any given year: that is at least 15 million men and women. Prior to puberty, males and females are equally affected; however, after puberty, the rates among women double, because of social or hormonal factors or both. The usual age of onset is late adolescence or early adulthood, although depression can begin at any time during the life span. Its common features are a persistently depressed mood lasting at least for a few weeks, disturbance of sleep and appetite, crying spells, and thoughts of self-harm. Vague bodily symptoms, such as headaches and fatigue, are common, as are problems at work and in marriage. In extreme cases death results from self-neglect or suicide. However, many mild cases go unrecognized. Chronic mild depression is labeled as 'dysthymia.' One of the main features of mild depression is irritability, which may be more pronounced in children than in adults. Apart from this difference, the symptoms of childhood depression are remarkably similar to those of adult depression. In the elderly, depression is more often accompanied by physical symptoms such as weight loss, preoccupation with bodily functions, feelings of guilt, and loss of self-esteem.

The cardinal feature of bipolar disorder is its cyclical nature. It is less common than major depression, occurring in about 1–2 per cent of the population. Both males and females are equally affected. Cycles of elation alternate with cycles of depressed mood. In younger patients, elation may be substituted by anger and irritability. Along with the mood disturbance, the patient typically shows an impairment of judgment leading to risk taking and other offending behaviors. Previously, it was believed that typical cycles of bipolar disorder lasted for several weeks; however, increasing evidence suggests that the cycles can be much shorter in duration, when the condition is labeled as a 'rapid cycling bipolar disorder.' Sometimes, these cycles can occur during the same day, making the diagnosis particularly difficult. Bipolar disorder itself is subdivided into at least two categories: bipolar I and bipolar II, depending on the severity. Other categories include cyclothymia and 'bipolar disorder not otherwise specified'. Most cases of bipolar disorder begin in early adulthood. Children suffering from bipolar disorder present with distinct features, including rage attacks ('affective storms'), a high comorbidity with Attention Deficit Hyperactivity Disorder (ADHD) and disruptive behavior disorders, and a chronic course. Depression is usually not the presenting symptom for children with bipolar disorder. Although the mean age of onset for a first manic episode is the early 20s, there is a growing trend to diagnose bipolar disorder in children, sometimes as young as 3 to 4 years of age. To what extent children so young can indeed suffer from bipolar disorder in the traditional sense – and reliably diagnosed – remains unclear and controversial.

Causes of depression

The causes of depression are several. Like other psychiatric disorders, these include a variety of genetic and environmental factors, with the bulk of the evidence pointing to a gene–environment interaction (Kendler, Karkowski and Prescott, 1999). Several family and twin studies have established the genetic roots of mood disorders. Adults with depression are more likely to have children with the same disorder, and depressed children are more likely to have depressed parents. Also, the earlier the onset of depression in children, the stronger is the likelihood of a family history of the disorder. Molecular genetic studies have highlighted areas of interest on several chromosomes, such as chromosomes 11, 21, and 22. Studies have long stressed the role of neurotransmitters in the etiology of depression. While a great deal of interest and attention have recently focused on the role of serotonin, other neurotransmitters, such as dopamine, are also involved. Imaging studies of the brain have revealed a wide array of abnormalities. While global atrophy of the brain is not often seen, a decrease in the volume of the frontal lobe, the cerebellum, and parts of the basal ganglia have been described in some types of depression (Soares and Mann, 1997). Changes in the volume of the amygdala and the hippocampus have also been reported. Unfortunately, as with most other psychiatric disorders, these findings are neither specific to mood disorders nor are they consistently seen in all patients. Several studies over the decades have also established the role of environmental stressors in the onset of depression. Painful and distressing life events, such as bereavement and divorce, can contribute to the disorder. Although the response to unpleasant life events itself can have genetic underpinnings, it should be noted that sometimes apparently pleasant events can also trigger a bout of depression. So far as the effect of life events on the pattern of symptoms is concerned, it is important to note that all cases of depression, whether or not precipitated by external events, have the same symptoms and respond to the same general treatments.

Course and treatment

Most types of mood disorders are self-limited in their course, while others tend to become recurrent and cyclical in nature. About 25 per cent of patients with major depression experience a switch to bipolar disorder during their lifetime. Sometimes, this switch is precipitated by the use of antidepressants or by significant life events. A substantial number of depressed patients suffer from other psychiatric disorders such as anxiety disorders and substance abuse. Although somewhat controversial, recent studies have suggested links between some forms of ADHD and bipolar disorder (Biederman *et al.*, 2000; Faraone *et al.*, 1997). Some authorities believe that severe ADHD that is accompanied by rage attacks and aggressive outbursts represents a distinct form of bipolar disorder.

The treatment of depression and other mood disorders includes a combination of medications and psychotherapy. Studies have shown that the response to treatment is better when both forms of intervention are combined. While several types of antidepressants exist, the most popular currently are the serotonin receptor uptake inhibitors (SSRIs), such as fluoxetine (Prozac), as discussed in Chapter 1.

The present chapter reviews the literature on the occurrence of mood disorders in persons with autism and Asperger syndrome. The focus is on major depression and, to a lesser extent, on bipolar disorder. Other types of mood disorders such as dysthymia, Seasonal Affective Disorder (SAD), and post-partum depression, are outside the scope of this book and are not discussed here.

Depression in people with autism and Asperger syndrome

There have been increasing reports of the occurrence of depression in persons with autism and Asperger syndrome. Although symptoms suggestive of depression can be gleaned from early case descriptions of autism, its presence was often dismissed as an incidental finding. For example, at least one child in Kanner's original series had a tendency to lapse into a 'momentary fit of depression' (Kanner, 1943, p.241). Also, many of the children described by Asperger (1944) had features suggestive of mild depression. While several recent reports have focused on this topic, most professionals who work in the field tend to miss the diagnosis (see Ghaziuddin and Greden, 1998; Lainhart and Folstein, 1994).

Prevalence

Systematic population-based studies of the prevalence of depression in persons with autism spectrum disorders have not been performed. However, reports from autism clinics and psychiatric units suggest that depression is probably the most common psychiatric disorder that occurs across the life span of an autistic person. This finding, in itself, is not surprising because of the fact that depression is the most common diagnosis in the general population. For example, in a case series of 64 children referred to a tertiary clinic, we found that depression was the most common diagnosis, affecting 2 per cent of the total sample (Ghaziuddin, Tsai and Ghaziuddin, 1992). This figure was probably an underestimate because the sample included a mixed group of both low- and high-functioning individuals and because the subjects were not interviewed directly. While depression can occur across the entire spectrum of autism, subjects who are higher functioning and those with Pervasive Developmental Disorder Not Otherwise Specified (PDDNOS) seem to be particularly affected. Thus, about 30 per cent of the sample in Wing's series of Asperger syndrome showed evidence of clinical depression (Wing, 1981) and depression was found to be the most common disorder in a series of 60 subjects with Asperger syndrome (Tantam, 1988). Another study of patients with Asperger syndrome using direct assessment methods found rates of about 30 per cent (Ghaziuddin, Weidmer-Mikhail and Ghaziuddin, 1998). Preliminary community-based studies have also found similar rates. For example, in a Canadian study, Kim and colleagues (2000) found high rates of depression and anxiety disorders in a sample of children with autism and Asperger syndrome. However, the increased rates of depression in high-functioning persons with autism spectrum disorders does not necessarily mean that they are more prone to depression, and may simply reflect the fact that the diagnosis of psychiatric disorders is more easily made in those who are verbal than in those who are severely handicapped.

Clinical features

The presentation of depression in autism and Asperger syndrome depends on the following factors: the age, level of intelligence, and level of verbal skills of the patient. As in the general population, the younger the child, the more difficult it is to obtain a reliable history and evaluate for the presence of depression. Patients with good verbal skills and a higher level of intelligence are able give a history of depressed mood and other features typical of the condition. These consist of a history of crying spells, sad affect, increasing social withdrawal, and a disturbance of sleep and of appetite. In addition, people with autism who get depressed show certain special features.

Special features of depression in people with pervasive developmental disorders (PDDs)

Increase in withdrawal

Autistic persons and those with pervasive developmental disorders who get depressed often show an increase in social withdrawal. Although autism is defined by aloofness and social isolation, care-givers are often able to point out what kind of aloofness is 'normal' for a particular individual. When depression sets in, the level of isolation and withdrawal gradually increases.

Increase in obsessive-compulsive behaviors

Sometimes an increase in ritualistic behaviors is seen with the onset of depression. This is especially true of persons who are verbal and higher-functioning. For example, an adolescent who has always been particular about his cleanliness may start washing his hands excessively. At times, this may be accompanied by feelings of distress and sadness.

Change in the character of the obsessions

Fixation on certain themes is typically seen in persons with autism, including those who are higher-functioning and in those who are diagnosed with Asperger syndrome. When these patients get depressed, the quality of their fixations and preoccupations often changes. For example, a verbal patient with autism was fixated on space exploration. With the onset of depression, his preoccupation assumed a depressive flavor. He started worrying about 'falling into the dark hole of space' and disappearing. When asked, he admitted to feeling sad and depressed and worried about recurrent thoughts of death.

Irritability

Persons with mental retardation and developmental disabilities become irritable when depressed. This is similar to the irritability that occurs in dysthymia. They tend to lose their temper for no apparent reason or after minimal provocation. This may or may not be accompanied by physical aggression, especially in those who suffer from the milder variants, such as PDDNOS. In some patients, self-injurious behaviors may accompany the irritability, particularly in those who suffer from severe forms of mental retardation.

Regression of skills

People who are lower-functioning and who suffer from severe mental retardation often do not express their sadness and unhappiness. Some of the features that suggest their depression are extreme regression of learned skills, weight loss, and incontinence. (In a few cases, an increase in eating and weight are seen.) Pollard and Prendergast (2004), for instance, described a 6-year-old girl with autism who presented with a regression of developmental skills, a depressed mood, and disturbed sleep and appetite, who responded to a course of antidepressants.

Psychotic behavior

Psychotic symptoms can also occur in depressed persons with PDDs. These often consist of a history of hearing voices, a tendency to be suspicious or paranoid of staff and care-givers, self-neglect, and aggressive behaviors. The voices are often disjointed and accusatory in nature, and the mood is typically depressed. A marked slowing of movements and thinking often complicates the clinical picture.

Bipolar disorder in people with autism/Asperger syndrome

Many patients with PDDs show problems in the regulation of affect which may lead to mood swings. At times, these mood swings may be severe enough to raise the possibility of bipolar disorder. Patients with bipolar disorder typically show alternating periods of depression and elation. A history of clear cyclical mood changes may be obtained in people with Asperger syndrome and those with high-functioning autism. Sometimes, the rambling one-sided manner of communication, with an active but odd manner of interacting with others, is confused with hypomania. Indeed, some authorities have suggested links between bipolar disorder and Asperger syndrome (DeLong and Dwyer, 1988). However, close attention should always be given to a patient's history. A clear history of onset of symptoms of mood instability or a qualitative change in the type of symptoms, along with a family history of bipolar disorder, should alert the clinician. This is particularly relevant to those patients who have deficits in communication or those who suffer from severe mental retardation. In such cases, symptoms such as irritability and aggressive outbursts along with a family history of bipolar disorder are especially important. If the symptoms are not diagnosed and treated in time, the patient may lapse into a manic state characterized by overactive, hostile, and disruptive behavior, and an irritable or elated mood. In some cases, psychotic symptoms, such as auditory hallucinations and delusions, may be present (Gillberg, 1985).

Case study: Tyler

Tyler is a 10-year-old Caucasian youngster living with his parents. He was admitted to the hospital after a series of temper tantrums and aggressive outbursts in school which resulted in his suspension. He carried a diagnosis of ADHD and impulsive control disorder. The school was threatening to expel him and wanted a full psychiatric evaluation before accepting him back. He had kicked and punched his teacher following a change of classrooms and this incident led to his referral.

On admission to hospital, his odd manner of relating to the other children became immediately apparent to the staff. He failed to read social cues. Instead of joining in with the other children, he either played by himself on the computer or with his puzzles or insisted on telling others what toys to play with. In the hospital-school, he was fixated on telling the teacher why the dinosaurs got extinct. He was active but odd, and had a lecturing quality to his conversation. His IQ testing revealed him to be functioning in the superior range, with his verbal IQ higher than his performance IQ. His parents reported that in addition to being overactive and impulsive, he had also become increasingly irritable since a change of classrooms. He lost his temper at the slightest excuse. His sleep and appetite were also disturbed.

Tyler's early developmental history was unremarkable. He spoke early and was putting sentences together by 2 years of age. Problems that first aroused his parents' concern when he was around 6 years of age were his hyperactivity and impulsivity. He was diagnosed with ADHD and started on stimulants (Adderall). Because of his habit of 'constantly arguing' and 'trying to teach the teachers,' he was also given an additional diagnosis of Oppositional Defiant Disorder (ODD) at the age of 7 years. He continued to have problems at school. He lectured on topics he considered important and claimed to know more than he actually did. He was articulate and verbal, but his eye contact was not predictable. At the age of 9 years, he developed tics (throat clearing); his stimulants were stopped because of this. Because of the history of temper tantrums and 'mood swings,' his psychiatrist suspected an additional diagnosis of bipolar disorder and requested a second opinion. His family history was positive for mood disorder. His father had a 39-year-old brother who was 'a lot like Tyler' in his social skills. Although he had a college education, he did not have a steady job and was described as being 'fixated' on mechanical objects.

On examination, Tyler appeared his stated age and was casually dressed. He was not overactive or impulsive, and showed no abnormal movements. He said he did not have any friends and admitted to feeling sad and angry. He spoke in a quiet tone, except when he was talking about his interests (dinosaurs and computer games), when he became excited and verbose. Although he said that he was good at playing computer games, he was not grandiose. There was no evidence of any psychotic ideas.

Based on the history and the examination, it was decided that this patient's symptoms fell along the spectrum of pervasive developmental disorders. A diagnosis of Asperger syndrome was considered most likely because of his intense intrusive interests, and his active but odd style of interacting and communicating. In addition, as required by the DSM-IV, he did not have a history of mental retardation or speech delay, and did not meet the full criteria for autistic disorder. Although Tyler had a history of mood symptoms, such as irritability and sadness, it was felt that the symptoms were not consistent with a diagnosis of bipolar disorder. Therefore, he was given a diagnosis of Asperger syndrome and mild depression. In addition, by history, he carried a diagnosis of ADHD.

Patients like Tyler are often seen in child psychiatric clinics and treatment centers. Initially they present with symptoms of hyperactivity and inattention and later, especially during adolescence, a history of mood swings and irritability emerges which raises the suspicion of bipolar disorder. However, when a detailed history is taken, focusing on the premorbid level of functioning and the quality of social interactions and intense preoccupations, it becomes apparent that the symptoms are more consistent with PDD and not with bipolar disorder. The diagnosis (of concurrent bipolar disorder and autism/Asperger syndrome) is difficult to make in children, especially in those younger than 10 years of age, and should be made with great caution because of the treatment implications. However, some patients with autism and Asperger syndrome do develop 'typical' symptoms of bipolar disorder, as illustrated by the case study below.

Case study: Chris

Chris is a 15-year-old male who was brought to the Psychiatry Emergency Room for displaying 'bizarre behavior.' He was diagnosed with ADHD and Asperger syndrome. Chris's parents reported that in the few weeks prior to his referral, he had become more disorganized. He was exhibiting unusual behaviors such as chasing cars and trying to decipher the meaning of the license plates. He believed that the license plates were giving him special messages. Different letters and colors on the license plates were conveying different meanings. He was elated in his mood. He believed that he had special talents (reading license plates) and appeared grandiose with respect to his intellectual abilities. He was not able to think clearly and he spoke fast in a pressured manner. He indicated that he had had increased energy and a decreased need for sleep over the last several weeks, as well as a difficulty in thinking clearly. Occasionally, he claimed to hear vague voices in his head.

The family history was positive for mood disorders. His father was said to be very much like his son, and was tentatively diagnosed as suffering from Asperger syndrome. His mother also had a history of depression. He had a younger sibling who had a diagnosis of OCD. His paternal grandfather was described as being 'cognitively slow' with a history of various phobias. His paternal great aunt had committed suicide.

Chris was admitted to the Child and Adolescent Psychiatry Inpatient Unit for clarification of diagnosis. Initially, a diagnosis of psychotic disorder with Asperger syndrome was made. He was started on an antipsychotic medication (Risperdal) that was gradually reduced over the course of a week. A mood stabilizer was also added subsequently. He was evaluated to rule out an organic cause of the psychotic behavior. The work-up included an MRI which was reported to be normal. Other tests included copper ceruloplasmin, ESR (erythrocyte sedimentation rate), TSH (thyroid stimulating hormone), ANA (antinuclear antibody), and a heavy metal screening, all of which were normal. A urine drug screen was also normal. The patient was stabilized and discharged after a week to intensive outpatient follow-up. Based on all the information available, his final diagnosis was bipolar disorder – recent episode manic with psychotic symptoms, Asperger syndrome, and a past history of ADHD.

Suicidal behavior in autism/Asperger syndrome

Suicidal attempts are not uncommon in persons with Asperger syndrome and autism. However, little systematic research has been done in this area. Completed suicide can also occur. A review of the literature on suicide in persons with mental retardation suggests that some of these patients may have suffered from autism spectrum disorders. Suicidal behavior needs to be differentiated from self-injurious behavior that occurs in some persons with severe mental retardation and autism. It can occur across the age span, as illustrated by the case study of Robert B.

Case study: Robert B

Robert B, a 12-year-old Caucasian male, was admitted to a child psychiatric unit, with recurrent thoughts of killing himself. He wanted to kill himself by jumping out of his bedroom window on the second floor. According to his parents, he had become increasingly withdrawn and depressed about six weeks prior to admission, and this coincided with the death of his hamster. He had no previous history of psychiatric illness, although his family history was positive for depression in both parents.

During the course of his hospital admission, it became apparent that Robert B was rather awkward in his social interactions. He often interacted with his peers in a one-sided manner, badgering them with information about birds and animals. He spoke in a lecturing tone, his prosody was somewhat mechanical, and his facial expression rather flat. He was an expert on animals, especially those beginning with the letter B. He had no close friends although he claimed to be popular in his class. His birth and early developmental history were unremarkable. All his milestones were reached at the expected time. He was bright and articulate, and single-minded in his interests. There was no history of seizure disorder.

During the course of the evaluation, it emerged that the death of his hamster was not accidental. Robert B said that he got 'mad' at his hamster, for no clear reason, and threw it against the cage which resulted in its death. Subsequently, he started feeling depressed and guilty, feelings which gradually increased. His plan to throw himself from the window was, in fact, an attempt to pay for what he had done to the hamster. Because of his history of social and communication deficits with rigid focused interests, it was apparent that Robert B was not only depressed, but also suffered from a pervasive developmental disorder. A diagnosis of major depression with Asperger syndrome was eventually made.

Suicidal behavior probably occurs more commonly in adults with high-functioning autism and Asperger syndrome than is generally recognized. Usually, the patients have a chronic history of depression, with only a partial response to antidepressants, as illustrated by the next case, that of Tony D.

Case study: Tony D

Tony D is a 25-year-old mechanical engineer. He was diagnosed with autism at the age of 3 years. His speech was delayed. However, as he grew older, he began to speak fluently. He finished college with some help, but was not able to find a suitable job because he did not do well in job interviews. He tried a string of odd jobs. It was around this time that he started feeling depressed. He felt angry and dejected. One day, he wrote a suicide note, saying how unhappy he was and how he had lost all hope in his future. He locked himself in his car, started the engine of the car, and put down the garage door. Fortunately, he was discovered by his parents in time, and his life was saved. He was well known to the local psychiatric services, and, at the time of the suicide attempt, he carried a diagnosis of depression and was already taking antidepressants.

Catatonia and depression in people with autism

Catatonia is a severe condition characterized by a disturbance of behavior and abnormalities of motor function. Its main features are immobility, extreme negativism, mutism, and peculiarities of voluntary movements; these are sometimes combined with echolalia and bursts of hyperactivity. If untreated, catatonia can cause death due to dehydration and renal failure. According to the DSM-IV (APA, 1994), it is often associated with schizophrenia, mood disorders, and general medical conditions, such as drug withdrawal and liver failure.

Catatonia is being increasingly recognized in persons with autism spectrum disorders, and in most cases depression appears to be either the underlying cause or a complicating factor. References to this condition can be found in earlier studies of autism. For example, Lockyer and Rutter (1970) found that 12 per cent of the subjects showed a regression during adolescence marked by a loss of language skills, inertia, and intellectual decline. In many cases, this was accompanied by seizures. Considering the symptoms described, it is possible that some of these subjects might have suffered from catatonia. In a more recent survey of 506 children and adults referred for a diagnostic evaluation of autism, Wing and Shah (2000) found that 30 subjects met the criteria of catatonia. A further eight individuals displayed some symptoms of the disorder without meeting all the criteria. The majority of the patients had their onset of catatonia between 15 and 19 years of age. The authors did not give details about the psychiatric aspects of their cases, but found that those who were language impaired and those who were passive in their social interactions were more vulnerable.

Realmuto and August (1991) described catatonia in three cases of autism and argued that the presence of psychiatric disorders increased the risk of catatonia emerging in persons with autism. Zaw and colleagues (1999) described a 14-year-old youngster with autism and catatonia. He displayed symptoms of mutism, akinesia, posturing, and rigidity. In addition to the symptoms of catatonia, he appeared depressed and showed nonspecific psychotic symptoms. A course of electroconvulsive therapy (ECT) improved the condition dramatically, although the core symptoms of autism were not affected. Thus, although most studies have not commented on the psychiatric comorbidity of patients with autism who later develop catatonia, it is likely that the underlying cause in a substantial number of patients is clinical depression.

Depression 'unmasking' PDD

Sometimes the treatment of depression unmasks an underlying autism spectrum disorder. For example, an adolescent may present with refractory depression. During the course of the treatment, it becomes apparent that there is 'something else' that needs to be investigated. The type of PDD that emerges in such cases is usually Asperger syndrome or a milder variant. This is illustrated by the case of RS.

Case study: RS

RS is a 21-year-old Asian male. He was referred for treatment of progressive worsening of mood accompanied by occasional suicidal thoughts. He was a freshman at a university and had no previous history of depression or any formal psychiatric disorder. He had become increasingly overwhelmed with stress after starting college, and was not able to cope. In particular, he had started missing his morning classes, and was often disorganized. The family history was strongly positive for depression and autism. There was no history of substance abuse or any medical factors to account for his worsening mood. On examination, his depression was confirmed. After the usual work-up and evaluation, he was started on an antidepressant. At the same time, he was also placed in individual therapy to help him cope with college.

A few months after starting medications and therapy, RS started to improve. He became brighter, and more talkative. Yet he continued to miss his classes. His therapy focused on issues of separation and autonomy. He blamed his parents for most of his symptoms and accused them of not being able to understand him. The therapist felt that there were cultural issues that needed to be addressed. However, after almost a year of therapy and medications, RS seemed to have reached a plateau. He still lived at home, refused to attend his classes, and when questioned, launched into long explanations about how his parents were not able to give him enough attention, and understand his problems. Yet, when asked, he was extremely vague about what exactly bothered him.

Because of the lack of progress, alternative possibilities were explored. RS's level of IQ was in the normal range. A closer look, however, revealed that RS had always had difficulties with social interactions. He was known as being aloof and withdrawn. He had never had any close friends, although he claimed that he had several. He spent most of the time on the computer, either reading or writing science-fiction short stories. He also had a history of language delay. He was tall, somewhat uncoordinated, and spoke too loud, especially on topics of his interest. People generally thought of him as being reserved, somewhat shy. However, in view of the history of lack of social relationships, rigid preoccupations on certain topics, and subtle pragmatic deficits, an impression of autistic spectrum disorder (most likely autistic disorder) was made. In addition, a diagnosis of major depression was also given because of the symptoms.

Causes of depression in people with autism/Asperger syndrome

As discussed in the introduction to this chapter, depression is caused by a combination of biological and environmental factors. Similar factors seem to operate in persons with autism spectrum disorders. For example, preliminary studies have shown that children with autism who suffer from depression are more likely to have a family history of depression (Ghaziuddin and Greden, 1998). Both parents and siblings may be affected. Also, the occurrence of depression in the family does not seem to be the result of the stress of raising a child with disabilities. Compared with parents of children with other handicapping conditions, such as Down syndrome, parents of autistic children seem to have an increased risk for depression (Piven and Palmer, 1999). This suggests that a specific link may exist between (some types of) depression and (some types of) autism spectrum disorders. DeLong and Dwyer (1988) have proposed such a relationship between Asperger syndrome and bipolar disorder. In a family study of autistic subjects grouped on the basis of language function, they found that the rate of bipolar disorder in the first-degree relatives of probands with high-functioning variants of autism, especially Asperger syndrome, was higher than that of the general population (DeLong and Dwyer, 1988). While depression does not appear to be part of the broader phenotype of autism (Bolton *et al.*, 1998), it is possible that autism with comorbid depression may index a distinct subtype, the nature of which is not clear at present. This comorbidity may be linked to dysfunction at a more basic level, because studies have shown that parents of autistic children who show altered serotonin levels themselves score high on depression and anxiety symptoms (Cook *et al.*, 1994).

Consistent with the findings in children without autism, depressed children with autism also experience unpleasant events before the onset of the disorder (Ghaziuddin, Alessi and Greden, 1995). The same is probably also true of adults with autism although no systematic studies have been done. Both high- and low-functioning people with autism show depressive symptoms in response to significant life events. Verbal individuals are often able to experience their feelings when asked. In those who are nonverbal, a marked change in the level of functioning may be suggestive. From a clinical point of view, therefore, it is important to elicit a history of changes and events, especially those that are negative in nature, when an autistic individual shows symptoms of sadness and depression. Although studies of life events and depression have not been performed in persons with Asperger syndrome, anecdotal experience suggests that this issue is of major importance.

Several recent publications have emphasized the importance of peer-victimization and loneliness in the onset of depression and anxiety disorder in the general population. Certain behavioral characteristics in children and adolescents may lead to them being regarded as odd or different. This may lead to rejection, loneliness, and problems with self-esteem. In a study of 96 eighth-graders, Sletta *et al.* (1996) found that loneliness was predicted by behavioral characteristics and low peer acceptance, and that loneliness often led to low self-esteem and negative social competence. Similar findings have been reported in persons with high-functioning autism and Asperger syndrome. Bauminger and colleagues examined 18 children with high-functioning autism. Compared to typically developing children, those with high-functioning autism showed a higher prevalence of loneliness (Bauminger, Shulman and Agam, 2003). Many patients with Asperger syndrome become aware of their limitations, especially during adolescence. Rejected by their peers, and often craving for their friendship, people with Asperger syndrome have to endure frequent teasing and bullying. In the absence of adequate support mechanisms, individuals with Asperger syndrome and autism develop depressive symptoms and show behaviors consistent with a diagnosis of clinical depression.

In addition to genetic and environmental stressors, co-existing medical conditions also play a role. It is known that the risk of depression, as indeed of other forms of psychiatric disorders, is increased in patients with epilepsy. Since at least a third of patients with autism suffer from epilepsy, it is reasonable to assume that this further adds to the risk of depression. The same applies to the presence of other psychiatric disorders. Patients with ADHD and anxiety disorders have an increased risk of depression. Therefore, whenever these disorders occur in persons with autism and Asperger syndrome, the risk for depression is also raised.

Complications

Depression affects both the patient and his family. Apart from feeling sad and lonely, a depressed teenager with autism or Asperger syndrome is more likely to be irritable and oppositional. These symptoms worsen the core deficits of autism, and make interventions difficult. Aggressive outbursts and temper tantrums may also occur, especially in those who have a limited ability to express themselves. At home, difficulties in getting along with parents and peers result in additional problems. Problems at school lead to a negative perception of the patient and make him feel more insecure and alienated. In a minority of cases, psychotic behavior may occur. The depressed patient loses touch with reality and may become preoccupied with paranoid ideas or delusional beliefs. In extreme cases, auditory hallucinations may also occur. These hallucinations are often derogatory in nature and add to the patient's distress. In a minority of cases, suicidal behavior may also occur.

Assessment

The key to assessment is to maintain a high index of suspicion. Any patient with autism or Asperger syndrome who presents with a history of behavioral problems, especially of a recent onset, should be evaluated for underlying depression. First, a complete physical examination should be performed. In particular, tests for thyroid function should be done because of the known association between depression and thyroid disorders. Other medical tests should also be done in order to provide a baseline. Any chronic infection can result in a change of mood. Details about social history focusing, in particular, on the presence of any significant life events should also be obtained.

A systematic psychiatric history should be obtained to clarify the onset and nature of symptoms, such as a history of regression of skills, presence of crying spells, loss of interest in enjoyable activities, fixation on morbid themes, change in the character of the fixations and preoccupations, and social withdrawal beyond what is regarded as normal for the patient. Evidence of weight and sleep disturbance should also be explored. Attention should be paid to complaints of increasing boredom and isolation, especially in higher-functioning individuals. Contrary to what is generally believed, most autistic patients, with the exception of those who are severely impaired, are able to describe their feelings of sadness and depression, if the questions are framed properly. Rating scales such as the Hamilton Depression Rating Scale (Hamilton, 1960) should also be used. Although experience is limited with the use of structured psychiatric interviews for persons with autism and Asperger syndrome, preliminary evidence suggests that they can be used.

Treatment

The treatment of depression in autism is based on a combination of psychopharmacological and psychological approaches, and does not differ from that in the rest of the population.

Psychopharmacological interventions

People with autism respond to antidepressants in the usual manner. There is no evidence that autistic persons are more prone to the side-effects of anti-depressants than the rest of the population. When they occur, side-effects are often due to the presence of co-existing medical complications such as seizure disorder. The choice of the antidepressant is influenced by the severity of the symptoms, the risk of side-effects, and the family history of a favorable response to the drug. In people with PDD, the available evidence indicates that the antidepressants that are most commonly used are the selective serotonin reuptake inhibitors (SSRIs) such as fluoxetine (Prozac) and sertraline (Zoloft). The doses used are generally the same as those in the rest of the population. Particular attention should be paid to the emergence of mood swings and symptoms of aggression, since antidepressants can occasionally precipitate hypomania in vulnerable patients. If one SSRI agent is not successful after a reasonable period of time (usually about a month), it is common practice to try another, or start an agent belonging to a different class of antidepressants as discussed in Chapter 1. In cases of refractory depression, other types of medications are often added. These include mood stabilizers, such as lithium, or anticonvulsants such as sodium valproate (Depakote).

Treatment of bipolar disorder in people with PDD depends on the type and severity of the symptoms. If the patient is in a manic state, he should be admitted to a hospital, with the objective of providing a safe environment and achieving a rapid stabilization of symptoms. The reasons that justify hospitalization include severe mood swings, aggressive outbursts, psychotic and bizarre behavior, and the risk of suicide or homicide.

It is usual to start the patient on an antipsychotic agent, such as haloperidol or risperidone. This is often combined with a mood stabilizer such as lithium carbonate or sodium valproate (Depakote). While lithium is a naturally occurring salt, sodium valproate is an anticonvulsant. Once the acute symptoms decrease, the dose of the medications can be titrated. In most cases, patients are continued on lithium or valproate with a low dose of the antipsychotic agent. If the patient is not in a manic state, and if his symptoms are not severe enough to place his or anyone else's safety at risk, he can be treated as an outpatient. The usual approach is to start a mood stabilizer, such as lithium or sodium valproate, and add an antipsychotic only if necessary. Many patients with bipolar disorder, during the course of their illness, develop depressive symptoms necessitating the addition of a small dose of an antidepressant. Side-effects should be monitored closely, especially when mood stabilizers and anticonvulsants are used. Regular monitoring of blood levels should be performed, preferably at six-monthly intervals.

Psychological interventions

Psychotherapy is often combined with medications. A variety of psychological therapies are currently used for the treatment of depression. For persons with autism, because of the cognitive and communicative impairments that are often present, therapy is often direct and supportive. Insight-oriented and psychodynamic psychotherapy that is aimed at uncovering inner conflicts is generally not useful, especially in the presence of psychotic ideas or behavior. Some higher-functioning autistic persons are able to engage in therapy. Cognitive behavioral approaches may also be tried depending on the level of functioning of the patient. In addition, traditional social work, consisting of helping the individual with the problems of everyday living, should be undertaken. This is especially important for adults living in supervised shelters who need help with shopping and other chores of daily living. At the same time, attention should be given to the presence of stressful events at home or in the community. Group therapy for adults with high-functioning autism and Asperger syndrome who suffer from additional depressive symptoms may be useful in those cases where the symptoms are mild or moderate. Group therapy is not indicated for those individuals who suffer from severe depression or for those who are suicidal or psychotic. Likewise, group therapy is also usually not successful in patients with manic symptoms.

Electroconvulsive therapy

Although it remains a controversial form of treatment, electroconvulsive therapy (ECT) is gaining in popularity. There is a growing recognition that ECT is a safe and effective treatment of refractory depression, and is particularly useful in cases of imminent suicide. A few reports have described the use of ECT with autistic persons (e.g. Zaw *et al.*, 1999). ECT is often considered when the patient has failed to respond to two or more trials of antidepressants, and if the intensity of depression is life-threatening. The author has known three cases of catatonia in persons with autism spectrum disorders, possibly secondary to depression, who responded to a course of electroconvulsive treatment. All were adolescents with a history of failure to respond to antidepressants and were at imminent risk of death through starvation.

Outcome

Studies have not examined the long-term outcome of persons with autism and depression. Clinical experience suggests that in a subset of patients with autism spectrum disorders, the depressive illness becomes chronic and refractory to treatment. Despite various medication trials, the illness appears to linger on in these patients, and they do not return to their previous level of functioning. Many such patients, anecdotally, have a strong family history of mood disorders, including one of completed suicide. While it is reasonable to assume that an early diagnosis leads to a better outcome, the exact nature of the factors that influence the prognosis is not clear.

Conclusion

Although bipolar disorder and other types of mood disorders can occur in persons with PDD, depression is by far the most common psychiatric disorder that affects persons with autism or Asperger syndrome across the life span. While the true prevalence in community samples is not known, clinic-based studies underscore its high prevalence. Depression can be reliably diagnosed in high-functioning persons using the usual diagnostic criteria. However, diagnosing those with severe cognitive and communication impairment is difficult. The symptoms of bipolar disorder are marked by cyclical mood changes and sometimes by aggression and disruptive behavior. It is important, therefore, to maintain a high index of suspicion, especially when there is history of a recent change in the level of functioning, often during adolescence. A variety of factors may contribute to the emergence of mood disorders in people with autism or Asperger syndrome. While in some cases this could occur by chance, in others the association could result from a combination of genetic or environmental factors or both. The presence of other medical disorders, such as seizure disorder, may also contribute to the etiology. Assessment of depression in lower-functioning persons should receive further study, as should the long-term follow-up of these disorders in older persons with autism. While treatment of depression and mood disorders does not cure the core symptoms of autism, it does result in a substantial degree of improvement in the quality of life of the affected person, and lessens the burden of care on the family.

References

APA (American Psychiatric Association) (1994) *Diagnostic and Statistical Manual of Mental Disorders, Fourth Edition* (DSM-IV). Washington, DC: APA.

Asperger, H. (1944) 'Die "autistischen Psychopathen" im Kindersalter.' *Archiv für Psychiatrie und Nervenkrankheiten, 117,* 76–136.

Bauminger, N., Shulman, C. and Agam, G. (2003) 'Peer interaction and loneliness in high-functioning children with autism.' *Journal of Autism and Developmental Disorders, 33,* 489–507.

Biederman, J., Mick, E., Faraone, S.V., Spencer, T., Wilens, T.E. and Wozniak, J. (2000) 'Pediatric mania: A developmental subtype of bipolar disorder?' *Biological Psychiatry, 48,* 6, 458–66.

Bolton, P.F., Pickles, A., Murphy, M. and Rutter, M. (1998) 'Autism, affective and other psychiatric disorders: pattern of familial aggregation.' *Psychological Medicine, 28,* 385–95.

Cook, E.H. Jr., Charak, D.A., Arida, J., Spohn, J.A., Roizen, N.J. and Leventhal, B.L. (1994) 'Depressive and obsessive-compulsive symptoms in hyperserotonemic parents of children with autistic disorder.' *Psychiatry Research, 52,* 25–33.

DeLong, R.G. and Dwyer, J.T. (1988) 'Correlation of family history with specific autistic subtypes: Asperger's syndrome and bipolar affective disease.' *Journal of Autism and Developmental Disorders, 18,* 593–600.

Faraone, S.V., Biederman, J., Mennin, D., Wozniak, J. and Spencer, T. (1997) 'Attention-deficit hyperactivity disorder with bipolar disorder: A familial subtype?' *Journal of the American Academy of Child and Adolescent Psychiatry, 36,* 10, 1378–87.

Ghaziuddin, M., Alessi, N. and Greden, J. (1995) 'Life events and depression in children with pervasive developmental disorders.' *Journal of Autism and Developmental Disorders, 25*, 5, 495–502.

Ghaziuddin, M. and Greden, J. (1998) 'Depression in children with autism/pervasive developmental disorders.' *Journal of Autism and Developmental Disorders, 28*, 2, 111–15.

Ghaziuddin, M., Tsai, L. and Ghaziuddin, N. (1992) 'Comorbidity of autistic disorder in children and adolescents.' *European Child and Adolescent Psychiatry, 1*, 4, 209–213.

Ghaziuddin, M., Weidmer-Mikhail, E. and Ghaziuddin, N. (1998) 'Comorbidity of Asperger syndrome: A preliminary report.' *Journal of Intellectual Disability Research, 4*, 279–83.

Gillberg, C. (1985) 'Asperger's syndrome and recurrent psychosis – a case study.' *Journal of Autism and Developmental Disorders, 15*, 389–97.

Hamilton, M. (1960) 'A rating scale for depression.' *Journal of Neurology, Neurosurgery, and Psychiatry, 23*, 56–62.

Kanner, L. (1943) 'Autistic disturbances of affective contact.' *Nervous Child, 2*, 217–50.

Kendler, K.S., Karkowski, L.M. and Prescott, C.A. (1999) 'Causal relationship between stressful life events and the onset of major depression.' *American Journal of Psychiatry, 156*, 837–41.

Kim, J.A., Szatmari, P., Bryson, S.E., Streiner, D.L. and Wilson, F.J. (2000) 'The prevalence of anxiety and mood problems among children with autism and Asperger syndrome.' *Autism, 4*, 2, 117–32.

Lainhart, J.E. and Folstein, S.E. (1994) 'Affective disorders in people with autism: A review of published cases.' *Journal of Autism and Developmental Disorders, 24*, 587–601.

Lockyer, L. and Rutter, M. (1970) 'A five to fifteen year follow-up study of infantile psychosis. IV. Patterns of cognitive ability.' *British Journal of Social and Clinical Psychology, 9*, 2, 152–63.

Piven, J. and Palmer, P. (1999) 'Psychiatric disorder and the broad autism phenotype: Evidence from a family study of multiple-incidence autism families.' *American Journal of Psychiatry, 156*, 557–63.

Pollard, A.J. and Prendergast, M. (2004) 'Depressive pseudodementia in a child with autism.' *Developmental Medicine and Child Neurology, 46*, 7, 485–9.

Realmuto, G.M. and August, G.J. (1991) 'Catatonia in autistic disorder: A sign of comorbidity or variable expression.' *Journal of Autism and Developmental Disorders, 21*, 517–28.

Sletta, O., Valas, H., Skaalvik, E. and Sobstad, F. (1996) 'Peer relations, loneliness, and self-perceptions in school-aged children.' *British Journal of Educational Psychology, 66*, 431–45.

Soares, J.C. and Mann, J.J. (1997) 'The anatomy of mood disorders – review of structural neuroimaging studies.' *Biological Psychiatry, 41*, 1, 86–106.

Tantam, D. (1988) 'Asperger's syndrome.' *Journal of Child Psychology and Psychiatry, 29*, 245–53.

Wing, L. (1981) 'Asperger's syndrome: A clinical account.' *Psychological Medicine, 11,* 115–29.

Wing, L. and Shah, A. (2000) 'Catatonia in autistic spectrum disorders.' *British Journal of Psychiatry, 176,* 357–62.

Zaw, F.K., Bates, G.D., Murali, V. and Bentham, P. (1999) 'Catatonia, autism, and ECT.' *Developmental Medicine and Child Neurology, 41,* 843–5.

CHAPTER 8

Anxiety Disorders in Autism and Asperger Syndrome

Introduction

It is normal to experience anxiety in certain situations, such as before an important meeting or an examination. While anxiety may be adaptive in the face of an impending threat, its excess leads to disability and impairment. In anxiety disorders a normal adaptive emotion is transformed into a handicapping condition that affects coping and results in distress. Excessive anxiety leads to a combination of physical and psychological symptoms. Psychological symptoms consist of a sense of impending doom and a feeling of tension or danger; while physical symptoms include palpitations, sweating, and stomach aches. Anxiety disorders occur in both children and adults, and are often associated with depression and other mood disorders. Females are more commonly affected. The DSM-IV divides anxiety disorders into several subtypes, the most common being Generalized Anxiety Disorder (GAD) and Obsessive-Compulsive Disorder (OCD). Other types include panic disorder, phobic disorder, and Post-Traumatic Stress Disorder (PTSD). The causes of anxiety disorders are several, ranging from a genetic predisposition to exposure to a severe traumatic event.

Symptoms of anxiety are often described in persons with autism spectrum disorders. People across the entire range of pervasive developmental disorders (PDDs) may present with these symptoms although they are more often reported by those who are higher-functioning and those with Asperger syndrome, probably because of their better-preserved verbal skills. These symptoms often manifest themselves as extreme distress at trivial changes in the environment, problems with change of schedules, and difficulties in adjusting to new people or surroundings, such as change of staff. These symptoms are often conceptualized as part of the autistic syndrome or as epiphenomena that go with the diagnosis of autism, based on the two core features described by Kanner (1943): aloofness and the desire for sameness. However, at times, these symptoms are severe enough to cause distress and impairment in the form of a range of physical and psychological symptoms. These consist of fears and phobias, vague bodily symptoms, avoidance of stressful situations, etc. In addition to general feelings of anxiety, people with autism and Asperger syndrome can also develop distinct anxiety disorders. The most common types of anxiety disorders in this population are OCD, PTSD, school refusal, selective mutism and social anxiety disorder. These are briefly discussed in this chapter.

Obsessive-Compulsive Disorder

Obsessions are thoughts that repeatedly intrude into a person's mind against his will. They usually involve such themes as sex, religion, cleanliness, and aggression. The patient is obsessed with thoughts and images that go against his moral values and personal beliefs. Usually, the more the patient tries to stop them, the more severe they seem to become. Compulsions are defined as acts and rituals that have to be carried out in a repetitive manner. They usually involve sequences of acts, such as getting out of a particular side of the bed, or checking the lights at night, or washing the hands repeatedly to ward off germs.

OCD is classified as an anxiety disorder. According to the DSM-IV (APA, 1994), it is characterized by intrusive thoughts, images, or worries (obsessions) and/or repetitive, nonfunctional behaviors or acts (compulsions), which are meant to suppress anxiety. Thus, to meet the criteria for OCD, the patient need not suffer from both obsessions and compulsions at the same time. In addition, during the course of the illness, the patient should recognize that the obsessions and compulsions are excessive or unreasonable. Although the patient regards these acts as senseless, he is not able to stop them. In extreme cases, obsessive slowing and incapacitation may occur. The symptoms of OCD are time consuming and distressing to both the patient and his family. Although patients with OCD may sometimes harbor suicidal ideas, they do not often carry them out, unless they are significantly depressed. The lifetime prevalence of OCD is around 2.5 per cent. It is more common in males than in females. While the most common age of onset is early adulthood, some researchers have suggested a bimodal age distribution: first, between 10 and 12 years; and the second, in early adulthood.

Obsessions and compulsions in people with autism

Compulsive rituals form an integral part of the clinical picture of autism (Gross-Isseroff, Hermersh and Weizman 2001). In Kanner's original series of 11 patients (Kanner, 1943), common symptoms consisted of verbal and motor rituals, obsessive questioning, fixation on routines and a preoccupation with details. Kanner believed that a desire for sameness formed an integral part of autism. However, it is not uncommon to see patients with autism, especially those who have a normal level of intelligence and reasonable verbal skills, to present mainly with an increase in compulsions and/or obsessions. The key to the diagnosis, therefore, lies in the exacerbation of symptoms. When the focus of clinical attention is the treatment of obsessive-compulsive behaviors, and when there is a clear history of onset or exacerbation of symptoms, it is justified to make an additional diagnosis of OCD.

While people with autism display a wide range of compulsive behaviors, obsessive thoughts tend to be uncommon. In addition, the compulsions of autism are not egodystonic, that is, they do not seemingly occur against the person's will. Some authorities have, therefore, suggested that the terms 'obsession' and 'compulsion' should not be used while describing these symptoms in persons with autism (Baron-Cohen, 1990). In addition, there are significant differences between the obsessive-compulsive behaviors of autistic persons and those displayed by nonautistic controls. For example, McDougle and colleagues (1995) compared 50 adults with a primary diagnosis of autistic disorder with 50 age- and sex-matched adults with OCD. Both the groups completed rating scales for autism and OCD. The authors found that adults with autism were more likely to show repetitive ordering, checking, lining up, hoarding, and touching. Likewise, their obsessive thoughts were less likely to involve the usual themes for OCD sufferers of aggression, religion, and sex. An interesting finding of this study was that none of the patients had a history of obsessions alone, and no compulsions (McDougle *et al.*, 1995). However, clinical experience and some reports suggest that obsessive thoughts without compulsions can occur in persons with high-functioning autism and Asperger syndrome. In the case of these persons, the 'obsessions' occur significantly more commonly in the domain of 'folk physics' (an interest in how things work), than in the domain of 'folk psychology' (an interest in how people work) (Baron-Cohen and Wheelwright, 1999).

Etiology

The reason why some patients with autism present with OCD is not clear. It may, as in most other psychiatric disorders, lie in a combination of genetic and environmental factors. As mentioned in Chapter 1, patients with autism more often have first-degree relatives with OCD compared to controls with other developmental disorders, such as Down syndrome (Bolton *et al.*, 1998). Factors relating to psychiatric comorbidity may also be important. For example, a significant number of patients with OCD, in the general population as well as in the autistic population, have an overlap with depression.

Indirect evidence for an association between autism and OCD comes from the studies of serotonin dysfunction in psychiatric disorders. Various studies have suggested that serotonergic abnormalities occur in both autism and OCD. In addition, medications that are effective in the treatment of OCD in the general population have been found to be useful in some patients with autism, especially in the control of the ritualistic behaviors (Cook and Leventhal, 1995).

Finally, some studies conducted in Sweden (Nilsson *et al.*, 1999) have suggested that other disorders, such as anorexia nervosa, that are characterized by obsessive-compulsive behaviors seem to be more common in persons with autism. However, these findings have not been replicated in other countries.

Prevalence

The prevalence of OCD in persons with autism spectrum disorders is not known. In one study, out of 64 patients with autism, only one met the criteria for OCD (Ghaziuddin, Tsai and Ghaziuddin, 1994). Reports based on referrals to autism clinics suggest that the two disorders exist in combination more commonly than generally assumed. This is especially the case with those autistic persons who initially present with depression. As is the case of persons without autism, the combination of autism and OCD appears to be more common in males than in females. It occurs across the whole range of autistic disorders, but is more commonly detected in those with higher levels of intelligence. Also, it is more easily detected in adolescents and young adults than in children with autism.

Clinical features

The presentation of OCD in the setting of autism depends mainly on two factors: the level of functioning and the age of the patient. In general, compulsions and rituals seem to be more common than pure obsessions.

It is extremely difficult to elicit a detailed history about those with mental retardation. This is particularly true of those with severe mental retardation. In the case of those with mild mental retardation, however, a history of a recent exacerbation of OCD-related behaviors can be obtained with the help of the care-givers.

It is more difficult to obtain a valid history of OCD symptoms from younger patients than from older patients. Although some patients with autism show evidence of ritualistic behaviors even before they reach the age of 3 years, the diagnosis of OCD cannot be reliably made at that age. Conversely, any child under 5 years of age who is referred with symptoms suggestive of OCD should be evaluated for autism because it is extremely rare for true OCD to emerge in the preschool years.

At times, patients with autism are specifically referred for the exacerbation of OCD symptoms. This is usually the case with older and higher-functioning patients. Usual referral symptoms consist of an increase in the type and severity of compulsive behaviors, often resulting in a significant degree of impairment.

Case study: Mathew

Mathew, a 25-year-old male with autism, was referred for increasing problems at work. He lived at home with his parents, and had recently lost his job as a cleaner at a local coffee shop. His level of intelligence was within the normal range.

According to his parents, about three months prior to the referral, Mathew started becoming obsessed with cleanliness. For no apparent reason, he started worrying about not cleaning the tables well. He would mop the tables repeatedly, making sure that not a speck of dirt remained on any of them. He would clean the tables a set number of times, only to repeat the ritual all over again. Eventually, he slowed down so much that he could not continue to work.

Mathew had no previous history of a psychiatric illness. However, his family history was strongly positive for depression and anxiety disorder. His medical history was unremarkable.

Examination revealed that Mathew was significantly distressed by his symptoms. He saw them as 'stupid' and wanted help. Although he had always had compulsions about cleanliness, and was known for his orderly life, the presenting symptoms were new, and represented a significant deterioration. It was for these reasons that an additional diagnosis of OCD was made. He was treated by a course of medications (clomipramine) and behavioral therapy to which he responded well.

Mathew's diagnosis was facilitated by his good verbal skills and his normal level of intelligence. Mathew recognized his symptoms as unusual and excessive, and was able to report accordingly. However, OCD symptoms can also present in autistic persons with additional mental retardation, when the diagnosis of OCD is difficult to make. This is illustrated by the following case study about Grant.

Case study: Grant

Grant is a 13-year-old Caucasian male with a diagnosis of autism and mild mental retardation (full-scale IQ 64). He was referred for a psychiatric evaluation because of a recent increase in his compulsive behaviors. Although he had always had a tendency to be a perfectionist, he had become increasingly fixated on doing things 'the best possible way.' For example, he would spend hours writing and re-writing his school assignments (most of these consisted of scribbling words over and over again). In addition, he had become obsessed with cleanliness. He would wash his hands repeatedly, sometimes counting the exact number of times, and get upset if asked to stop. His hands had become raw with persistent washing. His verbal rituals had also increased. In the past, he used to repeat sentences; but now, he insisted on others repeating his sentences in a certain way. He had always been fond of collecting things. For example, he had a collection of baseball cards, rocks, and pencils. However, for about a year, he had become fixated on collecting only paper clips.

The history revealed that Grant was doing reasonably well until about a year prior to the referral. He had been diagnosed as suffering from autistic disorder at the age of 5 years. He was well adjusted in his school, where he received services for autistic children. His behavior began deteriorating when he reached the age of about 12 years. He started becoming irritable, and at times would look sad and depressed. Around this time, he slowed down in performing his chores. Gradually, his compulsive behaviors became much more disabling and prompted the referral for psychiatric help.

His family history was positive for depression. Both his parents were on antidepressant medications. Apart from a history of febrile seizures at the age of 3, Grant's medical history was unremarkable. There was no past psychiatric history.

On examination, Grant was visibly anxious. His eye contact was poor. He responded to questions when directly asked. His mood was irritable and sad. He admitted to feeling the urge to collect certain kinds of articles like paper clips, and felt that he was unable to stop doing so. Based on the history and the examination, therefore, he was given a diagnosis of OCD, depression, autistic disorder, and mild mental retardation.

Despite his mental retardation, Grant was able to offer a coherent history of his symptoms, which underscores the fact that quite often autistic persons are able to talk about their worries. The fact that he was also clinically depressed stresses the importance of the common association between OCD and depression. Sometimes, severe OCD can lead to marked slowing and regression, justifying an additional diagnosis of catatonia. As discussed in Chapter 7, this is a severe, life-threatening condition in which the patient becomes progressively withdrawn and mute, with marked slowing of all movements. If not treated, death results due to emaciation. In many cases, depressive symptoms are also present. The important point is that in the case of some patients with autism, the symptom that suggests the onset of catatonia is a slowing of body movements that occurs in the context of increasing compulsions. This is illustrated by the following case study, describing Ken.

Case study: Ken

Ken is a 17-year-old Caucasian youngster. He carries a diagnosis of autism and mild mental retardation. He was admitted to hospital with a history of progressive weight loss, sleep disturbance, and refusal to eat. He had become increasingly withdrawn and isolated. In addition, he had developed urinary incontinence. Physical examination and biological tests failed to account for the progressive decline in Ken's functioning. The main symptom that alerted the parents to the imminent decline was his motoric slowing. He had started becoming slow in his movements, taking a long time to complete his chores, and finally reached the point when he would just sit and stare blankly, often holding his arms in an abnormal posture. He would get caught in complicated compulsive acts, such as arranging and re-arranging articles, or spending hours in the doorway, debating whether or not to enter his room. His past history was significant. He had been admitted to the hospital twice for similar complaints. His family history was positive for depression and suggestive of autistic traits.

During his admission, Ken was nonverbal. He looked sad and depressed, with occasional tearfulness. He would not eat a single meal during the day, and was progressively losing weight. In view of the above symptoms of progressive slowing of his body movements, his muteness, and his difficulty in taking care of himself, a diagnosis of catatonia was considered. Of relevance was the fact that the catatonia had started as a gradual increase in his compulsions and rituals which eventually led to admission to hospital.

Diagnosis

According to the DSM-IV (APA, 1994), the diagnosis of OCD requires the presence of obsessions and/or compulsions which the individual recognizes as being egodystonic, that is, distressing and unpleasant. For children, though, the criterion of egodystonicity is waived by the DSM-IV. This criterion cannot be applied with certainty to many people with autism, both adults and children, especially those who also suffer from mental retardation.

From a practical standpoint, the diagnosis of OCD in persons with autism is based on two criteria. First, the symptoms of OCD emerge *de novo* or change in their quality or intensity; and, second, they gradually deteriorate over time. Although a desire for sameness and a restricted range of interests constitute the main features of autism, when these increase in intensity, then the diagnosis of additional OCD is justified. Another reason that justifies the diagnosis is the fact that these symptoms form the main reason for referral and the basis for clinical intervention. Moreover, when autism is not complicated by additional OCD, the patient almost never complains about his compulsive rituals. On the other hand, when OCD complicates autism as a separate diagnosis, the patient often complains about these symptoms, and in most cases also tries to suppress them.

Assessment involves eliciting a detailed history focusing on the emergence of new rituals or the worsening of existing ones. Depressive symptoms should be carefully looked for. Rating scales should be used to provide a baseline of the symptoms and also to monitor the effectiveness of medications. Commonly used rating scales, such as the Yale Brown Obsessive Compulsive Checklist (YBOCS: Goodman *et al.*, 1986) can be adapted for use with patients with autism and Asperger syndrome. Intensity of depression, if present, should also be assessed with the help of scales such as the Hamilton

Depression Rating Scale (Hamilton, 1960). The main objective is to obtain a history establishing when and how the 'normal' obsessions/compulsions of autism became 'abnormal' and 'excessive.'

Differential diagnosis

Several conditions should be ruled out before considering a diagnosis of autism with OCD. These include the following:

- *Schizophrenia*: Patients with autism and OCD are sometimes misdiagnosed as suffering from schizophrenia. This is likely to happen when the patient, usually with good verbal skills, complains of intrusive thoughts. These thoughts are, however, the patient's own, and not alien, as in the case of schizophrenia. Sometimes the strategies that are adopted to cope with the obsessive thoughts may be so bizarre as to raise the question of schizophrenia. However, the typical features of schizophrenia – auditory hallucinations, delusions, and other forms of thought disorder – are not present. Many patients with severe mental retardation perform rituals that may be sometimes confused with schizophrenia. The most that can be done for such patients is to document the details of the behavior and try to treat the symptoms individually, because a proper diagnosis of schizophrenia or of OCD is extremely difficult to make in persons with severe mental retardation.

- *Depression*: Many patients with OCD suffer from additional symptoms of depression. Patients with autism who suffer from OCD are no exception. Quite often, the onset of depression is heralded by an increase in the type and frequency of compulsive behaviors. Thus, any patient with autism who presents with an increase in his compulsive behaviors should be screened for the presence of clinical depression.

- *Other anxiety disorders*: OCD is a form of anxiety disorder as defined by the official systems of classification, such as the DSM-IV. However, other anxiety disorders can also occur with OCD and should be differentiated. These include various types of phobias. Typically, a patient with a history of phobia experiences fear and avoidance of the anxiety-provoking object. Examples include the fear of riding on an elevator, or fear of needles.

However, the patient does not ruminate or obsess about the object, as in the case of someone with OCD.

- *Tourette syndrome:* Patients with OCD and autism/Asperger syndrome are sometimes misdiagnosed as suffering from Tourette syndrome (TS). This is because many patients with TS also show compulsive behaviors and stereotypic mannerisms. In addition, there is a significant degree of comorbidity between TS and autism. Therefore, in such cases, the patient should be evaluated for the presence of vocal and motoric tics.

- *PANDAS syndrome:* Psychiatric disorders that occur after infection with group A streptococcal infection are collectively termed as PANDAS (Paediatric Autoimmune Neuropsychiatric Disorders Associated with Streptococcal infection). These include tics and, sometimes, behaviors falling within the autistic spectrum. It is believed that antibodies induced after a group A streptococcal infection react with neurons in the basal ganglia of the brain and result in the features of PANDAS. Autistic patients may show an increase in their ritualistic behaviors after a streptococcal throat infection, in which case PANDAS should be suspected. A history of the emergence of OCD symptoms around the time of an upper respiratory infection should alert the clinician to consider a diagnosis of PANDAS (Giulino *et al.*, 2002).

Treatment

Treatment of OCD in autism spectrum disorders should focus on the two conditions separately. It can be broadly classified into two groups – psychological interventions and medications – although in practice, both medications and behavioral therapy are often combined.

PSYCHOLOGICAL APPROACHES

A variety of treatment approaches derived from the behavioral treatment of OCD in the general population have been adapted for use in persons with PDD. Since obsessions and ritualistic behaviors have a tendency to exacerbate at times of stress, it is important to pay attention to any environmental stressors that may be present. These stressors include change of schools, problems in the living situation, and family issues such as divorce. Howlin (1998) has outlined a set of behavioral guidelines for the control of obsessions and rituals in autism. These include establishing clear and consistent rules, introducing change gradually, exploring possible underlying factors and environmental precipitants, and making use of obsessive-compulsive behaviors as reinforcers for developing more productive activities. Psychological approaches can also be used to treat OCD with patients who have normal intelligence, such as those with Asperger syndrome. One popular method of treatment, cognitive-behavioral therapy (CBT), has also been used with some patients with PDD (Raven and Hepburn, 2003). In this form of treatment, which incorporates exposure and response prevention, the patient is taught to confront the OCD symptoms in a hierarchical manner.

USE OF MEDICATIONS

For a long time, behavior therapy was regarded as the first line of treatment. At present, though, the mainstay of treatment is the use of psychotropic medications. A variety of medications are used for this purpose. Common medications are the SSRIs (selective serotonin reuptake inhibitors), such as sertraline, fluoxetine and clomipramine. Occasionally, antipsychotic drugs, such as Risperdal, are also used. Risperdal has also been used in the treatment of PANDAS. A few patients with PANDAS may respond to immunotherapy; however, this form of treatment is reserved for a small group of patients on an experimental basis.

Course and prognosis

There are no long-term reports on the course of OCD in persons with pervasive developmental disorders. However, clinical experience suggests that the course depends to a large extent on the accompanying condition. If the symptoms of OCD arise in the context of depression, then treatment of depression also improves the OCD. However, if the OCD is independent, then the treatment is prolonged, and the course of the illness is marked by exacerbations. These exacerbations are often provoked by stress and changes in the environment. In some cases, the course of the OCD is progressively downhill. The symptoms increase to the extent that the patient becomes frozen in unusual and prolonged rituals. Marked posturing can also result. In such cases, as discussed above, electroconvulsive treatment (ECT) may be life-saving. Some patients require repeated ECTs to help them prevent lapsing into obsessional slowing and catatonia.

Conclusion

OCD often goes undetected in persons with autism and Asperger syndrome. This is largely because of the difficulty in delineating the symptoms of OCD from those of autism, since rigid ritualistic behaviors form an integral part of autistic symptoms. Another barrier to the diagnosis is the requirement that the patient recognize the symptoms as alien. However, in clinical practice autistic patients are sometimes referred with a clear history of an increase in ritualistic behaviors, accompanied by significant distress. These patients respond to a combination of behavioral and psychopharmacological interventions. Standard behavioral principles of treatment, such as exposure, redirection, and response prevention, can be modified for use. A wide variety of medications, including those that have recently been used for the control of OCD, such as the SSRIs, can be used. Patients often improve when treated aggressively, although long-term follow-up studies are not available at this time.

Post-Traumatic Stress Disorder

PTSD is being increasingly recognized in the general population. It is classified in the DSM-IV (APA, 1994) as a type of anxiety disorder. The critical feature of this disorder is that it involves exposure to a severe negative life event. Examples include witnessing a catastrophe such as an earthquake, being subjected to severe physical or sexual abuse, or being the victim of an armed robbery. The event, which is usually life-threatening, affects the person directly or someone close to him. Most of the literature on this topic has grown in the past few decades, partly because of increasing awareness and reports of this disorder among war veterans. The typical symptoms consist of efforts to avoid the incident or memories of the incident, coupled with a range of behavioral disturbances such as hallucinations, depressive symptoms, anxiety attacks, emotional acting out, and aggressive outbursts. In many cases, the symptoms are nonspecific, in that they can occur in a variety of other psychiatric disorders as well. What is characteristic is the history of exposure to a major event. The disorder is more prevalent in females than in males. The susceptibility in females tends to decrease with age, in that females may be more susceptible to this condition in their childhood than in their adolescence (Breslau et al., 1997). The disorder is labeled as acute (when the duration of symptoms is less than three months); chronic (when the symptoms last longer than three months); or delayed (when at least six months have passed between the traumatic event and the onset of symptoms).

PTSD and autism / Asperger syndrome

Although persons with developmental disabilities are physically and sexually abused more often than those without such disabilities (Ammerman *et al.*, 1989), few reports have described the occurrence of PTSD in persons with autism and Asperger syndrome. In a consecutive study of 150 patients with developmental disabilities admitted to a short-term psychiatric unit, about 40 per cent were found to have a history of physical or sexual abuse. Interestingly, those who were relatively less impaired were more vulnerable to the abuse. Ryan (1994) described the characteristics of 51 patients with developmental disabilities who met the criteria of PTSD. Studies have also suggested that those children who live in foster care are more vulnerable to abuse, and hence to trauma (Hobbs, Hobbs and Wynne, 1999). Cook and colleagues (1993) described an adolescent with autism and PTSD. After placement in a residential school, the subject reported being physically abused by a staff member. Psychiatric assessment revealed the presence of PTSD, including symbolic anxiety and repetition of the trauma. The authors stressed the need for ruling out a diagnosis of PTSD in children with developmental disorders, especially those who have been subjected to physical or sexual abuse.

Clinical features

The presentation is modified by the level of intelligence and verbal skills. A history of exposure to a catastrophic event is present. The patient may show signs of regression in his language and social skills. Those who are lower-functioning may lose weight and regress in their self-care skills. Depressive symptoms are often present accompanying the typical symptoms of PTSD. These consist of the individual avoiding the feared situation, showing signs of mounting agitation and anxiety when exposed to such a situation, and a general worsening in the level of functioning in other areas.

Diagnosis

It is not easy to make a diagnosis of PTSD in persons with autism, especially if verbal skills are not adequately developed. Howlin and Clements (1995) devised a method to assess the long-term effects of abuse in children with these disorders based on parental reports and retrospective review of records. They suggested that the diagnosis of PTSD and its effects can be reliably studied in persons with autism-related conditions. As it is extremely difficult in persons with lower levels of intelligence to make a diagnosis of PTSD, appropriate caution must be exercised not to over-diagnose this condition, particularly with the use of methods of assessment that have not been validated adequately.

Treatment

Treatment consists of a combination of psychotherapy, the choice of which depends on the patient's level of functioning – higher-functioning patients may respond to CBT – and medications. The types of medications that can be used include antidepressants and anti-anxiety agents, and clonidine, which dampens the level of excitability. Social interventions including appropriate placement should also be considered.

School refusal

Children who fail to attend school are traditionally divided into two groups: those who refuse to go to school because of fear or anxiety, and those who skip school because they defy authority. Children who belong to the former group are often anxious, shy, or depressed, while those who belong to the latter group are defiant and oppositional. Although clinically useful, this type of classification ignores the third group of children who show mixed features, of both anxiety and oppositional behavior. All the three types of patients show a wide range of formal psychiatric disorders, in particular, anxiety disorders, depression, oppositional disorder, and conduct disorder. A significant number of patients show evidence of multiple psychiatric disorders (Egger, Costello and Angold, 2003).

School refusal in people with autism / Asperger syndrome

Little systematic information is available about the prevalence of school refusal in children with autism spectrum disorders, although a few cases have been reported. Studies of school refusal often tend to exclude patients with mental retardation and other developmental disorders. In clinical practice, though, this problem is not uncommon, especially among those who suffer from Pervasive Developmental Disorder Not Otherwise Specified (PDDNOS) and other less severe variants of autism. The condition is difficult to diagnose in children with severe mental retardation, and, therefore, the diagnosis is seldom made in this population.

Clinical features

Kurita (1991) surveyed a group of youngsters with PDDs to ascertain the presence of school refusal. Out of 135 youngsters with autism and/or mental retardation, 30 with autism and 2 with mental retardation showed features consistent with a diagnosis of school refusal. As expected, patients with school refusal were characterized by a higher level of intelligence than the rest of the sample, and were also marked by a certain degree of obsessive behavior. Autism itself can sometimes present with school refusal. This seems to be particularly the case when the presenting diagnosis is selective mutism. Patients who present with selective mutism coupled with school refusal should be screened for autism, particularly the higher-functioning type.

Diagnosis

The diagnosis of school refusal rests on the central feature of the child's refusal or inability to attend school. Patients with autism spectrum disorders, especially those with PDDNOS and Asperger syndrome, should be screened for this condition. It is important not to dismiss this symptom as part of oppositional behavior. Other disorders that are commonly present, such as anxiety and depression, should also be excluded.

Treatment

The main goal of treatment is to return the child to the school. A trial of medications may help those children who are anxious or depressed. For children with normal intelligence, cognitive-behavioral therapy may be useful. Social skills training should be included as part of the treatment plan. In addition, if bullying and teasing are predisposing factors, these should also be corrected.

Selective mutism

Selective mutism is a psychiatric disorder characterized by a persistent failure to speak in certain social situations. It is typically diagnosed in childhood, and can last from a few months to several years. Girls are more commonly affected. The cause of the disorder is unclear, although it is often described as a form of anxiety disorder.

Some studies have focused on the role of developmental factors in selective mutism. For example, in a series of patients, Steinhausen and colleagues (Steinhausen and Adamek, 1996; Steinhausen and Juzi, 1997b) found a high prevalence of language disorders. Family history of other psychiatric disorders seems to be more common, thus underscoring the role of genetic factors in the etiology. Mutism can also occur in certain brain tumors affecting the cerebellum. A condition known as the posterior-fossa syndrome sometimes accompanies selective mutism along with such features as ataxia (an inability to coordinate muscular movements, often associated with damage to the nervous system) and cranial nerve paralysis (Gordon, 2001). Riva and Giorgi (2000) described a series of 26 children who had undergone surgery for the removal of cerebellar hemisphere or vermal tumors. Lesions in the vermis often led to mutism along with other speech abnormalities, irritability, and behavioral symptoms resembling autism.

Kristensen (2000) compared 54 children with selective mutism with 108 matched controls. Of the subjects with mutism, 68.5 per cent met the defined criteria for a developmental disorder/delay compared with 13.0 per cent in the control group. The criteria for any anxiety diagnosis were met by 74.1 per cent in the selective mutism group and for an elimination disorder (bedwetting or fecal soiling) by 31.5 per cent versus 7.4 per cent and 9.3 per cent, respectively, in the control group. On the whole, 46.3 per cent of the mute children met the criteria for both an anxiety diagnosis and a diagnosis reflecting developmental disorder/delay compared to 0.9 per cent of the controls. The author suggested that mutism often masked the presence of developmental problems in these children, and that children with selective mutism often met the criteria for both a developmental disorder and an anxiety disorder (Kristensen, 2000, 2002).

Although selective mutism is usually described as an uncommon disorder, recent work suggests that this is probably not the case. For example, Kopp and Gillberg (1997) surveyed children aged 15 years in two school districts in Göteborg, Sweden. Three girls and two boys met DSM-IV criteria for selective mutism and a further 25 had a combination of shyness and reticence that did not amount to clinical disorder. The authors estimated the rate of typical selective mutism to be 18 in 10,000 children. Shyness/reticence occurred in 89 in 10,000 children. They concluded that selective mutism was more common than generally believed.

Children with selective mutism often suffer from problems with anxiety and depression. Bergman, Piacentini and McCracken (2002) examined a large group of students attending kindergarten, first and second grades. Out of a total of 2256, 16 students were found to meet the DSM-IV criteria for selective mutism. Compared to age- and sex-matched controls, children with selective mutism scored higher on measures of social anxiety and internalizing symptoms.

The course of selective mutism is about six months, after which time most of the children improve. In a follow-up of 45 patients (23 boys and 22 girls) with selective mutism, the authors found that 12 years after the initial contact with the services, complete remission was seen in about 40 per cent of the cases, while the remaining continued to show residual communication abnormalities (Remschmidt *et al.*, 2001).

Selective mutism in people with autism / Asperger syndrome

The relationship between autism and selective mutism goes back to the early eighteenth century. Known for his efforts to habilitate the Wild Boy of Aveyron (who probably suffered from autism), Itard wrote on the different causes of 'intellectual mutism' (Cary, 1995). Studies have found an excess of language deficits, motor coordination problems, obstetric complications, and minor physical anomalies in people with selective mutism (Kristensen, 2002).

Selective mutism has also been described with patients who have chromosome abnormalities, some of which have also been reported in cases of autism. Grosso *et al.* described the case of selective mutism in a patient with deletion of the short arm of chromosome 18 (Grosso *et al.*, 1999). Selective mutism has also been found in patients with the Fragile X syndrome, a condition that bears some resemblance to autism. Hagerman *et al.* (1999) described a 12-year-old girl with selective mutism. This patient with heterozygous full mutation at FMR1 had a long history of social anxiety and shyness in addition to selective mutism. Interestingly, her sister also had the full mutation and a history of selective mutism that resolved in adolescence. A beneficial response to fluoxetine and psychotherapy was also described. Bankier *et al.* (1999) described a 25-year-old white male with a history of social deficits, selective mutism, and outbursts of temper. Careful examination showed the presence of the typical features of Asperger syndrome.

Sometimes, the child initially presents with selective mutism and is later diagnosed with PDD, as described in the case of AB.

Case study: AB

AB is a 9-year-old Caucasian youngster living with his mother and two younger siblings. He was referred to the community mental health center because his teachers had complained that he never spoke at school and never participated in any group activities. In addition, he was often irritable and sullen, and refused to follow directions.

History revealed that AB had spoken only once since he started school about three years prior to the referral. On that occasion, he had walked up to his teacher and asked her opinion about a certain construction firm that was building a site close to the school. He did not even look up at his teacher when he spoke, and quickly walked away without waiting for an answer.

Details about his behavior at school revealed significant areas of deficits. AB had no friends, and was known as a loner, who preferred to stay by himself and not join in any activities. He liked art, and spent his time drawing buildings. On his way back from school, he would sit by the railway track, watching construction crews at work. He knew the location and the builder of all construction sites in town. He seldom made eye contact, and wore a blank expression. At home, he spoke with his mother. However, his speech was minimal, limited only to his immediate needs. His interaction with his younger brothers was also limited.

AB's developmental history revealed that he had 'always been a shy child.' His mother believed that he would become more social once he started school, but that never happened. Instead, much to her disappointment, he continued to remain mute. She reported that even at home he preferred to be on his own, sometimes watching television programs about building sites, and sometimes drawing.

There was no family history of autism or related conditions, although his father was described as a loner. His mother had a history of depression.

On examination, AB appeared his stated age. He nodded occasionally but did not speak. His eye contact was poor, and his facial expression restricted. There were no abnormal movements. In view of the history of social and communication problems, in addition to his fixation on buildings and construction firms, the diagnosis of PDD was considered. Further evaluation revealed that although he did not meet the full criteria for autism, he fell along the autistic spectrum, and was therefore given a diagnosis of PDDNOS.

Diagnosis

The diagnosis rests on the typical feature of selective mutism: a difficulty in communicating in certain social situations although the patient is able to speak with close family members. The issue of comorbid autism should always be addressed in cases of selective mutism, especially if there is a history of social deficits and rigid ritualistic interests. In the case of AB discussed above, the history of fixations on certain interests, such as construction sites, supported the diagnosis. Rating scales and structured interviews should be performed in atypical cases to clarify the diagnosis.

Treatment

Treatment is often a combination of medications and behavioral therapy (Dow *et al.*, 1998). Individual psychotherapy based on psychoanalytic methods is not useful. Treatment consists of behavioral modification and cognitive intervention, and work with family and school authorities. Some reports have supported trials with antidepressants, especially the SSRIs (Lehman, 2002). In a double-blind study of five children with selective mutism, sertraline was found to be superior to placebo (Carlson, Kratochwill and Johnston, 1999). Similar results have been found with fluoxetine. Since anxiety symptoms are often present in patients with selective mutism, these should also form the focus of treatment (Dummit *et al.*, 1997).

Social anxiety disorder

Also known as 'social phobia,' social anxiety disorder is characterized by marked discomfort and distress in social situations such as meeting new people, speaking in public, or appearing for an interview. While most normal people experience some degree of discomfort in such circumstances, in social anxiety disorder the degree of discomfort is severe and often accompanied by a range of physical symptoms. If symptoms are not specific to any particular social situation, then the condition is said to be generalized. The disorder occurs slightly more commonly in females than in males. Although more common in adolescents and young adults, it can also occur in children. Depressive symptoms are often present. It overlaps considerably with avoidant personality disorder. As in the case of most psychiatric disorders, the etiology consists of a combination of genetic and environmental factors.

According to the DSM-IV, the diagnosis of social anxiety disorder should not be made if the symptoms occur in the context of a pervasive developmental disorder such as autism or Asperger syndrome, implying that symptoms of social anxiety are a part of these conditions. While this may be true in general, in clinical practice it is not uncommon to see higher-functioning people, especially adults with autism/Asperger syndrome, presenting specifically with the symptoms of social anxiety. This is illustrated by the following case study about Kristin.

Case study: Kristin

Kristin is a 19-year-old Caucasian woman living with her parents. She is an undergraduate in music and is particularly interested in musical instruments of the East. She referred herself for her increasing discomfort in social situations. She said that at least for the past six years, she has had a great deal of difficulty in speaking in public or interacting with unfamiliar persons. She rarely speaks in the class for fear of saying something inappropriate or embarrassing herself. She realizes that her fear is unfounded and excessive. In addition, she gets uptight and anxious at the time of playing her musical instruments in front of the class or in public. Apart from some physical symptoms of anxiety, such as excessive sweating of her hands, she is in good health. Her mood, sleep, and appetite are within the normal range.

Her mother reported, however, that Kristin was 'different' from her other child. She was always shy, reserved, and reticent. 'We just thought that was the way she was.' When Kristin was about 2 years of age, she went through a phase when she would become extremely upset when people laughed. This continued for a few years and subsided on its own, although she was seen by a psychologist. Her milestones were not delayed. However, again at about 2 years of age, she would go through periods when she would line up objects all the time. She was particularly fascinated by the letters of the alphabet; she would line them up from A to Z and back, over and over again. When she started her pre-school, she was so isolative and aloof that her teacher thought she had mental retardation. She did not play with the other children and was aloof and withdrawn. Since she did not have any major communication problems, apart from an inconsistent eye contact and a limited facial expression, people assumed that she was only shy! She did not play any pretend games, such as holding doll-parties or dressing-up games. She would dress-up only as a mermaid and insist on swimming.

From Kristin's second to fourth grade, she was fixated on space and the NASA program. She read only about these topics although she would talk only if asked. Conversation with her was limited, and to the point. Rarely did she talk about the interests of others, or show empathy or concern for others. For example, she did not console her mother if the latter was hurt or upset. She insisted on having the furniture and other objects arranged in a certain manner in her room, and did not like anything to be disturbed. She dressed casually but sometimes did not seem to have a clue about wearing appropriate clothes. Her main area of interest at the time of the evaluation was music; however, her mother did not feel that the interest was intrusive or overwhelming. Her family history was negative for depression or other disorders although a cousin on her maternal side appeared to have autism.

Her father, a computer analyst, was described as being social but awkward, given to organizing lists and cataloging music CDs.

Considering the above history, it was apparent that Kristin suffered from social anxiety disorder (social phobia). In addition, however, there was a history of social deficits (difficulty in making friendships), and mild communication deficits (poor eye contact, limited facial expression), with some suggestion of focused interests (music, space in the past) that raised the diagnosis of pervasive developmental disorder. However, the symptoms were not severe enough to meet the cut-off for autistic disorder or Asperger syndrome. Kristin was, therefore, given a diagnosis of PDDNOS. In addition, she met the criteria for social anxiety disorder.

It was recommended that Kristin's diagnosis of mild autism be taken into account during her educational planning. Specifically, attendance at a social skills training group for high-functioning persons with PDD was suggested, along with a trial of an anti-anxiety agent.

In clinical practice, treatment of such cases will involve an agent such as sertraline (Zoloft) or paroxitene (Paxil), along with appropriate behavioral therapy. This case study illustrates that although the diagnosis of social phobia is not generally given in persons with PDD, at times the symptoms cause great distress and discomfort to justify an additional diagnosis and treatment.

Conclusion

Symptoms of anxiety are often present in persons with autism and Asperger syndrome. Because of this, the diagnosis of anxiety disorders is often not made in this population. However, in a minority of cases, the symptoms become severe, resulting in a significant degree of distress to the individual and to the community, and interfering with academic and occupational adjustment. In such cases, an additional diagnosis of an anxiety disorder is justified. Preliminary reports have described a wide variety of anxiety disorders occuring among persons with autism and Asperger syndrome, the most common including OCD, social anxiety disorder, school refusal and selective mutism. In addition, simple phobias and social anxiety disorder also occur. The treatment of anxiety disorders in persons with PDD follows the general principles of the treatment of anxiety disorders and is based on a combination of behavioral therapy and medications.

References

Ammerman, R.T, Van-Hasselt, V.B., Herson, M., McGonigle, J.J. and Lubetsky, M.J. (1989) 'Abuse and neglect in psychiatrically hospitalized multihandicapped children.' *Child Abuse and Neglect, 13*, 3, 335–43.

APA (American Psychiatric Association) (1994) *Diagnostic and Statistical Manual of Mental Disorders, Fourth Edition* (DSM-IV). Washington, DC: APA.

Bankier, B., Lenz, G., Gutierrez, K., Bach, M. and Katschnig, H. (1999) 'A case of Asperger's syndrome first diagnosed in adulthood.' *Psychopathology, 32*, 1, 43–6.

Baron-Cohen, S. (1990) 'Do autistic children have obsessions and compulsions?' *British Journal of Clinical Psychology, 28*, 3, 193–200.

Baron-Cohen, S. and Wheelwright, S. (1999) '"Obsessions" in children with autism or Asperger syndrome. Content analysis in terms of core domains of cognition.' *British Journal of Psychiatry, 175*, 484–90.

Bergman, R.L., Piacentini, J.A. and McCracken, J.T. (2002) 'Prevalence and description of selective mutism in a school-based sample.' *Journal of the American Academy of Child and Adolescent Psychiatry, 41*, 8, 938–46.

Bolton, P.F., Pickes, A., Murphy, M. and Rutter, M. (1998) 'Autism, affective and other psychiatric disorders: Patterns of familial aggregation.' *Psychological Medicine, 28*, 385–95.

Breslau, N., Davis, G.C., Andreski, P., Peterson, E.L. and Schultz, L.R. (1997) 'Sex differences in posttraumatic stress disorder.' *Archives of General Psychiatry, 54*, 11, 1044–48.

Carlson, J.S., Kratochwill, T.R. and Johnston, H.F. (1999) 'Sertraline treatment of 5 children diagnosed with selective mutism: A single-case research trial.' *Journal of Child and Adolescent Psychopharmacology, 9*, 4, 293–306.

Cary, N.J. (1995) 'Itard's 1828 memoire on "Mutism caused by a lesion of the Intellectual functions:" A historical analysis.' *Journal of the American Academy of Child and Adolescent Psychiatry, 34*, 12, 1655–61.

Cook, E.H. Jr., Kieffer, J.E., Charak, D.A. and Leventhal, B.L. (1993) 'Autistic disorder and post-traumatic stress disorder.' *Journal of the American Academy of Child and Adolescent Psychiatry, 32*, 6, 1292–4.

Cook, E.H. and Leventhal, B.L. (1995) 'Autistic disorder and other pervasive developmental disorders.' *Child and Adolescent Clinics of North America, 4*, 2, 381–99.

Dow, S.P., Sonies, B.C., Scheib, D., Moss, S.E. and Leonard, H.L. (1998) 'Practical guidelines for the assessment and treatment of selective mutism.' *Journal of the American Academy of Child and Adolescent Psychiatry, 34*, 7, 836–46.

Dummit, E.S. 3rd, Klein, R.G., Tancer, N.K., Asche, B., Martin, J. and Fairbanks, J.A. (1997) 'Systematic assessment of 50 children with selective mutism.' *Journal of the American Academy of Child and Adolescent Psychiatry, 36*, 5, 653–60.

Egger, H.L., Costello, E.J. and Angold, A. (2003) 'School refusal and psychiatric disorders: A community study.' *Journal of the American Academy of Child and Adolescent Psychiatry, 42*, 7, 797–807.

Ghaziuddin, M., Tsai, L. and Ghaziuddin, N. (1994) 'Comorbidity of autistic disorder in children and adolescents.' *European Child and Adolescent Psychiatry, 1*, 4, 209– 13.

Giulino, L., Gammon, P., Sullivan, K., Franklin, M., Foa, E., Maid, R. and March, J.S. (2002) 'Is parental report of upper respiratory infection at the onset of obsessive-compulsive disorder suggestive of pediatric autoimmune neuropsychiatric disorder associated with streptococcal infection?' *Journal of Child and Adolescent Psychopharmacology, 12*, 2, 157–64.

Goodman, W.K., Price, L.H., Rasmussen, S.A., Riddle, M.A. and Rapaport, J.L. (1986) *Children's Yale-Brown Obsessive-Compulsive Scale.* Washington, CD: National Institute of Mental Health.

Gordon, N. (2001) 'Mutism: Elective or selective, and acquired.' *Brain Development, 23*, 2, 83–7.

Gross-Isseroff, R., Hermesh, H., and Weizman A. (2001) 'Obsessive compulsive behaviour in autism – towards an autistic-obsessive compulsive syndrome?' *World Journal of Biological Psychiatry, 2*, 4, 193–7.

Grosso, S., Cioni, M., Pucci, L., Morgese, G. and Balestri, P. (1999) 'Selective mutism, speech delay, dysmorphisms, and deletion of the short arm of chromosome 18: A distinct entity?' *Journal of Neurology, Neurosurgery and Psychiatry, 67*, 6, 830–1.

Hagerman, R.J., Hills, J., Scharfenaker, S. and Lewis, H. (1999) 'Fragile X syndrome and selective mutism.' *American Journal of Medical Genetics, 83*, 4, 313–17.

Hamilton, M. (1960) 'A rating scale for depression.' *Journal of Neurology, Neurosurgery, and Psychiatry, 23*, 56–62.

Hobbs, G.F., Hobbs, C.J. and Wynne, J.M. (1999) 'Abuse of children in foster and residential care.' *Child Abuse and Neglect, 23*, 12, 1239–52.

Howlin, P. (1998) 'Practitioner review: Psychological and educational treatments for autism.' *Journal of Child Psychology and Psychiatry, 39*, 3, 307–22.

Howlin, P. and Clements, J. (1995) 'Is it possible to assess the impact of abuse on children with pervasive developmental disorders?' *Journal of Autism and Developmental Disorders, 25*, 4, 337–54.

Kanner, L. (1943) 'Autistic disturbances of affective contact.' *Nevous Child, 2*, 217–50.

Kopp, S. and Gillberg, C. (1997) 'Selective Mutism: A population-based study: A research note.' *Journal of Child Psychology and Psychiatry, 38*, 2, 257–62.

Kristensen, H. (2000) 'Selective mutism and comorbidity with developmental disorder/delay, anxiety disorder, and elimination disorder.' *Journal of the American Academy of Child and Adolescent Psychiatry, 39*, 2, 249–56.

Kristensen, H. (2002) 'Non-specific markers of neurodevelopmental disorder/delay in selective mutism – a case-control study.' *European Child and Adolescent Psychiatry, 2*, 71–8.

Kurita, H. (1991) 'School refusal in pervasive developmental disorders.' *Journal of Autism and Developmental Disorders, 21*, 1, 1–15.

Lehman, R.B. (2002) 'Rapid resolution of social anxiety disorder, selective mutism, and separation anxiety with paroxetine in an 8-year-old girl.' *Journal of Psychiatry and Neuroscience, 27*, 2, 124–5.

McDougle, C., Kresch, L., Goodman, W.K. and Naylor, S.T. (1995) 'A case-control study of repetitive thoughts and behavior n adults with autistic disorder and obsessive-compulsive disorder.' *American Journal of Psychiatry, 152*, 3, 772–7.

Nilsson, E.W., Gillberg, C., Gillberg, I.C. and Rastam, M. (1999) 'Ten-year follow-up of adolescent-onset anorexia nervosa: Personality disorders.' *Journal of the American Academy of Child and Adolescent Psychiatry, 38*, 11, 1389–95.

Raven, J. and Hepburn, S. (2003) 'Cognitive-behavioral treatment of obsessive-compulsive disorder in a child with Asperger syndrome.' *Autism, 7*, 2, 145–64.

Remschmidt, H., Poller, M., Herpertz-Dahlmann, B., Hennighausen, K. and Gutenbrunner, C. (2001) 'A follow-up study of 45 patients with elective mutism.' *European Archives of Psychiatry and Clinical Neuroscience, 251*, 6, 284–96.

Riva, D. and Giorgi, C. (2000) 'The cerebellum contributes to higher functions during development: Evidence from a series of children surgically treated for posterior fossa tumours.' *Brain, 123*, Pt 5, 1051–61.

Ryan, R. (1994) 'Posttraumatic stress disorder in persons with developmental disabilities.' *Community Mental Health Journal, 30*, 1, 45–54.

Segal, N.L. (1999) 'Silent partners: Twins with selective mutism.' *Twin Research, 3*, 235–6, 238–9.

Steinhausen, H.C. and Adamek, R. (1997) 'The family history of children with elective mutism: A research report.' *European Child and Adolescent Psychiatry, 6*, 2, 107–11.

Steinhausen, H.C. and Juzi, C. (1996) 'Elective mutism: an analysis of 100 cases.' *Journal of the American Academy of Child and Adolescent Psychiatry, 35*, 5, 606–614.

CHAPTER 9

Schizophrenia and Other Psychotic Disorders

Introduction

Schizophrenia is a severe mental disorder characterized by a distinct pattern of signs and symptoms, and by a deteriorating clinical course. It affects all aspects of the personality and results in marked impairment of thought, mood, and perception. An important feature of the disorder is the presence of hallucinations in which the patient hears, sees, and feels things that do not exist. Delusions are also common. These are false beliefs, held despite evidence to the contrary, such as a belief that the environment is poisoned or the house is bugged by electronic devices. A variety of other symptoms also occur. Its prevalence rate is about 1 per cent of the population in western industrialized countries. It is a global disorder of major importance to public health that cuts across all countries and cultures. Males are more commonly affected than females.

While the disorder most frequently starts in early adult life, children and adolescents can also be affected (Kraeplin, 1919), although it is uncommon to find schizophrenia in children younger than 7 or 8 years of age, and its diagnosis in this age group remains controversial. While schizophrenia can be diagnosed in children using the same set of diagnostic criteria as in adults (Asarnow and Asarnow, 1994; Asarnow, Thompson and Goldstein, 1994), important differences exist between adult- and childhood-onset disorders. For example, childhood-onset schizophrenia is more often characterized by a poor premorbid adjustment, an insidious onset and a poor outcome (Asarnow *et al.*, 1994). Other studies have also found premorbid characteristics resembling those of autistic children, such as deficits of language, and delayed motor development, in children who later developed schizophrenia (Alaghband-Rad *et al.*, 1995; Russell, Bott and Sammons, 1989).

According to the DSM-IV, the diagnosis of schizophrenia requires at least two of the following symptoms: delusions, hallucinations, disorganized speech, grossly disorganized speech/catatonic behavior, negative symptoms (e.g., affective flattening (non-responsiveness of mood), alogia (lack of speech)). The diagnostic criteria also require that the disturbance lasts for at least six months and is accompanied by social and occupational dysfunction. In children and adolescents, this includes failure to achieve the expected level of academic or social achievement (APA, 1994).

Like other major mental disorders, schizophrenia is regarded as a multifactorial condition. While genetic factors play an important role, there is no single gene specific for schizophrenia. Schizophrenia is divided into several subtypes, with paranoid schizophrenia being the most common. Schizophrenia can also be divided into two main forms depending on the type of symptoms: positive and negative schizophrenia. The former is characterized by such features as hallucinations and delusions and with bizarre disturbances of behavior, while the latter presents itself as a deficit condition with poor thought and speech, a flat mood, and a decreased level of activity. A number of abnormal movements, such as rocking, mannerisms, and stereotypic behaviors, also occur. Inappropriate vocalizations and repetitive speech patterns are also sometimes observed. Although it is generally considered a single entity, schizophrenia can more accurately be described as a collection of disorders all of which are characterized by similar signs and symptoms.

Schizophrenia and autism: Differences

Although schizophrenia and autism are now regarded as two distinct conditions, they share an interesting history. Autism was initially described as 'infantile psychosis' which resulted in the belief that autism was a form of schizophrenia. Indeed, for a long time autism was regarded as synonymous with childhood schizophrenia. This was because the two disorders bore resemblance to each other in some of their clinical features. Even the term 'autism' had its origins in the description of schizophrenia. It was only in the late 1960s, almost 25 years after Kanner's description of autism, that serious attempts were made to separate the two conditions. Kolvin (Kolvin, 1971; Kolvin *et al.*, 1971) performed a series of studies in the UK to map out the differences. These studies outlined important differences between the two conditions focusing on their age of onset, pattern of symptoms, family history, course, and response to treatment. These are summarized in Table 9.1.

Table 9.1 The differences between autism and schizophrenia

	Autism	*Schizophrenia*
Age of onset	Less than 36 months	Adolescence or early adulthood
Symptoms	No hallucinations and delusions	Hallucinations and delusions are common
Mental retardation	Often present	No relationship with mental retardation
Seizure disorder	Common	No relationship with seizure disorder
Family history	Increased history of autism spectrum disorders	Increased history of schizophrenia spectrum disorders
Treatment	Medications palliative	Antipsychotic medications specific and effective
Course	Generally life-long. Few cases of 'recovery'	Generally life-long. But some cases recover more fully

As shown in Table 9.1, the main differences between autism and schizophrenia can be summarized as follows (Rutter, 1972).

First, autism is a childhood-onset disorder which almost always begins before 3 years of age, while schizophrenia more often arises in later adolescence or early adulthood.

Second, the pattern of symptoms is different. The characteristic symptoms of schizophrenia are hallucinations and delusions, which are not typically present in autism. However, some patients with autism present with what are regarded as overvalued ideas and cling excessively to certain topics of interest: astronomy, weather, pollution etc. These preoccupations – which are more likely to occur in higher-functioning individuals – have an 'as if' quality about them, that is, they resemble delusions but lack their fixed nature.

Third, there is a specific relationship between autism and mental retardation. At least half of patients with autism have mental retardation, defined as an IQ below 70 accompanied by problems with adaptive functioning. In contrast, there is no such relationship between schizophrenia and mental retardation, although patients with schizophrenia tend to have a somewhat lower IQ than the general population.

Fourth, autistic individuals often have a history of seizure disorder. About 30–50 per cent of individuals with autism, especially those with mental retardation, have a seizure disorder. There is no specific relationship between schizophrenia and seizure disorder, although some forms of epilepsy are more common in persons with psychosis. For example, psychotic behavior is particularly common in patients with temporal lobe epilepsy.

Fifth, important differences exist in so far as the family history is concerned. Patients with autism often have an excess of first-degree relatives with autism spectrum disorders and patients with schizophrenia have an excess of first-degree relatives with schizophrenia spectrum disorders.

Sixth, the response to psychopharmacological interventions is also different. While antipsychotic medications are more specific and effective in schizophrenia, their role in autism is largely limited to behavioral control.

Finally, the disorders also differ in their course and outcome. While the majority of patients with schizophrenia follow a deteriorating course, some recover completely, something that is extremely rare, if at all possible, in patients with autism.

Schizophrenia and autism: Similarities

Although schizophrenia and autism are generally regarded as two separate disorders, they do resemble each other in more ways than is generally recognized.

First, both the disorders are genetically heterogeneous categories, consisting of several subtypes, which occur not as distinct entities but as a range of abnormalities. Thus, autism is conceptualized as a spectrum disorder which ranges from traditional autism to mild variants of the disorder, such as Asperger syndrome and Pervasive Developmental Disorder Not Otherwise Specified (PDDNOS), while schizophrenia too is regarded as a spectrum disorder, whose boundaries include schizoid and schizotypal disorders. Of interest, schizoid personality disorder is sometimes regarded as synonymous with Asperger syndrome (Wolff, 1991).

Second, some patients with childhood schizophrenia show features of autism in their premorbid histories (McKenna et al., 1994). Thus, it has been shown that prior to the onset of psychosis these children give histories of poor social relationships, communication abnormalities (such as difficulties with eye contact), and motor abnormalities (such as clumsiness and deficits of coordination).

Third, many adults with autism show symptoms that resemble those of negative schizophrenia. These include poor social relatedness, anhedonia or lack of pleasure in activities, flat or constricted affect or ability to show emotions, restriction of facial expressions, poor use of gestures and diminished eye contact, alogia or poor speech, and the presence of stereotypic behaviors and mannerisms.

Fourth, some patients with Asperger syndrome and high-functioning autism sometimes resemble those with positive schizophrenia. The diagnosis of schizophrenia is based mainly on the presence of what is commonly known as 'thought disorder.' This is characterized by a variety of abnormalities of thinking, such as delusions, derailment, incoherence, and illogical thinking. However, such thought abnormalities are also often seen in persons with autism, especially those who are not mentally retarded, and are, therefore, able to describe their experiences adequately. Dykens, Volkmar and Glick (1991) studied features of thought disorder in a group of high-functioning autistic individuals. They used the Rorschach test, which is a projective test commonly used for psychological assessment. They found that high-functioning adults appeared more thought disordered than normal controls. Abnormalities such as poor reality testing, perceptual distortions, and areas of cognitive slippage were observed. Some of the abnormalities seen resembled those seen in schizophrenia. Ghaziuddin, Leininger and Tsai (1995) extended these findings to Asperger syndrome. They found that AS subjects demonstrated a trend towards greater disorganized thinking than those with high-functioning autism, and also tended to be more focused on their inner lives and fantasies.

Fifth, there is some anecdotal evidence of increased family history of schizophrenia in the first-degree relatives of some patients with Asperger syndrome. In this context, it is interesting to note that a recent molecular genetic study of Asperger syndrome found an overlap between the areas of Asperger syndrome and those linked to schizophrenia on the chromosomes (Ylisaukko-oja et al., 2004).

Finally, neuropsychological deficits, such as Theory of Mind and executive function deficits, are common to both the conditions. Thus, although schizophrenia and autism are generally regarded as two separate and distinct disorders, there are some superficial similarities between them. While the available evidence is not strong enough to suggest common underlying mechanisms, it is tempting to speculate that a subgroup of patients within the autistic spectrum, especially those who are higher-functioning, may be at an increased risk of developing schizophrenia.

Comorbid schizophrenia and autism

Although the association is rare, autism and schizophrenia sometimes occur together, as has been described in a few case reports. For example, Petty *et al.* (1984) described three autistic patients who later met the criteria for schizophrenia. All three developed sufficient communicative speech, had a full-scale IQ of over 70, and met the criteria for schizophrenia by the age of 13 years. Studies investigating the prevalence of schizophrenia in samples of children with autism are difficult to undertake because of the rarity of the fully diagnosed schizophrenic syndrome in younger children (Kydd and Werry, 1982). However, referral of children with autism and other pervasive developmental disorders (PDDs) for suspected schizophrenia is not uncommon in clinical practice. To ascertain how many children with PDD referred for psychotic behavior are given a diagnosis of schizophrenia, we studied a consecutive series of 43 children over a period of 18 months. Out of eight patients with PDD who were referred with psychotic symptoms (6 males; mean age: 11.8 years SD±1.1), four met the criteria for major depression. Diagnosis of schizophrenia was suspected in only one patient but was not confirmed. Thus, when psychotic behavior was the presenting symptom in autistic children, depression, and not schizophrenia, was the likely diagnosis, and failure to look for depression in autistic children, especially those who were higher-functioning, resulted in a mistaken diagnosis of schizophrenia (Ghaziuddin *et al.*, 1995).

Studies have also examined the presence of schizophrenia in adolescents in autism. Volkmar and Cohen (1991) studied 163 patients with autism referred to a special clinic. Children over 15 years of age were included. They found 41 patients in whom there was documentation of symptoms suggestive of schizophrenia. All the patients had communicative speech and a mean IQ of 58. Only one patient with mild mental retardation met the DSM-III-R (APA, 1987) criteria for schizophrenia. The authors concluded that there was no excess of schizophrenia in patients with autism.

Case study: Scott H

Scott H is a 17-year-old Caucasian youngster living with his biological parents. He was diagnosed with autism at the age of 3 years. He attended a program for autistic children in the public school system where he was described as a good student with an average level of functioning. His IQ was in the normal range. His main areas of interest were reading and running.

He had won several awards, including one for being the best runner in the city.

About three months prior to the referral, Scott H's behavior began to change. His coach noticed that he had become slower in his movements. At home, he started listening to music at full volume, much to the annoyance of his family. At times, he would put his ear close to the radio as if he was trying to listen to the music. When asked, he would say that he was trying to listen to 'a voice.' Gradually, he started complaining about hearing voices. These voices, both male and female, asked him to do 'things,' and sometimes talked about him. In addition, he became preoccupied with religious themes, worrying that his thoughts were 'getting out of control.' At times, he would worry about his thinking 'bad thoughts' about religion.

At the time of the evaluation, Scott H appeared anxious and fearful. He voiced concerns about his safety, and thought that something terrible was going to happen to him and to others. He made vague comments about a 'man who was trying to cause trouble' for him, but would not give any details. He believed that thoughts were being put in his head, and that he was being made to do things against his will. When asked to explain, he said that he was trying to get his thinking sorted out, but was not able to do so. He held his arms in odd postures, and sometimes looked around as if responding to voices. He said that the voices came out of his head; they asked him to do things and sometimes talked about him. He believed that other people were able to read his mind without talking to him. His mood was generally flat, and at times inappropriate and anxious. During the course of the interview, he would suddenly burst out singing, coining new words, and rhyming sentences. He would also compulsively rub between the toes of his right foot, a habit that had increased in the weeks preceding his evaluation.

There was no family history of psychiatric illness. Scott H's past psychiatric history was unremarkable. He was not on any medications and there was no history of substance abuse. Apart from the diagnosis of autism, he was in reasonably good health, although since the onset of his behavioral symptoms, he had not been eating and sleeping well. There was no evidence of a seizure disorder. All the investigations, including brain imaging, were normal. Based on the above history and the presentation, therefore, it appeared that schizophrenia was the most probable diagnosis. The main points in favor of this diagnosis were a history of hearing voices, having paranoid ideas and abnormal beliefs, and a gradual worsening of his behavior.

Comorbid schizophrenia and Asperger syndrome

Wolff (1991) described a group of children she labeled as 'schizoid.' They presented in middle rather than early childhood with a history of single-minded pursuits, solitariness, rigidity, and lack of empathy. In many ways, these patients resembled people with Asperger syndrome, although that diagnosis had not yet been introduced in the official systems of classification. About half of the patients described had some form of additional psychiatric disorder. Of the 32 subjects, 16 had problems with conduct and emotions. At adult follow-up, two patients gave a history consistent with schizophrenia.

In 1989, Szatmari and colleagues described a follow-up study of 45 high-functioning children with autism and related disorders. A high number of subjects showed comorbid psychiatric disorders. Although several gave a history of paranoid ideas and of hearing voices, only one was given a diagnosis of schizophrenia (Szatmari et al., 1989). None of the 35 patients with Asperger syndrome described in the study by Ghaziuddin, Weidmer-Mikhail and Ghaziuddin (1998) was given an additional diagnosis of schizophrenia.

Autism/Asperger syndrome presenting as schizophrenia

Patients with high-functioning autism and Asperger syndrome have characteristics that can lead to a mistaken diagnosis of schizophrenia and other psychotic disorders. These include eccentricities, social oddities, and a preoccupation with topics and interests that may be confused with other psychiatric disorders such as schizophrenia, bipolar disorder (manic depression), and Obsessive-Compulsive Disorder (OCD) (Ryan, 1992). However, each of these disorders present and develop differently. The importance of correctly diagnosing schizophrenia has been underscored in several studies. For instance, McKenna et al. (1994) examined 71 children and adolescents referred with a history of childhood-onset psychosis. Systematic clinical and structured interviews were done. Six patients with pervasive developmental (autism spectrum) disorders were identified. Although they had been referred with a history of psychotic symptoms, none of these six patients met the operational criteria for schizophrenia. Four of these patients were diagnosed with Asperger syndrome and two were diagnosed with PDDNOS. The patients with Asperger syndrome presented with a variety of psychotic symptoms such as visual hallucinations, unusual perseverations, and idiosyncratic utterances. The authors concluded that childhood-onset schizophrenia was often misdiagnosed, perhaps because of the 'rarity of the disorder and the ambiguity in applying the primary criteria' (McKenna *et al.*, 1994, p.636). In another study derived from the same sample, Gordon and colleagues (1994, p.636) found that the premorbid history of patients with childhood-onset schizophrenia was characterized by apparently normal to uneven developmental features such as delayed speech and sensory deficits.

Case study: Philip A

Philip A was seen at the age of 53 years. He was referred by the community mental health center because the treating psychiatrist felt that Philip's diagnosis of schizophrenia, which he had carried for about 30 years, did not seem to be accurate.

Philip A's history was as follows. He was noted to be somewhat unusual from a very early age. He spoke rather early, and seemed to enjoy initiating conversation with others at an early age. However, he related better with adults than with his peers. His topics of interest were unusual in that, even as a child, he was interested in geography, focusing on remote areas. He would talk incessantly, paying little regard to the social context or the needs of the listeners. His tone was odd, at times flat, and at other times robotic. After dropping out of school, he did a variety of odd jobs. He had no close friends and never had a sexual relationship. In his late 20s, he was diagnosed as having schizophrenia. The reasons given for this diagnosis were his social isolation, his preoccupation with geographic facts, and his odd manner of interaction with others. Because of his tendency to lecture on certain topics, he was described as having pressure of speech, and a diagnosis of bipolar disorder was also considered. He never had any hallucinations or delusions. His interest in geography was excessive.

Once diagnosed with schizophrenia, Philip A was treated by the county mental health system with a variety of medications, including antipsychotic drugs such as haloperidol. None of the medications changed his manner of relating to others. He was later re-diagnosed as suffering from Asperger syndrome because of the history of social deficits, his subtle communication impairment, and his excessive interest in certain topics. His general manner of interaction was active but odd, with a pedantic manner of speaking. Because of the lack of history of hallucinations and delusions, and other thought deficits characteristic of schizophrenia, that diagnosis was ruled out.

Case study: NS

NS is a 40-year-old male of Asian origin. Born in India, he moved to the US when he was in his 20s. Despite being somewhat awkward socially, he eventually obtained a master's degree in architecture from a well-known university. However, after graduation, he was not able to hold on to a stable job.

With some money from his family, NS started buying run-down apartments. Although this was meant for investment, it soon became apparent that this was not the sole reason. Rather, he seemed to be fixated on the idea of buying decrepit buildings. He would neither maintain them properly nor sell them off to cut his losses. His elderly mother, who lived with him, worried about his future because he not able to find a job, and was frequently getting into legal problems. In addition to his fascination with buildings, he was obsessed with the quality and the composition of air. When he met people socially, he would lapse into his favorite topic – a lecture on the importance of breathing pure air. He spoke in an odd, overly familiar manner with a fixed stare, sometimes lecturing. He had never had a girl friend or experienced any sexual relationship. Because of his mounting financial and legal troubles, he was referred to the local mental health services with a suspected diagnosis of schizophrenia/OCD.

NS's family history was negative for autism or for Asperger syndrome. However, his older sister suffered from schizhophrenia and was on medications. Although his past history did not reveal any mental illness, it was recorded that NS had always been rigid and awkward, even as a child. His eye contact was inconsistent; in the middle of a sentence, he would suddenly start staring the examiner intently for no apparent reason. His mood was mildly depressed without any suicidal ideas or plans.

Initially, a diagnosis of schizophrenia was made based on the bizarreness of NS's thinking, his difficulty in relating to people, his odd demeanor etc. However, because there were no clear hallucinations, and no other features typical of schizophrenia, this diagnosis was later changed to that of Asperger syndrome. The points in favor of Asperger syndrome were a history of odd social interactions since early childhood, a lack of language delay with a tendency to pedantry, and single-minded pursuits. He did not meet the criteria for autism.

PDDNOS and psychotic disorder

As explained elsewhere, PDDNOS is a residual category that includes those patients whose symptoms do not meet the criteria of a specific disorder such as autism or Asperger syndrome. Quite often, these patients suffer from mild social and communication deficits, with or without rigid isolated interests. The main distinction of PDDNOS from autism/Asperger syndrome lies in the fact that either two of the three cardinal symptoms (reciprocal social deficits, communication impairment, and rigid ritualistic interests) of autism are present, or all three are present in a mild form. At least one of the symptoms must be the presence of reciprocal social deficits.

Although systematic studies are lacking, there is ample clinical evidence that many patients with PDDNOS go through periods of affective dysregulation and disorganization. In addition, some of them may show brief psychotic features in response to an actual or perceived change in routines. (Sometimes, these patients are referred to as suffering from multiplex developmental disorder.) Repeated episodes of disorganization in thinking are common (Towbin *et al.*, 1993). However, the symptoms are not severe enough to meet the criteria for any psychotic disorder, such as schizophrenia.

Since little information is available on the long-term aspects of this condition, it is unclear if there is any association with schizophrenia, although some studies have suggested an association. In one such study, the authors compared 19 children with 'multidimensionally impaired disorder' with two control groups of children with schizophrenia and Attention Deficit Hyperactivity Disorder (ADHD). Patients with multidimensionally impaired syndrome and patients with very early-onset schizophrenia shared a similar pattern of early transient autistic features, post-psychotic cognitive decline, and an elevated risk of schizophrenic spectrum disorders among their first-degree relatives (Kumra *et al.*, 1998). However, more information is needed on the diagnostic validity of this condition and its relationship with schizophrenia before any generalizations can be made.

Psychotic depression presenting as schizophrenia

Depression can sometimes lead to psychotic features. The patient presents with symptoms, such as auditory hallucinations, which resemble those of schizophrenia. There is often a past history of depression. The patient's mood is depressed with evidence of suicidal ideas. These features are more easily elicited from those with high-functioning autism and Asperger syndrome than those who are low-functioning. The hallucinations that are present often have a depressive content. For example, the voices may call derogatory names to the patient and tell him to kill himself. The quality of the voices is also different, in that, in psychotic depression, the voices often talk to the person, addressing him directly; whereas in true schizophrenia, the voices often talk about the person. The family and past history are also suggestive of depression.

Case study: Samuel U

Samuel U, a 16-year-old youngster with autism, was referred for psychiatric treatment for increasing behavioral problems. He was reported to have become socially withdrawn, spending long periods of time locked up in his room. He believed that he was going to fall into the 'dark hole in space' and disappear. At times, he appeared to talk to himself, and respond to outside voices. His ability to take care of his basic hygiene had deteriorated. He was not eating or sleeping properly.

The onset of Samuel U's symptoms was about six months prior to the referral. This seemed to coincide with the family's move to a new house. Further history revealed that he had become irritable, getting angry for trivial reasons, and started losing interest in his studies. His main area of interest was science and space. However, he had gradually become preoccupied with depressive themes, worrying about the ozone layer, and finally, coming to believe that he was going to fall into what he called the dark hole in space.

Samuel U had no previous psychiatric history. He had been diagnosed as autistic in his pre-school; his level of intellectual functioning was average. There was no evidence of seizures. His family psychiatric history was negative. Also, there was no history of recent drug or alcohol abuse. When he was seen in the emergency room, a diagnosis of schizophrenia was made, based on his deteriorating behavior, history of hearing voices, preoccupation with bizarre scientific themes such as the ozone layer, and a general decline in his self-care skills. However, a closer evaluation on follow-up strongly suggested that the primary problem was one of depression, and that the psychotic behavior was the result of the underlying mood disorder and not of schizophrenia.

Bipolar disorder resembling schizophrenia

Patients with high-functioning autism and Asperger syndrome sometimes present with features consistent with bipolar disorder. There is evidence of cyclical mood changes, alternating periods of depressed mood and elation, periods of grandiosity, and disturbance of sleep and appetite. In extreme cases, the patient may lapse into a manic phase. This phase is characterized by a distinct period of elevated or irritable mood which may lead to hospitaliza-tion. During this period, the following features may be present: grandiosity, decreased need for sleep, extreme talkativeness, flight of ideas, racing thoughts, distractibility, psychomotor agitation, an increase in goal-directed activity, and an excessive involvement in pleasurable activities. Hallucinations and disordered thought patterns may be present, leading to the suspicion of schizophrenia; but the key to the diagnosis of a manic episode is the mood disturbance, and the history of a long-standing cyclical mood disturbance. A family history of a mood disorder also helps in the differential diagnosis.

Autism, schizophrenia, and mental retardation

Schizophrenia can occur in the setting of mental retardation. Kraeplin (1919) estimated that from 3.5 to 7 per cent of all cases of what he called 'dementia precox' (later called schizophrenia) were due to 'idiocy' or mental retardation. 'Propfschizophrenia' is the term given to describe schizophrenia superim-posed or engrafted on mental retardation. It is characterized by hebephrenic[1] or catatonic features, a paucity of delusions, which are often transitory and naive in nature, recurrent episodes of psychosis often precipitated by signifi-cant life events, and presence of stereotypies and movement disorders. Propfschizophrenia differs from childhood-onset schizophrenia in that the symptoms of the latter disorder are similar to those of adult-onset schizo-phrenia, except for the age of onset. Propfschizophrenia, on the other hand, is marked by a lack of clear delusions in the presence of hebephrenic or catatonic features. The presence of stereotypies in this condition underscores the need to separate it from autism. However, in those patients who have severe mental retardation and verbal deficits, it is almost impossible to distin-guish between autism and schizophrenia.

Assessment and treatment

The first step in the management of a patient with PDD with superimposed psychosis is to establish the diagnosis and ensure safety. Ideally, the patient should be seen by a psychiatrist and admitted to hospital for the diagnosis to be clarified, and to provide a safe environment for the patient and his family.

---

1   Marked disorganization of the personality, including incoherence, loosening
       of affect, and grossly disorganized behaviours.

Information should be collected from all sources, especially the school. Care should be taken to assess the quality of change. A comprehensive and reliable history focusing on the premorbid level of functioning is, therefore, critical. A history of substance abuse should be looked for. Patients with high-functioning autism and those with Asperger syndrome sometimes indulge in substance abuse, though this topic has not been studied systematically. Particular attention should be given to the family history because a history of schizophrenia in the family increases the risk of that disorder. Information should be obtained about mood disorders because, as discussed earlier, symptoms resembling schizophrenia are sometimes present in psychotic depression and bipolar disorder. Medical investigations should be performed depending on the presentation. In all cases, some of the baseline laboratory tests that should be performed include blood counts to rule out infections, and tests to assess thyroid and kidney functions. Investigations, such as the CT scan and the MRI, should be reserved only for those who have a history of head injury or of symptoms suggesting a neurological disorder.

Irrespective of the underlying cause, the immediate goal of treatment is to treat the psychosis and stabilize the behavior. As discussed elsewhere, the mainstay of treatment in this phase is the antipsychotic group of medications. These include the older medications such as haloperidol (Haldol) and chlorpromazine (Thorazine), and the newer drugs such as risperidone (Risperdal). Other newer antipsychotic medications that are used include olanzapine and quetiapine. It should be noted, however, that an immediate response to antipsychotic drugs does not confirm a diagnosis of schizophrenia. This is because irrespective of the diagnosis, antipsychotic medications have a calming effect. In clinical practice, antipsychotic medications are often combined with mood stabilizers.

Conclusion

Schizophrenia sometimes occurs in patients with autism and Asperger syndrome. The diagnosis is likely to be made in higher-functioning patients who are able to give a verbal account of their illness. The most common presenting features are disturbed behavior, chaotic thinking, and a history of auditory hallucinations. In the majority of cases, the psychotic behavior is the result of an underlying mood disorder, such as psychotic depression or mania, rather than schizophrenia. True schizophrenia occurring in the context of autism or Asperger syndrome is uncommon. However, a subgroup of patients within the autistic spectrum may be at an increased risk of developing psychotic disorders, including schizophrenia. The key to the diagnosis lies in the history. History of an onset of deterioration, along with presence of true hallucinations and delusions, is supportive of a diagnosis of schizophrenia superimposed on autism/Asperger syndrome. Treatment consists of ensuring safety, evaluating the risk for self-harm, stabilizing the disturbed behavior, and treating the distorted thinking. Antipsychotic medications, often combined with mood stabilizers, form the mainstay of treatment.

References

Alaghband-Rad, J., McKenna, K., Gordon, C.T., Albus, K., Hamburger, S., Rumsey, J., Frazier, J., Lenane, M. and Rapoport, J.M. (1995) 'Childhood-onset schizophrenia: The severity of premorbid course.' *Journal of the American Academy of Child and Adolescent Psychiatry, 34*, 1273–83.

APA (American Psychiatric Association) (1987) *Diagnostic and Statistical Manual of Mental Disorders, Third Edition, revised* (DSM-3-R). Washington, DC: APA.

APA (American Psychiatric Association) (1994) *Diagnostic and Statistical Manual of Mental Disorders, Fourth Edition* (DSM-IV). Washington, DC: APA.

Asarnow, R.F. and Asarnow, J.R. (1994) 'Childhood-onset schizophrenia: Editors' introduction.' *Schizophrenia Bulletin, 20*, 4, 591–7.

Asarnow, J.R., Thompson, M.C. and Goldstein, M.J. (1994) 'Childhood-onset schizophrenia: A follow-up study.' *Schizophrenia Bulletin, 20*, 599–617.

Dykens, E., Volkmar, F. and Glick, M. (1991) 'Thought disorder in high-functioning autistic adults.' *Journal of Autism and Developmental Disorders, 21*, 291–301.

Ghaziuddin, M., Leininger, L. and Tsai, L. (1995) 'Thought disorder in Asperger syndrome: Comparison with high-functioning autism.' *Journal of Autism and Developmental Disorders, 25*, 3, 311–17.

Ghaziuddin, M., Weidmer-Mikhail, E. and Ghaziuddin, N. (1998) 'Comorbidity of Asperger syndrome: A preliminary report.' *Journal of Intellectual Disability Research, 42*, 4, 279–83.

Gordon, C.T., Frazier, J.A., McKenna, K., Giedd, J., Zametkin, A., Zahn, T., Hommer, D., Hong, W., Kaysen, D. and Albus, K.E. (1994) 'Childhood-onset schizophrenia: An NIMH study in progress.' *Schizophrenia Bulletin, 20*, 4, 697–712.

Kolvin, I. (1971) 'Studies in the childhood psychoses. I. Diagnostic criteria and classification.' *British Journal of Psychiatry, 118*, 381–4.

Kolvin, I., Ounsted, C., Humphrey, M. and McNay, A. (1971) 'The phenomenology of childhood psychosis.' *British Journal of Psychiatry, 118*, 385–95.

Kraeplin, E. (1919) *Dementia praecox and paraphrenia*. Translated by R.M. Barclay from the 8th German edition of the Textbook of Psychiatry. Edinburgh, UK: Churchill Livingstone.

Kumra, S., Jacobsen, L.K., Lenane, M., Zahn, T.P., Wiggs, E., Alaghband-Rad, J., Castellanos, F.X., Frazier, J.A., McKenna, K., Gordon, C.T., Hamburger, S. and Rapoport, J.L. (1998) '"Multidimensionally impaired disorder": Is it a variant of very early-onset schizophrenia?' *Journal of the American Academy of Child and Adolescent Psychiatry, 37*, 1, 91–9.

Kydd, R.R. and Werry, J.S. (1982) 'Schizophrenia in children under 16 years.' *Journal of Autism and Developmental Disorders, 12*, 343–57.

McKenna, K., Gordon, C.T., Lenane, M., Kaysen, D., Fahey, K. and Rapoport, J.L. (1994) 'Looking for childhood-onset schizophrenia: The first 71 cases screened.' *Journal of the American Academy of Child and Adolescent Psychiatry, 33*, 5, 636–44.

Petty, L.K., Ornitz, E.M., Michelman, J.D. and Zimmerman, E.G. (1984) 'Autistic children who become schizophrenic.' *Archives of General Psychiatry, 41*, 2, 129–35.

Russell, A.T., Bott, L. and Sammons, C. (1989) 'The phenomenology of schizophrenia occurring in childhood.' *Journal of the American Academy of Child and Adolescent Psychiatry, 28*, 399–407.

Rutter, M. (1972) 'Childhood schizophrenia reconsidered.' *Journal of Autism and Childhood Schizophrenia, 2*, 315–37.

Ryan, R.M. (1992) 'Treatment-resistant chronic mental illness: Is it Asperger's syndrome?' *Hospital and Community Psychiatry, 43*, 8, 807–11.

Szatmari, P., Bartolucci, G., Bremner, R., Bond, S. and Rich, S. (1989) 'A follow-up study of high-functioning autistic children.' *Journal of Autism and Developmental Disorders, 19*, 213–25.

Towbin, K.E., Dykens, E.D., Pearson, G.S. and Cohen, D.J. (1993) 'Conceptualizing "borderline syndrome of childhood" and "childhood schizophrenia" as a developmental disorder.' *Journal of the American Academy of Child and Adolescent Psychiatry, 32*, 4, 775–82.

Volkmar, F.R. and Cohen, D.J. (1991) 'Comorbid association of autism and schizophrenia.' *American Journal of Psychiatry, 148*, 12, 1705–707.

Wolff, S. (1991) '"Schizoid" personality in childhood and adult life. 1. The vagaries of diagnostic labelling.' *British Journal of Psychiatry, 159*, 615–20.

Ylisaukko-oja, T., Nieminen-von Wendt, T., Kempas, E., Sarenius, S., Varilo, T., von Wendt, L., Peltonen, L. and Jarvela, I. (2004) 'Genome-wide scan for loci of Asperger syndrome.' *Molecular Psychiatry, 9*, 161–8.

CHAPTER 10

Autism, Tic Disorders, and Tourette Syndrome

Introduction

Tic disorders are a group of conditions characterized by a range of jerky movements (tics) involving the body. According to the DSM-IV, a tic is a sudden, rapid, recurrent, stereotyped motor movement or vocalization (APA, 1994). Although tics are experienced as irresistible, they are often exacerbated by stress, suppressed during sleep and absorbing activities, and postponed for varying lengths of time by distraction. When tics affect the muscles responsible for the production of speech, they give rise to grunts, or to attempts at throat clearing, and are then termed as vocal tics. Tics which affect movements, such as those of the head and neck or of the limb muscles, are labeled as 'motor tics.' Both motor and vocal tics can be simple or complex. Common simple motor tics are eye blinking and neck jerking, while common complex motor tics include grooming behaviors and facial gestures. Simple vocal tics consist of such behaviors as throat clearing, grunting, snorting, and sniffing; while complex vocal tics include repeating words or phrases out of context, uttering obscenities (coprolalia), and repeating the last heard sound, word, or phrase (echolalia) (APA, 1994).

Tics and Tourette syndrome (TS) are sometimes differentiated from stereotypic movements, but the distinction is neither easy nor particularly useful clinically. The terms are, therefore, often used interchangeably. Tic-like movements can complicate the use of psychotropic medications – a fact that should be remembered while assessing any patient presenting with tics.

When a patients presents with both vocal and motor tics that occur at any one point in time, the diagnosis of Tourette syndrome is made. TS is the main condition within the spectrum of tic disorders. Other conditions that are included in this category are chronic motor or vocal tic disorder and transient tic disorder. Tics that do not meet the full criteria of Tourette syndrome or of any of the other tic disorders are grouped under tic disorder NOS (not otherwise specified). The symptoms of TS last for anything between several months to years. To meet the criteria for TS one has to have both vocal and motor tics, which can be as simple as eye blinking and throat clearing. The prevalence of TS is about 10 individuals per 10,000. This figure is probably an underestimate, especially if milder versions of the condition are included in the diagnosis. About 10 per cent of children suffer from transient tics, and the true prevalence rate of TS may be higher than what is generally believed. The disorder occurs about three times as frequently in males as in females. About 50 per cent of tics disappear by the age of 18 years.

The underlying cause is biologic. Tic disorder and TS cluster in families. In addition, disorders such as Obsessive-Compulsive Disorder (OCD) and trichotillomania (compulsive hair pulling) are common in the first-degree relatives. Imaging studies have pointed to abnormalities in the basal ganglia-thalamo-cortical network. As well as genetic factors, medications, such as stimulants, can precipitate tics, although some researchers believe that stimulant-induced tics are likely to occur only in those patients who are genetically vulnerable.

Tics and Tourette syndrome in autism spectrum disorders

The association of autism with tics is well established. People with autism often show tics and mannerisms such as facial grimacing, throat clearing, and eye blinking. These are often considered part of autism and, therefore, not given any special attention. However, sometimes they increase in severity and may then affect other aspects of the patient's life and areas of functioning, such as behavior in school or adjustment in the community. For example, a teenager with autism may become the object of ridicule if he jerks his shoulders or clears his throat inappropriately. When this happens, tics and mannerisms should be categorized as distinct disorders and treated appropriately.

Several reports have documented the occurrence of tic disorders in autism in clinic samples (see Barabas and Matthews, 1983; Kano et al., 1988; Realmuto and Main, 1982). Community-based studies have also shown similar findings. For example, Baron-Cohen and colleagues assessed the presence of tics and Tourette syndrome in a group of 447 children. Using family interviews, the authors proposed that at least 4 per cent of the children met the criteria of TS, and several more presented with a variety of tics (Baron-Cohen et al., 1999).

Some studies have described multiple conditions in children with autism who have tic disorders. Cases of autism and TS with bipolar disorder have been reported. For example, Kerbeshian and Burd (1996) described four cases of autism with TS and bipolar disorder. The authors suggested that common factors are involved in the etiology of TS, bipolar disorder, and autism. Another condition that often clusters with autism and TS is Attention Deficit Hyperactivity Disorder (ADHD). In addition to psychiatric disorders such as bipolar disorder, medical conditions, such as syndromes with mental retardation, also cluster in those autistic patients who have TS. For example, in the case series of patients with both autism and Down syndrome described by the author, several patients had additional symptoms of tics and TS (Ghaziuddin, 1997). Tourette syndrome may also form one of the defining features of autistic persons with savant syndrome (Moriarty, Ring and Robertson, 1993).

Although tics and TS seem to be less common in Asperger syndrome than in traditional autism, a few clinic-based reports have described the association. Ringman and Jankovic (2000) examined a group of 12 children with autism spectrum disorders referred to a movement disorders clinic. Of the eight patients with Asperger syndrome, seven had tics and six met the criteria for TS. Three of these patients also had symptoms of severe sensory deficits. Nass and Gutman described five boys with Asperger syndrome and TS (1997). All were characterized by clumsiness and exceptional verbal skills, with numerous motor and vocal tics. The authors underscored the importance of treating the tics in order to improve the social skills of the patients. Although the evidence is only suggestive, several patients with Pervasive Developmental Disoerder Not Otherwise Specified (PDDNOS) who were referred to psychiatric clinics suffered from mild to moderate tics. Anecdotally, this seems to be particularly true of those patients who suffer from severe temper tantrums and aggressive outbursts, and are often admitted to psychiatric units.

Prevalence

Few prevalence studies have examined the comorbidity of tics/TS with autism spectrum disorders. In a study of primary-school children in Sweden, Kadesjo and Gillberg (2000) examined the pattern of comorbidity in TS. They found that both ADHD and autism spectrum disorders were extremely common, affecting as many as 75 per cent of the entire sample, and they underscored the importance of making a correct diagnosis of the pattern of psychiatric comorbidity in this population.

Clinical features

The presence of tics and TS in patients who already carry a diagnosis of autism or Asperger syndrome is often viewed as part of the pervasive developmental disorder (PDD) and usually ignored. In these circumstances, the onset of the tics is not clear. Parents often report that the tics have been present for 'as long as they can remember.' Yet tics are seldom the earliest symptoms of autism in young children. It is rare for autistic children to be referred for the evaluation of tics alone, although some patients with Asperger syndrome are first referred to clinicians because of symptoms suggestive of TS. A usual presentation is that of a pre-pubertal child with a diagnosis of ADHD, who later presents with tics. When a detailed history is taken, areas of social deficits and rigid, focused interests become apparent, which then raise the question of a PDD. Tics that occur in the setting of PDD wax and wane in their severity and do not often need to be treated actively. However, some children experience them as increasing in frequency to the extent that treatment becomes necessary.

At times, the diagnosis of Tourette syndrome is made first, and features of autism and PDD are detected later. It is not uncommon to have a teenager with Tourette syndrome referred for management of refractory tics, when, on close evaluation, he is found to have features of autism or Asperger syndrome. These patients usually have a normal IQ and are given a variety of other diagnoses before autism is suspected. The features that suggest the diagnosis are resistance to change and fixation on certain themes and topics.

Case study: Jason D

Jason D, a 13-year-old Caucasian youngster, was referred with a history of uncontrolled tics. He had previously been diagnosed with Tourette syndrome and been treated. However, for about six months prior to his referral, the symptoms had increased in frequency. His tics involved snorting, throat clearing, and making jerky movements of his neck. There was a family history of tics, such as excessive eye blinking.

On evaluation, it emerged that, apart from his tics, a source of major concern was Jason D's lack of social skills. He did not have any close friends and tended to stand out in a group of his peers. His main area of interest was making model planes. He would spend the whole day making planes if allowed to do so. He insisted on reading about them, and showing off to his schoolmates the amount of knowledge he had in this area. He talked excessively about this topic, even when his schoolmates showed no interest, and tended to be somewhat pedantic. His facial expression was restricted.

This presentation raised the possibility of autism spectrum disorder. The points in favor of this diagnosis were Jason D's history of social deficits, mild communication deficits in the social use of language, and excessive focus on making airplane models. Additional details about his early development and social history were obtained. This revealed that Jason D had always been rather odd in his social relationships, a feature that was attributed to his tics. (The tics had started when he was around 7 years of age.) There was no history of any cognitive or language delay. Based on the DSM-IV, he was given a diagnosis of Asperger syndrome with Tourette syndrome.

Patients with autism sometimes present with an exacerbation of tics when their general level of functioning deteriorates. This usually happens in the setting of clinical depression. When the depression worsens, the intensity of tics also seems to increase. Similarly, when the mood improves, the tics also decrease in intensity.

Tics may sometimes emerge after the use of stimulants and other medication-related events, such as the withdrawal of neuroleptics (drugs used in the treatment of psychotic disorders). While the emergence of tics is a recognized side-effect of stimulants, there are no firm data on the extent of the problem. Sometimes the tics decrease after the offending medication is withdrawn, while at other times the use of stimulants does not appear to have any effect on tics. Other medications have also been implicated in giving rise to symptoms of TS in patients with PDD. Littlejohns, Clarke and Corbett (1990) described an 8-year-old boy with Asperger's syndrome who was given haloperidol to control agitation and aggressive outbursts. When the drug was withdrawn after two years the boy began to experience Tourette-like symptoms. Subsequently, neither haloperidol nor a second antipsychotic drug altered the boy's core features of Asperger syndrome, although they did suppress his movement disorder. Perry, Nobler and Campbell (1989) described a similar case in a 5-year-old boy with autism who developed TS after neuroleptic withdrawal. The authors highlighted the need for baseline assessment of functions before starting neuroleptic therapy with autistic children.

Common biologic mechanisms

Chromosome abnormalities have been reported in cases with combined autism and Tourette syndrome. Hebebrand and colleagues (1994) described a

14-year-old male with partial trisomy 16p and autistic disorder. He showed complex motor and vocal phenomena, including simple tics that had first appeared in childhood. These simple tics were of subclinical significance, but the later development of complex motor and vocal tics justified the additional diagnosis of Tourette syndrome. The authors stressed the importance of chromosome 16p as a possible candidate region for both autism and TS.

Family genetic studies have also suggested common underlying mechanisms between the two conditions. Sverd (1991) described a case series of ten patients with concurrent TS and PDD. Family history data were presented. The author proposed that TS contributes significantly to the etiological heterogeneity of autistic disorder and that a few cases of autism may actually be the result of homozygosity for the TS gene. In addition, some of the families showed comorbid affective disorders supporting the hypothesis that TS may be responsible for a subgroup of families with co-existing affective and autistic disorders. Some authors have suggested wider links between TS, PDD, and OCDs. Comings and Comings (1991) reviewed the existing literature on the two conditions and presented additional data on 16 families with both TS and autism. They found a high frequency of alcoholism, drug abuse, and obsessive-compulsive and other behavior disorders in the relatives of these patients. Stern and Robertson (1997) reviewed the literature on TS and PDD, and concluded that in a subgroup of cases with both TS and PDD, an excess of tics and TS was observed in the family members. This suggests that TS may be responsible for some of the genetic heterogeneity seen in autism spectrum disorders (Stern and Robertson, 1997).

Diagnosis

The diagnosis of tic disorder or Tourette syndrome in the setting of autism/Asperger syndrome should only be given if the symptoms are severe enough to interfere with functioning. Tics that are mild and infrequent are best ignored. Various rating scales are available that can give a comprehensive assessment of the pattern and severity of tics, and also serve as tools to monitor the effects of medications. These include the Yale Global Tic Scale (Leckman *et al.*, 1989), Tourette syndrome global scale (Harcherik *et al.*, 1984), and the Yale-Brown Obsessive Compulsive Scale (Goodman *et al.*, 1989). Tics often have a waxing and waning quality, a fact that should be remembered when initiating treatment.

Tourette syndrome should be differentiated from a variety of conditions including general medical conditions that can cause tics (for example, Wilson's disease), medication-induced movement disorder, and stereotypic movement disorder (APA, 1994). The latter is an interesting condition that is sometimes confused with autism spectrum disorder as in the case of Christopher, described below.

Case study: Christopher

Christopher is a 21-year-old Caucasian male referred by his parents for a diagnostic evaluation to rule out Asperger syndrome. He had a habit of flapping his hands whenever he was excited or upset. The onset of the symptom was in early childhood and it continued through childhood. There were no complaints about his social functioning or his verbal skills. However, his parents were concerned about his difficulty in reading social cues and situations. There was no history of language delay. According to his parents, Christopher had some special interests, such as wrestling, about which he often talked with his friends.

At interview, Christopher said that he had no complaints. He described his hand flapping as a 'stress-reliever.' He said that whenever he watched certain TV shows, or read an emotional passage in a book, he would feel like 'shaking his hands.' While he was able to control his impulse for some time, this was not always possible. At times, when in public, he would go to the nearest bathroom and flap his hands. He had a circle of friends and seemed to enjoy going out and socializing. He denied having any focused excessive interests. He did not have a girlfriend, something that upset him immensely.

On examination, Christopher was pleasant and cooperative. He was able to relate to the examiner in an appropriate manner. His eye contact, body language, and the tone of his voice appeared to be within normal limits. He described his mood as being depressed, perhaps mildly so, without any suicidal ideas or plans. Based on this history and the examination, he did not seem to fall within the autistic spectrum. His condition best seemed to fit the description of stereotypic movement disorder with a comorbid mild depressive illness.

Treatment

Management of tics and Tourette syndrome in autism should focus on the treatment of both disorders simultaneously. Treatment of the tics is essentially psychopharmacological. The most commonly used – and the most effective –

medications are the antipsychotic group of drugs, of which the most frequently used at present are the atypical antipsychotic agent Risperdal, and the older agent Haldol. Other medications that are sometimes used include clonidine and pimozide. Clonidine is a medication used for the treatment of hypertension and has been found to be useful in some cases of ADHD and also in TS. Pimozide is an antipsychotic that is used as a second line of drug if trials with Risperdal and Haldol are not successful. When patients' tics develop or worsen after starting stimulants, it is good clinical practice to discontinue the stimulants and try the patient on a medication like Clonidine or the newer drug, Strattera.

Outcome

Some authors have suggested that development of TS in autism may indicate a good outcome in autism (Burd *et al.*, 1987). However, no systematic studies have explored this issue. If outcome is narrowly defined in terms of adjustment in the community, then the presence of vocal and physical tics has a negative impact on the course of the disorder.

Conclusion

Tics commonly occur in persons with autism and related disorders. Some studies have suggested more than a casual association between autism and Tourette syndrome. Although most research has focused on the association of tics with autism and Asperger syndrome, clinical experience suggests that tics commonly occur in patients with PDDNOS. The decision to treat depends on the severity of the symptoms and the degree of distress and impairment they cause to the patient. Milder tics need not be treated, in part because many of them disappear with time. Treatment usually consists of a combination of medications, such as neuroleptics, and behavioral therapy. Counseling should also be given to those who are higher-functioning to help them cope better with their disability.

References

APA (American Psychiatric Association) (1994) *Diagnostic and Statistical Manual of Mental Disorders, Fourth Edition* (DSM-IV). Washington, DC: APA.

Barabas, G. and Matthews, W.S. (1983) 'Coincident infantile autism and Tourette syndrome: A case report.' *Journal of Developmental and Behavioral Pediatrics, 4*, 280–1.

Baron-Cohen, S., Scahill, V.L., Izaguirre, J., Hornsey, H. and Robertson, M.M. (1999) 'The prevalence of Gilles de la Tourette syndrome in children and adolescents with autism: A large scale study.' *Psychological Medicine, 29*, 1151–9.

Burd, L., Fisher, W.W., Kerbeshian, J. and Arnold, M.E. (1987) 'Is development of Tourette disorder a marker for improvement in patients with autism and other pervasive developmental disorders?' *Journal of the American Academy of Child and Adolescent Psychiatry, 26*, 162–5.

Comings, D.E. and Comings, B.G. (1991) 'Clinical and genetic relationships between autism, pervasive developmental disorder and Tourette syndrome: A study of 19 cases.' *American Journal of Medical Genetics, 39*, 180–91.

Ghaziuddin, M. (1997) 'Autism in Down's syndrome: Family history correlates.' *Journal of Intellectual Disabililty Research, 41*, 87–91.

Goodman, W.K., Price, L.H., Rasmussen, S.A, Mazure, C., Fleischmann, R.L., Hill, C.L., Heninger, G.R. and Charney, D.S. (1989) 'The Yale-Brown Obsessive Compulsive Scale. I. Development, use, and reliability.' *Archives of General Psychiatry, 46*, 11, 1006–1011.

Harcherik, D.F., Leckman, J.F., Detlor, J. and Cohen, D.J. (1984) 'A new instrument for clinical studies of Tourette's syndrome.' *Journal of the American Academy of Child and Adolescent Psychiatry, 23*, 2, 153–60.

Hebebrand, J., Martin, M., Korner, J., Roitzheim, B., de Braganca, K., Werner, W. and Remschmidt, H. (1994) 'Partial trisomy 16p in an adolescent with autistic disorder and Tourette's syndrome.' *American Journal of Medical Genetics, 15*, 54, 268–70.

Kadesjo, B. and Gillberg, C. (2000) 'Tourette's disorder: Epidemiology and comorbidity in primary school children.' *Journal of the American Academy of Child and Adolescent Psychiatry, 39*, 548–55.

Kano, Y., Ohta, M., Nagai, Y., Yokota, K. and Shimizu, Y. (1988) 'Tourette's disorder coupled with infantile autism: A prospective study of two boys.' *Japanese Journal of Psychiatry and Neurology, 42*, 49–57.

Kerbeshian, J. and Burd, L. (1996) 'Case study: Comorbidity among Tourette's syndrome, autistic disorder, and bipolar disorder.' *Journal of the American Academy of Child and Adolescent Psychiatry, 35*, 681–5.

Leckman, J.F., Riddle, M.A., Hardin, M.T., Ort, S.I., Swartz, K.L., Stevenson, J. and Cohen, D.J. (1989) 'The Yale Global Tic Severity Scale: Initial testing of a clinician-rated scale of severity.' *Journal of the American Academy of Child and Adolescent Psychiatry, 28*, 4, 566–73.

Littlejohns, C.S., Clarke, D.J. and Corbett, J.A. (1990) 'Tourette-like disorder in Asperger's syndrome.' *British Journal of Psychiatry, 156*, 430–3.

Moriarty, J., Ring, H.A. and Robertson, M.M. (1993) 'An idiot savant calendrical calculator with Gilles de la Tourette syndrome: Implications of the savant syndrome.' *Psychological Medicine, 23*, 4, 1019–21.

Nass, R. and Gutman, R. (1997) 'Boys with Asperger's disorder, exceptional verbal intelligence, tics, and clumsiness.' *Developmental Medicine and Child Neurology, 39*, 691–5.

Perry, R., Nobler, M.S. and Campbell, M. (1989) 'Tourette-like symptoms associated with neuroleptic therapy in an autistic child.' *Journal of the American Academy of Child and Adolescent Psychiatry, 28,* 93–6.

Realmuto, G.M. and Main, B. (1982) 'Coincidence of Tourette's disorder and infantile autism.' *Journal of Autism and Developmental Disorders, 12,* 367–72.

Ringman, J.M. and Jankovic, J. (2000) 'Occurrence of tics in Asperger's syndrome and autistic disorder.' *Journal of Child Neurology, 15,* 394–400.

Stern, J.S. and Robertson, M.M. (1997) 'Tics associated with autistic and pervasive developmental disorders.' *Neurology Clinics, 15,* 345–55.

Sverd, J. (1991) 'Tourette syndrome and autistic disorder: A significant relationship.' *American Journal of Medical Genetics, 39,* 173–9.

CHAPTER 11

Other Psychiatric Disorders

In addition to the disorders described in the previous chapters, persons with autism or Asperger syndrome may experience several miscellaneous psychiatric conditions: these include anorexia nervosa and eating disorders, sleep disorders, severe self injurious behaviour, gender identity disorder and substance abuse. This chapter discusses these psychiatric conditions in conjunction with autism.

Anorexia nervosa and eating disorders

Introduction

Anorexia nervosa is the main category in a group of disorders characterized by altered food intake and disturbance of weight. Its main features are a refusal to maintain body weight at or above a minimally normal weight for age and height, intense fear of gaining weight or becoming fat, disturbance in the way in which the patient's body weight or shape is experienced, and in females, amenorrhea or absence of at least three consecutive menstrual cycles. The patient is obsessed with food, and often has a distorted sense of body image. Even if she is emaciated, she may see herself as being overweight. Specific parts of the body, such as the thighs and abdomen, are perceived as being fat and unsightly. Several physical complications result, and if untreated, the disorder may result in death.

Much more common in females than in males, by a proportion of nine females to one male, the disorder is often accompanied by surreptitious attempts to lose weight (by vomiting, purging, abusing laxatives or diet pills, etc.). The disorder is far more prevalent in industrialized countries, such as the US and the countries of western Europe, than in third world countries of Asia and Africa. This difference has been attributed to the cultural factors which promote a thin female figure as the ideal in the western world. The disorder often begins after puberty. Associated psychiatric disorders are common, especially in those cases where the disorder begins before puberty. The mortality rates are high, at least in those who are admitted to teaching hospitals, and approach about 10 per cent. The cause of death is often starvation or suicide. As is the case for all major psychiatric disorders, several causes have been proposed for anorexia nervosa. There is an increased risk of the disorder in the first-degree relatives of patients with anorexia nervosa and also of mood disorders such as depression.

Anorexia nervosa and pervasive developmental disorder (PDD)

An important symptom of anorexia nervosa is an obsession with food. The patient may perform rigid and ritualistic behaviors and feel a desire for sameness. Patients are often described as having perfectionist personality traits. A superficial resemblance to autism is apparent in such cases, although patients do not have the other deficits characteristic of autism, namely, the social and communication deficits.

Some reports have described the co-occurrence of autism and anorexia nervosa. Over the years, Gillberg, Rastam and colleagues have presented data showing that a subgroup of patients with anorexia nervosa suffers from features justifying a diagnosis of autism spectrum disorders. In one study, they found that the cognitive profile of patients with anorexia nervosa resembles that of autism/Asperger syndrome (Gillberg et al., 1996). In another study, in a ten-year follow-up of adolescents diagnosed with anorexia nervosa living in the community, the investigators found that a substantial number had symptoms of autism/Obsessive-Compulsive Disorder (OCD), and that these patients were particularly vulnerable to a poorer outcome (Rastam, Gillberg and Wentz, 2003). Although the association of anorexia nervosa and autism suggested by the Scandinavian studies has not been supported by other researchers, it is possible that the two disorders are linked at some level because of the common association with obsessive-compulsive behavior. For example, the occurrence of obsessive-compulsive traits is well documented in the first-degree relatives of patients with autism or anorexia nervosa. Patients with anorexia nervosa themselves meet the criteria for OCD in some cases. For example, Milos and colleagues examined the relationship between these two disorders in a follow-up study of patients with eating disorders (including anorexia nervosa). They found that almost a third of their sample met the criteria for OCD (Milos et al., 2002). However, the presence of autistic traits/disorder in patients with anorexia nervosa may apply only to a small subgroup, because anorexia nervosa itself may be composed of a broader spectrum of disorders than previously believed (Anderluh *et al.*, 2003).

Since a certain degree of cognitive maturity is critical to the development of the disordered thinking characteristic of anorexia nervosa, it follows that when this condition occurs in the setting of autism, the patient is usually of normal or near-normal intelligence. The case of ER below describes an adolescent who was admitted for anorexia nervosa. During the course of her hospital stay, a range of behaviors emerged that raised the question of an accompanying autism spectrum disorder.

Case study: ER

ER is a 16-year-old Caucasian girl with a diagnosis of anorexia nervosa. She was admitted to the psychiatric unit with the complaints of food restriction and progressive weight loss. This was her second admission. Although she was compliant with the eating disorders protocol, her greatest problem soon emerged in the area of social interaction. She was aloof in therapy groups, and tended to 'talk down' to people, without taking part in any of the group activities. Some of her peers regarded her as annoying while others thought of her as being snobbish. Her room in the hospital was arranged in a remarkable manner and gave a hint of deficits that reached beyond her eating disorder. She had a row of Barbie dolls arranged in a straight line on her window. This was followed by a row of little boxes containing play-dough. She insisted on lining them up in straight lines and made sure that no one touched them or disturbed the arrangement in any way.

ER had no family history suggestive of autism or of related disorders. Regarding her developmental history, no delay or abnormalities suggestive of autism were noted. On clinical examination, ER came across as somewhat awkward in her ability to relate. Her eye contact and other nonverbal behaviors appeared to be within the normal limits. She denied any intrusive thoughts or a desire to perform any rituals. However, she said that she insisted on having things arranged in a particular way in her room. She said she labeled articles in her room (she had a labeling machine), and said that she had a collection of store bags from all over the world (she had two plastic tubs full of such bags). Her other 'interests' consisted of cleaning her room repeatedly. There was no history of a medical disorder such as epilepsy. Based on the above history and examination, a diagnosis of autism spectrum disorder (Pervasive Developmental Disorder Not Otherwise

Specified (PDDNOS)) was made since she did not meet the full criteria for autism.

Other eating disorders

Many autistic individuals show distinct patterns of unusual and abnormal eating behaviors. These include a tendency to eat certain kinds of foods, rituals around meal times, and insistence on eating from certain types of plates. Most of these behaviors do not lead to significant impairment. Apart from anorexia nervosa, other eating disorders that may occur in persons with autism include pica (indiscriminate eating), water intoxication (polydipsia), and bulimia nervosa. Pica usually occurs in autistic persons with severe mental retardation. The indiscriminate eating of inedible objects can lead to serious problems, such as lead intoxication. In a retrospective study of children screened at a lead treatment program, 17 children with autism were identified (Shannon and Graef, 1996). The authors stressed the need for early identification and continued monitoring of children with developmental delays because of the high risk of recurrence. Earlier studies also found increased levels of lead in the blood of children with autism (Cohen, Johnson and Caparulo, 1976). Another disorder that sometimes occurs in persons with autism and mental retardation is polydipsia. In this condition, the patient drinks an excessive amount of water which results in severe electrolyte imbalance (Deb et al., 1994). Apart from pica and polydipsia, autistic people do experience other forms of unusual eating behaviors. These include over-eating, especially in those who also suffer from superimposed depression (O'Brien and Whitehouse, 1990).

Relatively little is known about the occurrence of bulimia nervosa in persons with autism. In this condition, the person goes through periods of binge eating followed by vomiting and other compensatory behaviors. To qualify for this diagnosis, the binge eating and the inappropriate compensatory behaviors must occur at least twice a week. Although, when strictly defined, cases of bulimia nervosa are hard to find in persons with autism spectrum disorders, clinical experience suggests that binge eating is not uncommon in this population. A 'binge' is defined as eating, in a discrete period of time, an amount of food that is definitely larger than most individuals would eat under similar circumstances. (An emerging entity called 'binge-eating disorder' has been described in the DSM-IV, in which episodes of binges are not accompanied by compensatory behaviors as is the case in bulimia nervosa.)

Diagnosis

Patients with anorexia nervosa should be routinely evaluated not only for the presence of conditions such as depression and OCD, but also for the presence of autism spectrum disorders. A history of reciprocal social deficits predating the onset of the eating disorder should be looked for, especially with the presence of rigid ritualistic interests and communication impairment of the autistic kind. The important issue is to maintain a high level of suspicion. Screening instruments such as the Autism Behavior Checklist (Krug, Arick and Almond, 1980) may be used with persons with eating disorders, especially in those uncommon instances when the onset is before puberty, particularly in males. In more difficult cases, a structured interview for the diagnosis of autism spectrum disorders, such as the Autism Diagnostic Interview (Lord, Rutter and Le Couteur, 1994), should be performed. In addition, attention should also be paid to the possible presence of depression and other mood disorders, which are commonly experienced by persons with eating disorders.

Treatment

The treatment of anorexia nervosa in the setting of autism is essentially based on the principles of treatment of the former disorder. Treatment in a specialized inpatient unit is often required. It is important to start the patient on an eating disorder protocol and gradually monitor and increase the food intake. Attention should be given to the presence of physical complications. Whenever any accompanying mood disturbance, such as depression, is present, it should be aggressively treated. The role of antipsychotic drugs in the control of symptoms of body distortion and self-image is not proven. In addition to these measures, treatment of autism based on the usual modalities, such as social skills training, should continue. Other eating disorders, such as rumination (a tendency to chew repeatedly) and pica, should be treated with appropriate behavioral methods.

Sleep disorders

Introduction

In the last decade, there has been a growing recognition of the importance of sleep disorders in the general population. Sleep parameters are increasingly being used to define and investigate the neurobiology of common psychiatric conditions such as depression. Studies have been carried out on both children and adults. It is known, for instance, that depressive illness is characterized by reduction in the amount of sleep, mid- and early morning awakening, and deficits occurring in the REM sleep cycle.

Sleep disorders can be either primary or secondary. Primary sleep disorders consist of sleep apnea, narcolepsy, cataplexy, pathologic daytime sleepiness, etc. Secondary sleep disorders complicate other physical and psychological conditions. For example, Parkinson's disease is associated with excessive daytime drowsiness, whereas storage diseases, such as the San Filippo syndrome, are characterized by insomnia.

In the DSM system of classification, sleep disorders are divided into four broad categories depending on the presumed underlying cause:

- Primary sleep disorders are thought to result from abnormalities in the sleep–wake cycle.

- Sleep disorders related to another mental disorder are those that occur generally in conditions such as anxiety disorders and depression.

- Sleep disorders can also occur from general medical conditions.

- Finally, substance-induced sleep disorders result from the concurrent use of both legal and illegal drugs.

Sleep disorders are not psychiatric disorders in the traditional sense. However, disturbed sleep is often seen in a variety of psychiatric conditions. Patients with sleep disorders sometimes present with what appear to be psychiatric and behavioral symptoms. For example, a child who does not sleep well at night may present with daytime irritability and tantrums. Also, disorders such as sleep apnea can mimic psychiatric and behavioral symptoms such as hyperactivity, irritability, and impulsivity.

Sleep disorders in people with autism and Asperger syndrome

Problems of sleep disturbance are commonly seen in children with mental retardation including those with autistic disorder (Stores, 2001). In general, the greater the level of mental retardation, the less time spent in rapid eye movement sleep (REM sleep), and greater the sleep disturbance (Harvey and Kennedy, 2002). Abnormalities of sleep architecture are known to occur in persons with autism and related disorders. For example, Harvey and Kennedy (2002) compared the polysomnographic findings of patients with autism, with those of Fragile X syndrome and Down syndrome. They found greater levels of undifferentiated sleep in patients with autism. Richdale and Prior (1995) examined the sleep patterns of two groups of children with autism, those with mild mental retardation and those with moderate/severe mental retardation. Compared with children without autism, those with autism had a higher prevalence of sleep abnormalities. They suggested that most children with autism experience some form of sleep disturbance before they reach 8 years of age. These include lengthy periods of sleep waking (waking up during the night), shortened night sleep, and early morning waking. Some studies have claimed that people with Asperger syndrome are particularly vulnerable to sleep disorders. For example, Tani and colleagues (2004) suggested that insomnia is common in Asperger syndrome probably because of these patients' 'inherent anxiety.'

Disorders of sleep in people with autism spectrum disorders occur due to a variety of reasons. One important reason is a change of routines and schedules. People with autism and Asperger syndrome are fixated on routines, and any change in their usual set of activities around the time of going to bed may cause a disturbance of sleep. Younger children sometimes show a tendency to carry certain objects such as a teddy bear. If, for some reason, the object is left behind, the patient may find it hard to go to sleep. Another cause of disturbed sleep in persons with autism and Asperger syndrome is sleep apnea. This disorder is being increasingly diagnosed these days. If left untreated, it can result in a variety of symptoms including fatigue, daytime drowsiness, problems with attention and concentration during the day, and a host of effects on the cardiovascular system. The presence of other disorders, such as depression, can also result in sleep disturbance. The patient may have difficulty in falling asleep and may wake up earlier than usual. A diminished need for sleep is sometimes seen in persons with emerging bipolar disorder. The effect of medications, especially of stimulants, should be carefully examined.

Assessment and treatment

Treatment of the sleep disorder should include a good sleep history focusing on sleep habits, the use of over-the-counter medications, and a detailed medical and psychiatric examination. In the first instance, the treatment should be behavioral. The patient should be encouraged to sleep at the same time every day, and to stay away from all distractions (such as watching TV or playing video games) before going to bed. In some cases, the symptoms may be so severe as to justify the addition of medications such as Benadryl or Trazodone. Some patients respond to a small dose of melatonin given an hour before sleep. However, all medications (including melatonin) have side-effects that should be considered. More specialized treatments, such as positive pressure breathing for sleep apnea, can be tried depending on the level of functioning of the patient. The role of prescribed medications should also be examined. Stimulants should not be given late in the afternoon to avoid their interfering with sleep.

Severe self-injurious behavior

Introduction

Severe self-injurious behavior is an extremely difficult problem to manage and treat. It is characterized by severe forms of self-injury of a repetitive nature persisting over time, and is generally not responsive to the usual pharmaco-logical and behavioral interventions. The self-inflicted injuries can be disfig-uring and, in some cases, life-threatening. Examples consist of severe self-digging of skin leading to exposure of bone, biting of lips resulting in their total loss, pulling of hair resulting in infection, and enucleation of eyes. The exact prevalence of this kind of behavior, which can more appropriately be described as self-mutilation, is not known. Among the subtypes of autism, the problem is higher in those who have severe mental retardation and multiple pathologies.

Various theories have been proposed to explain this kind of self-injurious behavior. Two types of theories are popular – the pain theory and the addiction theory, both of which center on the role of chemical substances called opioids being released in the brain. According to the pain theory, brain opioids are significantly elevated in severe self-injurious behavior resulting in analgesia. According to the addiction theory, self-injurious behavior induces the production of endorphins, to which the brain gets addicted. A disturbance of the endorphin system has been proposed to explain the deficits of autism, including serious self-injury (Panksepp and Sahley, 1987; Willemsen-Swinkels et al., 1996). Similar results have not been found in people with mild self-injurious behaviors suggesting that there may be different subtypes in this group of patients.

Clinical features

The onset of the severe self-injurious behavior is in early childhood and its emergence is gradual, as opposed to the pattern of other cases of self-injury, as in Lesch Nyhan syndrome (Hall, Oliver and Murphy, 2001).

The patient is often severely impaired and often has severe to profound degrees of mental retardation. In some cases, the level of intelligence cannot be estimated. Many patients are nonverbal. Higher-functioning persons with autism, that is, those persons with an average or above-average IQ, do not often present with severe self-injurious behaviors. Likewise, severe self-injurious behavior is uncommon in persons with Asperger syndrome.

In a few cases, a cyclical pattern can be observed. The patient may go through periods when the tendency to self-injure may be minimal. Exacerbations may occur without any reason, or in some cases, appear to be precipitated by life events, such as changes and moves. The mood is often irritable, with either constant whining or screaming. Sleep disturbance is also commonly present. Both sexes are affected, and many suffer from superimposed seizure disorder. In several cases, overlapping features of other genetic syndromes of mental retardation, such as Cornelia de Lange syndrome, may be present. The course of the severe self-injurious behavior is variable. In some cases, the problem decreases in intensity, especially in later adulthood. In most cases, however, it persists and goes through periods of exacerbation and remission.

Case study: Brad

Brad is a 14-year-old Caucasian youngster with autism, severe mental retardation, and herpes encephalitis. He was first seen at the age of 4 years because of severe aggressive behavior towards himself and others. Specifically, he would pull out his hair, exposing large areas of his scalp. Over time, this evolved into other similar behaviors. One spot on his body that was particularly affected was the nape of his neck. He would dig into his neck repeatedly, and at times, expose the underlying muscles. His choice of site changed over the years, and so did the intensity of his behavior. At times, he would hit himself so hard on his head that only a helmet could protect him from potentially severe injury. At other times, his arms needed to be padded at the elbows to stop him from reaching his bone through repeated digging. A variety of behavioral interventions and medication trials over the years have affected the intensity of Brad's injuries, but have not totally eliminated the behaviors.

Case study: Nathan

Nathan is a 16-year-old Hispanic male with Asperger syndrome. He was referred at the age of 14 years with a variety of diagnoses, including Oppositional Defiant Disorder (ODD), OCD, and Attention Deficit Hyperactivity Disorder (ADHD). In brief, apart from his social deficits, he presented with an unusual problem. He would try to shake his teeth and attempt to uproot them, and over the years, had lost two of his front teeth in this fashion. In addition, he suffered from other forms of self-injurious behaviors, such as repeatedly peeling off his scabs.

Nathan had a focused interest in sports, and was an authority on the Detroit Tigers and the Red Wings. He had a phenomenal memory for sport-related statistics, and had a tendency to ramble on his topics of interest in a pedantic manner. His self-injurious behaviors showed a decline over time during the two-year period that he was followed. It is not clear if this was the result of the use of medications or a case of natural remission.

Assessment and treatment

The management of patients with autism and severe self-injurious behavior is often difficult and frustrating. Special inpatient units are sometimes needed to take care of these individuals. These units employ a very high level of staffing and use a predominantly behavioral approach.

Possible underlying causes should also be examined (Cox and Schopler, 1993). A variety of techniques involving standard behavioral interventions have been tried. These include extinction, time-out, differential reinforcement, alternative forms of stimulation, sensory deprivation, and physical restraint (see Howlin, 1993). All approaches center round a detailed functional analysis of the behavior.

Medications have a limited role. Agents that are useful in the control of OCD (such as clomipramine or fluoxetine) can be tried because the behaviors are often compulsive in nature (King, 2000). In a few instances, antidepressants are beneficial, especially when the behavior is accompanied by a significant degree of irritability. The problem is often compounded by the fact that the patient is nonverbal and also by the innate disturbance in pain perception from which some autistic persons suffer. Several open-label trials involving a range of medications have been used. These include paroxetine, mitrazapine, and others (Davanzo et al., 1998; Posey et al., 2001). Most of these studies, however, are based on small case numbers.

In a minority of cases, unconventional drugs such as naltrexone can be tried. This medication is often used in the treatment of drug dependence. The rationale for its use stems from the belief among some researchers that severe self-injurious behavior and drug addiction bear some resemblance to each other. Naltrexone is said to act on the endorphin system that mediates this type of activity in the brain. However, there is no consistent evidence of its efficacy in autistic persons with severe self-injurious behavior. Some studies have reported a dramatic improvement not only in the level of self-injury but also in social relatedness (Walters *et al.*, 1990), while others have found no benefit at all (Willemsen-Swinkels *et al.*, 1995). In fact, some studies have warned against its use, citing an exacerbation of the very symptoms that it purports to treat (Benjamin *et al.*, 1996).

Gender identity disorder

Introduction

Gender identity disorder (GID) is a condition in which a person, usually a male, believes that he belongs to the opposite sex. He takes a great deal of delight and pleasure in dressing up accordingly, and adopting the mannerisms and habits of the female sex. According to the DSM-IV, the main clinical features of GID consist of a repeated desire to belong to the opposite sex, a preference for cross-dressing in boys, and a persistent preference for playmates of the opposite sex (APA, 1994). As is the case with any other psychiatric disorder, all the symptoms do not need to be present simultaneously. In general, boys are more commonly affected than girls.

Problems of gender identity are sometimes reported in persons with autism. While clinical experience suggests that boys with autism spectrum disorders not uncommonly go through phases when they dress like girls and seem to have a fascination for female clothes, few cases meeting the criteria of GID have been described in persons with autism and Asperger syndrome. In one such report, Mukaddes (2002) described two boys, aged 10 and 7 years of age, both with borderline intelligence, who developed symptoms consistent with a diagnosis of GID. In both the cases, despite a combination of treatments, the cross-dressing and other behaviors characteristic of GID persisted. In an earlier report, Landen and Rasmussen (1997) described a girl with high-functioning autism and gender identity problems and wondered if autistic persons are at an increased risk of developing gender dysphoria. More recently, Perera, Gadambanathan and Weerasiri (2003) described a girl with Asperger syndrome who had additional features of GID and OCD.

Clinical features

While systematic studies have not explored this issue, gender identity problems appear to be under-reported in persons with autism and Asperger syndrome. The author is aware of at least two cases of Asperger syndrome where the predominant fixation was on wearing female clothes and playing with dolls. The cross-dressing seems to start early in life, as early as 4 to 5 years of age. In some cases, sensory issues appear to play a role. For example, the patient may enjoy the feel of nylon stockings. With time, this may evolve into wearing stockings and acquiring mannerisms more commonly associated with the opposite sex. In other cases, the act of spinning around may show an overlap with cross-dressing behaviors. For example, one youngster with high-functioning autism liked to spin wearing a long skirt; the feel of the skirt blowing up in the wind reinforced his fixation on wearing female dresses. In some cases, other psychiatric symptoms, such as anxiety disorder, may be present.

Assessment and treatment

Patients with GID should be screened for the presence of autistic traits. The treatment of GID itself is unsatisfactory. Patients who cross-dress often continue to do so. Behavioral interventions and redirection works in a limited manner. There are no medications that work, unless the symptoms are the result of a psychotic disorder or a mood disturbance. The best approach is to redirect the youngster to more gender-specific activities, and encourage him to build appropriate social skills. Another option is acceptance of the person's behaviour.

Substance abuse

Although cases of substance abuse are sometimes seen in persons with autism spectrum disorders, almost nothing is known about this topic. Anecdotal reports of alcohol and substance abuse among adults with Asperger syndrome have been described. A recent report sought to propose a link between a family history of alcoholism, especially in mothers, with autism in children, especially when the autism was associated with loss of language (Miles *et al.*,

2003). Some youngsters, especially those with normal intelligence and those with Asperger syndrome and PDDNOS, experiment with drugs such as marijuana during adolescence. Cases of substance abuse have also been reported in persons with mental retardation, some of whom suffer from comorbid autism. At this time, however, no systematic studies have been performed. Assessment and treatment should follow the usual guidelines established for the treatment of substance abuse.

References

Anderluh, M.B., Tchanturia, K., Rabe-Hesketh, S. and Treasure, J. (2003) 'Childhood obsessive-compulsive personality traits in adult women with eating disorders: Defining a broader eating disorder phenotype.' *American Journal of Psychiatry, 160*, 2, 242–7.

APA (American Psychiatric Association) (1994) *Diagnostic and Statistical Manual of Mental Disorders, Fourth Edition* (DSM-IV). Washington, DC: APA.

Benjamin, S., Seek, A., Tresise, L., Price, E. and Gagnon, M. (1996) 'Case study: Paradoxical response to naltrexone treatment of self-injurious behavior.' *Journal of the American Academy of Child and Adolescent Psychiatry, 34*, 2, 238–42.

Cohen, D.J., Johnson, W.T. and Caparulo, B.K. (1976) 'Pica and elevated blood levels in autistic and atypical children.' *American Journal of Diseases of Children, 130*, 1, 47–8.

Cox, R.D. and Schopler, E. (1993) 'Aggression and self-injurious behaviors in persons with autism – the TEACCH (Treatment and Education of Autistic and related Communications Handicapped Children) approach.' *Acta Paedopsychiatrica, 56*, 85–90.

Davanzo, P.A., Belin, T.R., Widawski, M.H. and King, B.H. (1998) 'Paroxetine treatment of aggression and self-injury in persons with mental retardation.' *American Journal on Mental Retardation, 102*, 5, 427–37.

Deb, S., Bramble, D., Drybala, G., Boyle, A. and Bruce, J. (1994) 'Polydipsia amongst adults with a learning disability in an institution.' *Journal of Intellectual Disabililty Research, 38*, 359–67.

Gillberg, I.C., Gillberg, C., Rastam, M. and Johannson, M. (1996) 'The cognitive profile of anorexia nervosa: A comparative study including a community-based sample.' *Comprehensive Psychiatry, 37*, 1, 23–30.

Hall, S., Oliver, C. and Murphy, G. (2001) 'Self-injurious behaviour in young children with Lesch-Nyhan syndrome.' *Developmental Medicine and Child Neurology, 43*, 745–9.

Harvey, M.T. and Kennedy, C.H. (2002) 'Polysomnographic phenotypes in developmental disabilities.' *International Journal of Developmental Neurosciences, 20*, 443–8.

Howlin, P. (1993) 'Behavioural techniques to reduce self-injurious behaviour in children with autism.' *Acta Paedopsychiatrica, 56*, 2, 75–84.

King, B.H. (2000) 'Pharmacological treatment of mood disturbances, aggression, and self-injury in persons with pervasive developmental disorders.' *Journal of Autism and Developmental Disorders, 30*, 5, 439–45.

Krug, D.A., Arick, J. and Almond, P. (1980) 'Behaviour checklist for identifying severely handicapped individuals with high levels of autistic behaviour.' *Journal of Psychology and Psychiatry, 21*, 3, 221–9.

Landen, M. and Rasmussen, P. (1997) 'Gender identity disorder in a girl with autism – a case report.' *European Child and Adolescent Psychiatry, 6*, 3, 170–3.

Lord, C., Rutter, M. and Le Couteur, A. (1994) 'Autism Diagnostic Interview – Revised: A revised version of a diagnostic interview for caregivers of individuals with possible pervasive developmental disorders.' *Journal of Autism and Developmental Disorders, 24*, 5, 659–85.

Miles, J.H., Takahashi, T.N., Haber, A. and Hadden, L. (2003) 'Autism families with a high incidence of alcoholism.' *Journal of Autism and Developmental Disorders, 33*, 4, 403–15.

Milos, G., Spindler, A., Ruggiero, G., Klaghofer, R. and Schnyder, U. (2002) 'Comorbidity of obsessive-compulsive disorders and duration of eating disorders.' *International Journal of Eating Disorders, 31*, 3, 284–9.

Mukaddes, N.M. (2002) 'Gender identity problems in autistic children.' *Child: Care, Health and Development, 28*, 6, 529–32.

O'Brien, G. and Whitehouse, A.M. (1990) 'A psychiatric study of deviant eating behavior among mentally handicapped adults.' *British Journal of Psychiatry, 157*, 281–84.

Panksepp, J. and Sahley, T.L. (1987) 'Possible brain opioid involvement in disrupted social intent and language development of autism.' In E. Schopler and G.B. Mesibov (eds) *Neurobiological Issues in Autism.* New York: Plenum Press.

Perera, H., Gadambanathan, T. and Weerasiri, S. (2003) 'Gender identity disorder presenting in a girl with Asperger's disorder and obsessive compulsive disorder.' *Ceylon Medical Journal, 48*, 2, 57–8.

Posey, D.J., Guenin, K.D., Kohn, A.E., Swiezy, N.B. and McDougle, C.J. (2001) 'A naturalistic open-label study of mirtazapine in autistic and other pervasive developmental disorders.' *Journal of Child and Adolescent Psychopharmacology, 11*, 3, 267–77.

Rastam, M., Gillberg, C. and Wentz, E. (2003) 'Outcome of teenage-onset anorexia nervosa in a Swedish community-based sample.' *European Child and Adolescent Psychiatry*, supplement 1, 12, 178–90.

Richdale, A.L. and Prior, M.R. (1995) 'The sleep/wake rhythm in children with autism.' *European Child and Adolescent Psychiatry, 4*, 175–86.

Shannon, M. and Graef, J.W. (1996) 'Lead intoxication in children with pervasive developmental disorders.' *Journal of Toxicology and Clinical Toxicology, 34*, 177–81.

Stores, G. (2001) 'Sleep-wake function in children with neurodevelopmental and psychiatric disorders.' *Seminars in Pediatric Neurology, 8*, 4, 188–97.

Tani, P., Lindberg, N., Nieminen-von Wendt, T., von Wendt, L., Virkkala, J., Appelberg, B. and Porkka-Heiskanen, T. (2004) 'Sleep in young adults with Asperger syndrome.' *Neuropsychobiology, 50,* 147–52.

Walters, A.S., Barrett, R.P., Feinstein, C., Mercurio, A. and Hole, W.T. (1990) 'A case report of naltrexone treatment of self-injury and social withdrawal in autism.' *Journal of Autism and Developmental Disorders, 20,* 2, 169–76.

Willemsen-Swinkels, S.H., Buitelaar, J.K., Nijhof, G.J., van England, H. (1995) 'Failure of naltrexone hydrochloride to reduce self-injurious and autistic behavior in mentally retarded adults. Double-blind placebo-controlled studies.' *Archives of General Psychiatry, 52,* 9, 766–73.

Willemsen-Swinkels, S., Buitelaar, J.K., Weijnen, F.G., Thijssen, J.H., Van Engeland, H. (1996) 'Plasma beta-endorphin concentrations in people with learning disability and self-injurious and/or autistic behavior.' *British Journal of Psychiatry, 168,* 105–109.

CHAPTER 12

Violence in Autism and Asperger Syndrome

Introduction

There is a growing perception that persons with autism spectrum disorders, especially those with Asperger syndrome (AS), are prone to violent behavior. Recent media reports have reinforced the view that autistic persons pose an increased risk of violence to society. However, before we examine the relationship between violence and autism/Asperger syndrome, it is important to clarify what exactly is meant by 'violence.' Researchers have defined violent behavior in several ways. Some have equated verbal threats with violent behavior, while others have advocated a more stringent approach that should include only those acts that result in criminal conviction (Modestin and Ammann, 1996). Most studies, however, tend to group certain types of offending behaviors under the rubric of violence. These include homicide, assault, robbery, fire-setting, illegal possession of a weapon, sexual crime, and domestic violence, etc. (Kandel and Mednick, 1991; Raine, Brennan and Mednick, 1997). All other behaviors, such as theft, blackmail, fraud, and driving offences, are excluded. For the purpose of this chapter, therefore, 'violent behavior' is defined as any physically aggressive behavior that results in either serious injury or death to others or leads to criminal prosecution (Kandel and Mednick, 1991, Raine et al., 1997).

Violence results from a variety of causes and mechanisms. These often include impulsivity, psychopathy, or deficient fear processing (Hoptman, 2003). In impulsive aggression, the individual responds to the precipitating trigger in an overwhelming manner. Trivial stimuli elicit an unusually strong reaction. Psychopathy is characterized by a lack of empathy; the individual is not able to understand the emotions and feelings of others. There is little regard for the rights of others, and a lack of guilt or remorse. Deficient fear processing involves the failure of the individual to understand fearful situations; he may not be aware of circumstances in which his behavior causes fear in others. Studies have implicated a variety of areas of the brain in the etiology of violence, especially parts of the frontal and temporal lobes.

Violence and mental disorder

Although society itself has become more violent over the last few decades, it is the violent behavior of persons with mental disorders that continues to generate much public interest and attention. The popular image of a mentally ill person is that of someone who is unpredictable and dangerous. Media reports of crimes allegedly committed by mentally disordered persons serve to perpetuate this stereotype.

Researchers have studied the association of violence with mental disorder in several ways. The first strategy focuses on investigating the occurrence of violent behavior in persons with identified psychiatric disorders. A sample of patients with a known psychiatric disorder is taken, and the prevalence of violent behavior shown by this group is studied systematically. For example, patients with a known psychiatric diagnosis such as schizophrenia or Asperger syndrome are identified, and the pattern of violence committed by them is studied. For this purpose, two methods are often used: cross-sectional studies and cohort studies. Cross-sectional studies are concerned with the study of the prevalence of violent behavior in the identified group, at any one point in time. Typically, studies of this nature focus on acts of violence committed by patients admitted to hospital, or those committed after discharge from hospital. Cohort studies follow up a group of patients with a particular disorder – matched for age, sex, and other factors – for long periods of time, up to 10–20 years, to detect the emergence of criminal behavior. The second strategy consists of studying psychiatric disorders in a sample of forensic patients. In this type of study, prevalence of a known disorder, such as depression or schizophrenia, is studied in different types of forensic settings – prison inmates, persons referred for psychiatric examination after committing an offence, and persons convicted of a particular crime, such as homicide. In the third strategy, criminal behavior in community samples is studied. Here, information on unselected samples of persons living in the community is collected. Studies may focus on whole groups of people with the selected diagnosis living in the community at a given point in time, and matched systematically for demographic factors such as race, age, and sex (Wessely, 1997).

A variety of psychiatric disorders has been found in certain populations, such as sentenced prisoners. Factors which influence the occurrence of violent behavior in such populations include male sex, poverty, school failure, family psychiatric history, childhood antisocial disorder, and hyperactivity. While these reports suggest that some mentally disordered persons are at an increased risk of violence, they also underscore the fact that the majority of persons with psychiatric disorders are not prone to violence. In addition, they emphasize the importance of factors other than psychiatric illness that independently increase the risk of violent behavior.

Several flaws characterize the methods used in the investigation of violence in general, and that of violence in psychiatric disorders in particular: the definition and measurement of violence, definition of psychiatric disorder, selection criteria used, and the recruitment of subjects, for example. Few studies have been clear in the definition of violence or in the diagnostic boundaries of mental disorders, and fewer still have focused on the nature of individual psychiatric symptoms. Measurement of violence has also not been standardized in general. Some studies have used self-reports and case-notes, while others have relied on official records. Methods of subject selection and recruitment have also varied widely across studies. Selection bias may be a factor. For example, some patients may not consent to participate in a study because they are prone to violent outbursts. Others may not be referred to the criminal justice system, because they are deemed to be mentally ill. Other possible biases include the manner of conducting interviews and ignoring the role of social class (Walsh, Buchanan and Fahy, 2002). To minimize this problem, cross-sectional studies in community samples, with both treated and untreated psychiatric disorders, should be carried out, ideally including those who are known to the forensic system.

Despite these caveats, the bulk of evidence suggests that the risk of violence is increased in persons with psychiatric disorder, and leads to the following tentative conclusions. First, most authorities now agree that there is a moderate but reliable association between mental disorder and violence (Eronen, Angermeyer and Schulze, 1998). Second, the tendency to commit violence is strongly associated with the nature of the psychiatric disorder. Among major psychiatric disorders, the risk for violence is the highest for antisocial personality disorder and substance abuse disorder. Other disorders, such as schizophrenia and psychotic depression, lead to a moderately increased risk, while the risk appears to be the lowest for anxiety disorders. Third, much of the violence observed in persons with psychiatric disorders does not occur at random, but is influenced and precipitated by the *nature* of psychiatric symptoms. Symptoms of a paranoid nature, such as persecutory delusions, are especially dangerous, as are acute and more intense symptoms.

For example, in persons with schizophrenia, acutely ill patients are more prone to violence than those who are chronically ill (Modestin and Ammann, 1996). Thus, it is the presence of psychosis, combined with antisocial personality disorder and substance abuse, that tends to confer the largest risk of violence.

Violence in mental retardation

Studies of violence in mental retardation are relevant to understanding violent behavior in autism and pervasive developmental disorders. This is because most people with autism also suffer from co-existing mental retardation. As already discussed in previous chapters, up to 75 per cent of people with autism suffer from mental retardation. About 30 per cent of persons with severe mental retardation and about 10 per cent of those with mild mental retardation show features of autism (Steffenburg, Gillberg and Steffenburg, 1996). Thus, the relationship between autism and mental retardation is not only close but also specific.

Since mental retardation is defined primarily on the basis of the level of IQ and adaptive functioning, it forms a heterogeneous category consisting of several entities, some of which are indexed by distinct biological factors, such as Fragile X syndrome and Down syndrome. Some persons with mental retardation show a variety of maladaptive behaviors, including aggression and violence. Studies have documented the role of low IQ as a contributing factor in the occurrence of crime in general; for example, the mean IQ of convicted prisoners as a group is below average (Eysenck and Gudjonsson, 1989). However, the relationship between violence and mental retardation is not straightforward, as discussed in detail elsewhere (see, for example, Murphy and Mason, 1999).

To a large extent, the offending behavior in mentally retarded individuals depends on their level of functioning. Persons with severe mental retardation are often not involved with the criminal justice system because they usually lack the capacity to stand trial. Those with mental retardation tend to be young men, with mild to moderate degrees of mental retardation. Those with borderline intelligence, that is, those who have an IQ between mild mental retardation and normal intelligence, seem to be particularly affected. They often have a family history of violent behavior, and tend to come from socially deprived environments. Their offending behavior often starts in early childhood. Although a wide variety of offences can occur, certain kinds of offences, such as sexual offences, are particularly common.

Studies have found a high prevalence of psychiatric disorders in those mentally retarded persons who commit acts of violence (Day, 1988). While several types of psychiatric disorders have been described, the prevalence of autistic spectrum disorders among offenders with mental retardation is not known with certainty. Some studies derived from special hospitals and secure units have found a wide range of estimates. O'Brien (2002) compared the type of offences committed by autistic individuals with those of mentally retarded persons without autism, admitted to a medium secure unit. A survey of the first 100 admissions revealed that offences committed by autistic individuals often lacked a clear personal motive and were less often influenced by the use of alcohol and substance abuse. Also, autistic individuals tended to commit their acts of crime during the day, while the non-autistic controls showed no such clear pattern. In all, over 40 per cent of the sample had a formal psychiatric diagnosis, including that of autism (O'Brien, 2002). However, most of these studies have been derived from highly selected sources, such as high-security hospitals and prisons, and cannot, therefore, be generalized to the rest of the population.

Violence in people with autism spectrum disorders

Persons with autism/Asperger syndrome who commit violent acts can be divided into two groups depending on their level of functioning. Those who are low-functioning, that is, those who suffer from mental retardation, indulge in acts that are often unpredictable, and are of a varying degree of severity. Sometimes, medical factors, such as seizures, can compound the violence. Aggressive acts committed by lower-functioning people often lack detailed planning, and are usually viewed in the context of 'challenging behaviors.' However, it is the violence committed by higher-functioning individuals, especially those with Asperger syndrome, that has generated an immense degree of interest.

Violence in people with Asperger syndrome

Increasing claims have been made over the years of an association between violence and pervasive developmental disorders (PDDs), in particular Asperger syndrome. These claims are based on two types of studies: case descriptions of individuals with autism/Asperger syndrome referred for psychiatric/psychological services, and studies of patients derived from forensic settings such as hospitals and remand prisons. It was Asperger himself who first suggested a possible association between the condition he described under the title 'autistic psychopathy,' and violence. All four children he described had a history of conduct problems such as physical aggression, fascination with blood, graphic description of violent fantasies, or obsession with poisons (Asperger, 1944).

Other authors have also described violent behavior in patients with characteristics of Asperger syndrome. For example, in the follow-up study of children with schizoid personality disorder – widely regarded as overlapping with Asperger syndrome – Wolff and Cull (1986) commented on the presence of conduct disorders. They found that while the incidence of conduct disorders in their sample was the same as that in the control group, patients who indulged in antisocial acts showed little empathy. Several patients in the series described by Wing (1981) showed violent tendencies, which ranged from sudden outbursts to injury caused to others because of fixations on chemical experiments. Mawson, Grounds and Tantam (1985) described a 44-year-old male with Asperger syndrome and a long history of violent behavior and psychiatric admissions. His violent acts included stabbing a girl in the wrist with a screwdriver because he did not like her.

Baron-Cohen (1988) described a 21-year-old man referred for an assessment of social difficulties. He had never been diagnosed with autism before. The main reason for the referral was his history of violence directed at his 71-year-old 'girlfriend.' In addition, he had a history of difficulties in adapting to change, an inability to fit in any particular group, and an obsession with his jaw. His birth and early developmental history were unremarkable. Despite a lack of language delay, his conversational use of language was impaired. He had an obsessional interest in record charts, and could remember long lists. After a few foster home placements and hospital admissions, he moved in with a 71-year-old woman, whom he described as his 'girlfriend.' It was the frequent violence directed at this woman that resulted in his referral. On examination, he showed an abnormal verbal–performance discrepancy (verbal IQ 92, performance IQ 69, full-scale IQ 80). Although he sometimes lashed out at others for no apparent reason, most of his violence was directed at his 'girlfriend,' and seemed to be related to his preoccupation with his jaw. He would look at his jaw frequently, and sometimes ask her if his jaw looked all right. His father also reported that his son would hit others when he felt frustrated or 'paranoid' about his jaw, and any change of routine would make the aggression worse. The author hypothesized that the patient's violent behavior was the result of his inability to read other people's emotions and feelings. Although the patient had a history of depression (his mother committed suicide) and his own behavior suggested the presence of irritability, anxiety and paranoia, no details were given about the patient's comorbid psychiatric diagnosis, if any, and its treatment.

Everall and Le Couteur (1990) described a 17-year-old male who had been diagnosed with Asperger syndrome at the age of 10 years. The reason for his referral was fire-setting, which started at the age of 16 years. He was expelled from school for this reason. Initially, the fires were 'small experimental bracken fires,' then he 'progressed to setting hay and straw stack fires.' He chose his target carefully, planning the fire during the night, and watching it from a distance to avoid being detected. His early history was typical of Asperger syndrome. His speech was not delayed. He spoke in a pedantic manner, and had a special interest in water and plastic pipes. In addition, he was fascinated by trees and by square-rigged sailing ships. On examination, he showed little understanding of the consequences of his actions, and of the distress his fire-setting caused others. His intelligence was in the lower range of normal. It is of interest, though, that his fire-setting did not appear to be related to his special interests, nor was there any evidence of a mood or psychotic disorder. The authors emphasized that although the patient displayed a disorder of conduct, he did not meet the full description of conduct disorder, as currently understood. Yet, the fact that he tried to conceal his actions cleverly, and that his fire-setting was not the result of his special interests or fixations, raises this possibility.

Studies of forensic settings

A few studies have attempted to explore the link between violence and autism/Asperger syndrome in forensic settings. In an oft-cited study, Scragg and Shah (1994) surveyed the entire male population of Broadmoor Hospital, a well-known high-security hospital in the UK. The purpose of the survey was to examine the rates of Asperger syndrome. Identification of cases was carried out in three stages: first the entire population of the hospital was screened, then a semi-structured interview was administered to the key nurses, and finally, the patients suspected of having Asperger syndrome were directly interviewed. Early childhood information was not available in all cases. Six patients were diagnosed with definite Asperger syndrome and three more with probable Asperger syndrome. The prevalence of the disorder was found to be higher than that expected for males in the general population. However, as pointed out by Hall and Bernal (1995), it is difficult to comment on the validity of these findings because the subjects and the controls came from two totally different population samples.

Siponmaa and colleagues (2001) studied a group of juvenile young adult mentally disordered offenders. The aim was to assess the prevalence of child psychiatric disorders with particular reference to autism and related PDDs. The referrals were made to the forensic department in Stockholm, from 1990 to 1995, often for a variety of criminal offences, mostly of a violent nature. Diagnosis of PDD was made on the basis of a retrospective chart review. Out of a total of 127 subjects aged 15 to 22 years, 15 per cent had a definite diagnosis of PDD and another 12 per cent had a probable diagnosis of that group of disorders. None of the subjects met the criteria for autism. In all, 13 subjects had a diagnosis of Asperger syndrome; 4 had a definite diagnosis and the remaining had a probable diagnosis. None of the patients had a diagnosis of autism, presumably because patients with autism are often diagnosed early in life and cared for in alternate settings (Siponmaa et al., 2001). When the diagnosis was compared with the type of crime, the only significant relationship that was found was between Pervasive Developmental Disorder Not Otherwise Specified (PDDNOS) and arson.

Factors contributing to violence in people with autism/AS

Precipitants

A variety of precipitants can trigger acts of aggression and violence in persons with autism/AS. At times, these precipitants are often trivial; for instance, a precipitant might be a change of routines, especially in school settings. These outbursts are more likely to occur in those autistic patients who also suffer from mental retardation. In the case described by Baron-Cohen (1988) above, for example, the violent episodes were precipitated by the subject's frustration, and by the threat of change of routines. In lower-functioning individuals, the precipitants of violence may originate in common physical complaints, such as constipation, which the subjects are not able to describe. In other cases, biological factors, such as seizures, may contribute to the violent outbursts. Sometimes, no obvious precipitating factors can be found as in the case of arson described by Everall and Le Couteur (1990).

Types of violent acts

ARSON

Fire-setting or arson is a major symptom of antisocial personality disorder, and can occur in a variety of psychiatric settings, including depression and schizophrenia. Persons with autism and Asperger syndrome may start fires as an isolated antisocial act or as part of a special fascination for and interest in fires. Apart from the case described by Everall and Le Couteur (1990), two of the cases in the follow-up series of Wolff and Cull (1986) also showed a history of fire-setting. Siponmaa *et al.* (2001) also suggested that there was a specific link between fire-setting and pervasive developmental disorders. In their sample, out of the 16 persons who had committed arson, 10 had a diagnosis of PDD (Asperger syndrome and PDDNOS). The diagnosis of PDDNOS and Asperger syndrome was statistically more frequent in the arson group than it was in the other groups, such as Attention Deficit Hyperactivity Disorder (ADHD) and mental retardation. Another point to note was that two of the PDD individuals who committed arson had a history of alcohol abuse, which suggests the possible role of substance abuse in this type of offending behavior. In the Broadmoor Hospital study, of the six men diagnosed with Asperger syndrome, one had committed arson (Scragg and Shah, 1994). Sometimes, patients with autism spectrum disorders first come to professional attention because of repeated arson, as in the case described below.

Case study: AB

AB is a 15-year-old Caucasian youngster with mild mental retardation who is awaiting trial for arson. He was referred for a psychiatric evaluation because he had broken into two homes in the neighborhood and started fires. His level of retardation was mild to moderate, and his full-scale IQ, when last examined, was 66. There was no previous diagnosis of autism although AB carried a diagnosis of conduct disorder and ADHD. AB would start fires at home and watch them intently. During the course of the assessment, it emerged that he had always been fascinated by fire. He liked to sit and watch things burn. In addition, he was fixated on electrical and mechanical gadgets. At times, he would insert objects, such as pencils, into the electrical outlets. He had no friends. He stood out as being 'different' even in his classroom of other adolescents with mental retardation. His eye contact was unusual because he seldom blinked. Also, he had a habit of pulling out his eyebrows, which gave him a staring look. At one time, in his early childhood, he had been given the diagnosis of Obsessive-Compulsive

Disorder (OCD). He spoke in a high-pitched voice, and had a fixed expression on his face, which seldom changed with the social context. He was 'active but odd' and took particular delight in lecturing about the mechanics of desk chairs! He walked in a clumsy manner and seemed to lack the ability to read social cues.

After evaluation, AB was given a diagnosis of autistic spectrum disorder, because of the clustering of the three main features of reciprocal social deficits, communication impairment, and rigid ritualistic interests. A change in his school placement was suggested and the need for close supervision and structure emphasized.

MURDER

Some cases of persons with autism and Asperger syndrome who commit murder have been reported. Such crimes are probably more common among those who are higher-functioning and those with Asperger syndrome. In the Siponmaa study cited above (2001), although 28 of the 126 referrals were for murder/manslaughter, it was not clear how many of these were eventually given a diagnosis of Asperger syndrome or PDDNOS. Scragg and Shah (1994) reported that out of the six patients with AS, three had committed murder for a variety of reasons including matricide and 'erotomania.' The rather high rate in this study reflects the fact that it was conducted in a special hospital for the criminally insane.

Murder can be the result of an autistic individual's special interests and idiosyncratic fixations. For example, a student who is obsessed with chemical experiments may come up with an idea to try his concoction on one of his classmates and cause death even without intending to do so. One of the subjects in the Scragg and Shah (1994) study was fascinated with murder books and another collected knives and weapons.

At times, seemingly trivial reasons can trigger murderous acts. A 13-year-old boy in Bristol, England, stabbed his baby brother to death. It later emerged that the boy had been upset with his mother. He stabbed his brother after an argument with his mother. According to the newspaper reports, he then changed his blood-stained clothes, walked into a police station and told officers he had stabbed his brother with a kitchen knife. When asked why he had stabbed his brother, he replied: 'I want to be with my mum' (BBC News Online, 2001).

More frequently, however, murder has more to do with other factors than with Asperger syndrome. Barry George, a man with Asperger syndrome, was charged with murder (Daily Telegraph, 2001). He had six personality disorders in addition to being diagnosed with Asperger syndrome. As a young boy he had been diagnosed with ADHD, and showed a variety of psychiatric symptoms. He was also obsessed with celebrities, weaponry and women, which was probably the reason why he was given a diagnosis of Asperger syndrome. His crime seemed to be more a result of his personality disorders, ADHD, and other psychiatric disorders, rather than of Asperger syndrome.

SEXUAL OFFENCES

Some recent reports have claimed that persons with Asperger syndrome are prone to committing sexual offences. It has been argued that, since sexual offenders are often fixated on certain themes to the exclusion of others, and are socially impaired, they may suffer from PDDs, particularly Asperger syndrome. This is not only inaccurate but also simplistic. If this argument were to be accepted, then every serial killer and sexual offender could claim to have Asperger syndrome. However, some persons with autism and Asperger syndrome do commit sexual offences. In those who are lower-functioning, the common types of behaviors include sexual acting out in public places (such as masturbation). These behaviors result from a lack of understanding of social rules. At times, people with autism are fascinated by the touch of objects, especially if the objects are soft and fluffy. The author is reminded of a youngster with autism who was fixated on touching pantyhose. He would walk up to strangers, and touch their legs, more to get a 'feel,' than to harass them sexually.

Because of their social naivety, persons with autism spectrum disorders may find themselves in situations that are mistaken for sexual harassment. A 25-year-old adult with autism, with a full-scale IQ of about 70, was fired from his job at a local grocery store because he would keep staring at his customers because he wanted to be 'friendly' with them. His attempts to socialize with others were mistaken for sexual harassment. Another individual who worked in a used car dealership lost his job because he would constantly ask personal and rather intrusive questions of his colleagues and customers, both male and female. There is no evidence that sexual offences, such as rape or deliberate assault, are common in persons with autism and Asperger syndrome. Such cases have more to do with conduct disorder and antisocial personality disorder than with autism or Asperger syndrome.

AGGRESSIVE OUTBURSTS AND TEMPER TANTRUMS

Persons with autism and related disorders, including Asperger syndrome, are prone to aggressive outbursts and temper tantrums. These occur across the entire spectrum, and tend to occur more frequently in younger children and in those with mental retardation. In those with severe mental retardation, aggressive outbursts may be unpredictable and unprovoked. Such children and adults are often cared for in specialized inpatient units, and require a variety of pharmacological and behavioral interventions. Older individuals, especially those who are of normal or near-normal intelligence, do not often present with episodes of serious aggression. Surprisingly, patients who fall within the PDDNOS category tend to be over-represented in clinic samples and in general child psychiatric inpatient units.

Patients with autism and Asperger syndrome can sometimes present with a history of assault and battery directed against staff and family. These incidents are often provoked by a change in a routine of which the staff may not be aware. For example, a 25-year-old male with autism had a tendency to run across a busy road to his favorite McDonald restaurant, at the same time every day, and order the same meal (cheese burger with french fries). He would get extremely combative and violent if interrupted during his ritual. Another 15-year-old individual with high-functioning autism and seizure disorder presented for an assessment because he was expelled from school for having assaulted his teacher. The reason was that the youngster insisted on having his desk arranged in exactly the same manner every day, and was slow to follow the teacher's directions to clean it up. This led to frequent resistance and finally to an aggressive outburst and an assault on the teacher.

Targets of violent acts

The violence of people on the autistic spectrum can be directed against inanimate objects as well as living creatures. The latter can be further divided into animals and human beings (both strangers as well as known persons). The targets of their violence can be inanimate objects, especially as regards those who are lower-functioning, and sometimes property may be destroyed and fires started. Breaking furniture and throwing objects can sometimes occur, leading to admission to secure units. Those who are higher-functioning may target their violence differently, depending on the level of intelligence and other factors. The aggression of those who are lower-functioning may be nonspecific, in that it can be directed against anyone.

Idiosyncratic interests

As stated, the violent behavior of persons with autism and Asperger syndrome often results from their special interests getting 'out of hand.' This is more commonly seen among higher-functioning persons with autism and those with Asperger syndrome. For example, a patient with Asperger syndrome may be unusually interested in collecting guns; another example would be that of a youngster with Asperger syndrome who develops a fascination for making pipe bombs (with the information obtained from the internet). However, an important point to remember is that there is seldom a real attempt on the part of the autistic individual to conceal his behavior. On the contrary, most people with conduct disorder try to conceal their motives – a point that may help in the assessment and diagnosis (Green *et al.*, 2000).

Psychiatric factors

The offending behavior of people with autistic spectrum disorders often index the occurrence of another form of psychiatric disorder, commonly depression and psychotic behaviors. Thus, the youngster who took his homemade pipe bomb to school admitted to feeling depressed, and feeling like blowing up the school. Therefore, when offending behaviors occur in the setting of autism/PDD, it is important to exclude other psychiatric conditions, because these can independently raise the risk of offending. A study done in the UK of all special hospitals confirmed this view. In a survey of offending behaviors committed in the UK by adults with PDD, the authors found that often it was not the PDD but the presence of other psychiatric disorders that accounted for the behaviour (unpublished data). Several individual cases reported in the literature seemed to have suffered from undiagnosed psychiatric problems. For example, Tantam (1988) noted the high prevalence of additional psychiatric disorders in a group of adults with Asperger syndrome and violent behavior.

DISRUPTIVE BEHAVIOR DISORDERS

Behavioral problems, especially aggression, can sometimes occur in the setting of disruptive behavior disorders, which include Oppositional Defiant Disorder (ODD) and conduct disorder. According to the DSM-IV (APA, 1994), ODD is diagnosed when a child displays a persistent or consistent pattern of defiance, disobedience, and hostility toward various authority figures including parents, teachers, and other adults. It is characterized by such behaviors as persistent fighting and arguing, being touchy or easily annoyed, and deliberately annoying or being spiteful or vindictive to other people. Children with ODD may repeatedly lose their temper, argue with adults, deliberately refuse to comply with requests or rules of adults, blame others for their own mistakes, and be repeatedly angry and resentful. Stubbornness and testing of limits are common. These behaviors cause significant difficulties with family and friends and at school or work (APA, 1994).

Conduct disorder is a much more serious condition. It is characterized by such behaviors as intimidating, physically assaulting, sexually coercing, and/or being cruel to people or animals. Fire-setting and other acts of deliberate destruction of property are common, as are theft, truancy, and early tobacco, alcohol, and substance use and abuse, as well as precocious sexual activity. Girls with a conduct disorder are prone to running away from home and may become involved in prostitution. The behavior interferes with performance at school or work, so that individuals with this disorder rarely perform at the level predicted by their IQ or age. Their relationships with peers and adults are often poor. They have higher injury rates and are prone to school expulsion and problems with the law. Sexually transmitted diseases are common. If they have been removed from home, they may have difficulty staying in an adoptive or foster family or group home, and this may further complicate their development.

Children and adolescents with autism and Asperger syndrome are sometimes given the above diagnoses, especially that of ODD, even when the criteria are not fully met. While some patients with PDD do indeed show persistent patterns of maladaptive behavior, the risk of using loose diagnostic criteria is that any child who is temperamental and rather assertive runs the risk of being labeled as having an ODD or, worse, as having a conduct disorder. It is the author's view that the diagnosis of a disruptive behavior disorder be used sparingly in persons with PDD. This is because these conditions are often regarded as lying on a continuum with ODD on one end and criminality/antisocial personality disorder on the other.

Medical factors

Persons with mental retardation, especially those with problems in communication, sometimes get aggressive when their demands are not met, or when they are trying to communicate. Sometimes, even common physical conditions can result in behavior that is described as 'acting out.' However, in general, little attention has been paid to the presence of medical factors that might contribute to the emergence of violent behavior in persons with autism and Asperger syndrome. For example, a substantial number of persons with these disorders suffer from epilepsy, the prevalence of which rises with the level of mental retardation. Yet it is not known how the presence of epilepsy relates to the onset of aggressive behavior in people with autism/Asperger syndrome.

Family factors

Family factors that predispose to violence in persons with autism/Asperger syndrome can be divided into two groups: general factors and specific factors. General factors include low social class, poor parental control, and a chaotic environment. Specific factors include a family history of mental illness and criminality. In addition, family factors can also play a role by decreasing the likelihood of violence by increasing a patient's compliance with treatment. Another way in which the family exerts its role is through 'expressed emotion.' Research has shown that an atmosphere at home characterized by hostility and over-involvement can trigger a relapse, especially in the case of people with schizophrenia. Although such research has not been done in the case of people with autism/Asperger syndrome, it is reasonable to assume that similar factors operate in triggering violence in this population.

Autistic patients as victims

The discussion so far has dwelt on the forensic aspects of AS and autism. However, these patients are often the victims themselves of aggression and violence. In the younger age group, especially in the middle school (ages 9–13 years), autistic children find themselves the target of practical jokes. As they step into adolescence, patients with autism, even if they are higher-functioning, are often unable to deal with issues of sexuality, and this could easily lead to violence and aggression, sometimes of a sexual nature. Cases are on record of adolescents with AS being mugged and robbed by others. In their adult years, higher-functioning people, including those with AS, sometimes face sexual harassment and discrimination in the workplace; this may be violent in nature. In addition, because of their social naivety, they may be led into committing criminal acts (Howlin, 1997).

Assessment of violence

The assessment of the violent behavior of persons with autism/AS begins with a detailed history. Factors that need to be taken into account include the level of functioning, history of precipitants, use of medications and drugs, a detailed history of medical factors, such as seizures, and presence of psychiatric symptoms. Before a detailed assessment is undertaken, it is important to determine the degree of risk to the patient and/or to others. If there is any concern that the patient's safety or that of others is compromised, immediate referral either to the police or, if appropriate, to the hospital for an inpatient admission, should be considered.

The other part of the assessment should deal specifically with the presence of psychiatric factors. An effort should be made to look for the presence of psychotic symptoms. Since depression is usually associated with irritability and anger, patients should be evaluated for the presence of depression.

It is often said that the best predictor of future behavior, in so far as violent behavior is concerned, is past behavior. If the patient's preoccupations increase in intensity or become morbid in nature, these should serve as warning signs. However, the assessment of dangerousness is an inexact science. Generalizations made at a group level do not always hold true at an individual level, and do not necessarily contribute to making accurate predictions or initiating treatments. For example, knowing that some people with Asperger syndrome indulge in violent behavior does not help us in predicting which AS patients will resort to violence during their life, and which should be targeted for interventions. All that can be done is to assess each patient individually, evaluate the precipitating and contributing factors, and intervene in a timely manner.

Treatment and interventions

The treatment of aggression in persons with autism and Asperger syndrome should target the underlying causes. The level of functioning and the degree of overall functioning determine the type of intervention that should be adopted. No single modality of treatment works in all cases. At the individual level, a detailed behavioral analysis should be done to determine the precipitants of aggression. Medical and psychiatric issues should be addressed adequately. At the family and community level, efforts should be made to modify the emotional environment at home. Similar changes should be made in the school and work settings.

The importance of behavioral and psychological treatments stems from the fact that in a substantial number of cases, the origins of the aggressive behavior lie in changes of routines and schedules. The desire for sameness is an important symptom of autism spectrum disorders, and quite often persons with these disorders react in an aggressive manner to any perceived threat to their personal or immediate environment. Thus, it is important that particular attention be paid to an individual's ritualistic behaviors at the time of treatment programming. Frequently, a main objective of treatment programs is to decrease or stop the patient's rituals and compulsions. This is not always possible or necessary.

There are no specific medications for the treatment of aggression and violence in persons with autism or Asperger syndrome, although several medications are currently used (McDougle, Stigler and Posey, 2003). In general, medications are used if there are features suggestive of a complicating psychiatric condition, such as psychosis or depression. In such cases, the standard psychopharmacological approaches are used, since the role of medications in the treatment of these conditions is well established. Sometimes, however, the use of psychopharmacological agents is justified even if there are no clear signs of an additional psychiatric illness. For example, some reports suggest the utility of agents such as the Selective Serotonin Reuptake Inhibitors (SSRIs). Although most of these reports are anecdotal in nature, the severity of violence sometimes exhibited by this population justifies the use of such agents. Other medications that are commonly used are the anticonvulsants. These drugs, which are used to treat epilepsy, are sometimes used as mood stabilizers, on the assumption that this might have a beneficial effect on the violent behaviors. Lithium is another medication that has been used with persons with these disorders. Last but not least, threat of legal action may be necessary. At times, it may be more appropriate to prosecute a high-functioning adult with autism who deliberately resorts to aggression against others than to let him avoid the consequences of his actions.

Conclusion

While several reports have suggested a link between criminal behavior and autism spectrum disorders, especially Asperger syndrome, most of these assertions are either based on single case reports or derived from forensic samples such as assessment centers for offenders or maximum-security hospitals (Ghaziuddin, Tsai and Ghaziuddin, 1991). No community-based study has investigated this issue. Since people with a variety of psychiatric disorders, ranging from schizophrenia to conduct disorder, can behave violently it is unclear to what extent people with autism spectrum disorders should be singled out as being particularly vulnerable to offending behavior. This does not mean, however, that violent behaviors, including indictable offenses, do not occur in people with autism. They sometimes do. And when this occurs, the underlying reason may be a psychiatric disorder, such as major depression or psychosis. In addition, the offending behaviors of persons with PDD have certain specific characteristics, such as those emanating from their special interests, which help in the assessment and diagnosis. Treatment consists of the judicious use of medications, where necessary, combined with structure, consistency, and supervision. At times, referral to the legal system may be necessary, especially in cases of repeated offences and where other interventions fail.

References

APA (American Psychiatric Association) (1994) *Diagnostic and Statistical Manual of Mental Disorders, Fourth Edition* (DSM-IV). Washington, DC: APA.

Asperger, H. (1944) 'Die "autistischen Psychopathen" im Kindersalter.' *Archiv für Psychiatrie und Nervenkrankheiten, 117,* 76–136.

Baron-Cohen, S. (1988) 'An assessment of violence in a young man with Asperger syndrome.' *Journal of Child Psychology and Psychiatry, 29,* 3, 351–60.

BBC News Online (2001) 'Boy with Asperger syndrome killed baby brother.' *BBC News Online,* 13 February.

Daily Telegraph (2001) 'The psychology: Six personality disorders.' *www.telegraph.co.uk.* 3 July.

Day, K. (1988) 'A hospital-based treatment programme for male mentally handicapped offenders.' *British Journal of Psychiatry, 153,* 635–44.

Eronen, M., Angermeyer, M.C. and Shulze, B. (1998) 'The psychiatric epidemiology of violent behavior.' *Social Psychiatry and Psychiatric Epidemiology, 33,* S13–23.

Everall, I.P. and Le Couteur, A. (1990) 'Firesetting in an adolescent boy with Asperger's syndrome.' *British Journal of Psychiatry, 157,* 284–7.

Eysenck, H.J. and Gudjonsson, G.H. (1989) *The Causes and Cures of Criminality.* London: Plenum Press.

Ghaziuddin, M., Tsai, L. and Ghaziuddin, N. (1991) 'Violence in Asperger syndrome: A critique.' *Journal of Autism and Developmental Disorders, 21,* 349–54.

Green, J., Gilchrist, A., Burton, D. and Cox, A. (2000) 'Social and psychiatric functioning in adolescents with Asperger syndrome compared with conduct disorder.' *Journal of Autism and Developmental Disorders, 30,* 4, 279–93.

Hall, I. and Bernal, J. (1995) 'Asperger's syndrome and violence.' *British Journal of Psychiatry, 166,* 262–8.

Hoptman, M.J. (2003) 'Neuroimaging studies of violence and social behavior.' *Journal of Psychiatric Practice, 9,* 4, 265–78.

Howlin, P. (1997) *Autism: Preparing for Adulthood.* London: Routledge.

Kandel, E., and Mednick, S.A. (1991) 'Perinatal complications predict violent offending.' *Criminology, 29,* 519–29.

Mawson, A., Grounds, A. and Tantam, D. (1985) 'Violence and Asperger's syndrome: A case study.' *British Journal of Psychiatry, 147,* 566–9.

McDougle, C.J., Stigler, K.A. and Posey, D.J. (2003) 'Treatment of aggression in children and adolescents with autism and conduct disorder.' *Journal of Clinical Psychiatry, 64,* Supplement 4, 16–25.

Modestin, J. and Ammann, R. (1996) 'Mental disorder and criminality: Male schizophrenia.' *Schizophrenia Bulletin, 22,* 69–82.

Murphy, G.H. and Mason, J. (1999) 'People with developmental disabilities who offend.' In N. Bouras (ed.) *Psychiatric and Behavioral Disorders in Developmental Disabilities and Mental Retardation.* Cambridge: Cambridge University Press.

O'Brien, G. (2002) 'Dual diagnosis in offenders with intellectual disability: Setting research priorities: A review of research findings concerning psychiatric disorder (excluding personality disorder) among offenders with intellectual disability.' *Journal of Intellectual Disabililty Research, 46,* Supplement 1, 21–30.

Raine, A., Brennan, P. and Mednick, S.A. (1997) 'Interactions between birth complications and early maternal rejection in predisposing individuals to adult violence: Specificity to serious, early-onset violence.' *American Journal of Psychiatry, 154,* 1265–71.

Scragg, P. and Shah, A. (1994) 'The prevalence of Asperger's syndrome in a secure hospital.' *British Journal of Pschiatry, 165,* 679–82.

Siponmaa, L., Kristiansson, M., Jonson, C., Nyden, A. and Gillberg, C. (2001) 'Juvenile and young adult mentally disordered offenders: The role of child neuropsychiatric disorders.' *Journal of the American Academy of Psychiatry and the Law, 29,* 4, 420–6.

Steffenburg, S., Gillberg, C. and Steffenburg, U. (1996) 'Psychiatric disorders in children and adolescents with mental retardation and active epilepsy.' *Archives of Neurology, 53,* 904–12.

Tantam, D. (1988) 'Lifelong eccentricity and social isolation. I: Psychiatric, social and forensic aspects.' *British Journal of Psychiatry, 153,* 777–91.

Walsh, E., Buchanan, A. and Fahy, T. (2002) 'Violence and schizophrenia: Examining the evidence.' *British Journal of Psychiatry, 180,* 490–5.

Wessely, S. (1997) 'The epidemiology of crime, violence and schizophrenia.' *British Journal of Psychiatry, 170,* 32, 8–11.

Wing, L. (1981) 'Asperger's syndrome: A clinical account.' *Psychological Medicine, 11,* 115–29.

Wolff, S. and Cull, A. (1986) '"Schizoid" personality and antisocial conduct: A retrospective case note study.' *Psychological Medicine, 16,* 677–87.

CHAPTER 13

Psychiatric Comorbidity of Autism Spectrum Disorders: The Task Ahead

Introduction

The preceding chapters have given an overview of the common psychiatric disorders that occur in persons with autism spectrum disorders. Since research in this area is still in its early stages, the main purpose was to underscore the importance of psychiatric comorbidity of autism and Asperger syndrome, and stress the need for early diagnosis and treatment.

Current status

The risk of psychiatric disorders is increased in persons with autism spectrum disorders. Carrying a diagnosis of autism and Asperger syndrome does not confer immunity against other medical or psychiatric disorders. Although systematic community studies have not been performed, clinic rates confirm the high rates of psychiatric disorders in this population.

A variety of psychiatric disorders occur in persons with autism and Asperger syndrome. Depression is probably the most common disorder that occurs across the life span of an individual with these disorders. Although comparison studies have not been done, this seems to mirror the prevalence of depression in the general population. The other common condition is Attention Deficit Hyperactivity Disorder (ADHD). Problems of inattention and hyperactivity are commonly seen in children with Pervasive Development Disorder (PDD) and are often either missed or ignored. Although the DSM and the ICD allow for the recording of additional psychiatric disorders in persons with PDD, in several conditions, such as ADHD and social phobia, it is not easy to apply the diagnostic criteria. There does not appear to be an association between schizophrenia and autism. However, clinical experience suggests that patients with Asperger syndrome sometimes go through psychotic episodes, and since both PDD and schizophrenia are spectrum disorders, there may be a subgroup within the PDD spectrum that is particularly prone to developing psychosis, including schizophrenia. Other conditions seen in persons with autism and Asperger syndrome include anxiety disorders and eating disorders.

Psychiatric disorders occur across the entire spectrum of autism. People with traditional autism are affected as well as those with Asperger syndrome. At this time, it is not clear if patients with autism and Asperger syndrome differ in the pattern and rate of psychiatric comorbidity. People with Asperger syndrome seem to report more symptoms, possibly because of their better preserved verbal skills. A condition that is being increasingly diagnosed in child psychiatric hospitals, especially in inpatient settings, is Pervasive Developmental Disorder Not Otherwise Specified (PDDNOS). Although it is a poorly defined miscellaneous category, it is overrepresented among severely behaviorally disturbed children admitted to inpatient units. Again, the evidence for this is only anecdotal at this stage.

The reasons for the association of autism spectrum disorders with other psychiatric disorders are varied and depend on both genetic and environmental factors. The reasons why some people within the PDD spectrum develop psychiatric disorders may lie in a combination of genetic and psychosocial factors, as in the rest of the population. It is not clear why some conditions, such as depression and ADHD, are more common than others. People with PDD are vulnerable to environmental stressors and life events. Since almost all psychiatric disorders have genetic underpinnings, similar factors may operate in persons with autism and Asperger syndrome. The association may be the result of coincidence in some cases, while in others it may suggest the existence of distinct subtypes within the autism spectrum.

The presentation of psychiatric symptoms varies across the autistic spectrum. To a large extent, it depends on the level of intelligence and the sophistication of verbal skills. Higher-functioning individuals, such as those with Asperger syndrome, are able in most cases to give a detailed and coherent account of their illness. However, in those with mental retardation, especially if they have only partially developed language, psychiatric assessment is difficult, and is more dependent on the reports of care-givers. In general, two factors emerge as the main clues to the presence of psychiatric disorders: appearance of new maladaptive behaviors, and a worsening of 'old' symptoms.

While the diagnosis of psychiatric disorders in persons with PDD can often be made on the basis of conventional diagnostic criteria, in the case of some conditions such as depression, the presence of 'special features' may assist in the assessment. Also, in lower-functioning individuals, observed behavioral data and vegetative features, such as weight loss, help in the diagnosis. At the same time, it is important to underscore that although the traditional method of psychiatric diagnosis remains categorical, the approach to patients with PDD is often symptom-based. That is, even when a formal psychiatric diagnosis has not been made for persons with PDD, the symptoms (such as aggression and hyperactivity) often form the main focus of clinical attention.

The main purpose of diagnosis is to assist in treatment. The treatment of psychiatric disorders in persons with autism spectrum disorders does not have a direct effect on the core symptoms of autism, such as communication and play. The impact, however, is indirect but important. For example, a child with severe hyperactivity and impulsivity responds better to behavioral interventions and interacts better with his peers if these symptoms are brought under control. Thus, the treatment of additional psychiatric disorders in the autistic population is critical to improving the quality of life of the patients and lessening the burden of care on the families.

Future directions

Research over the last few decades has shown that most psychiatric disorders do not occur as pure entities. Psychiatric comorbidity is often the rule and not the exception in the case of persons with autism spectrum disorders. For research to progress in this often neglected area, the following steps are necessary.

First, a high index of suspicion should be maintained for the presence of psychiatric disorders, and the level of awareness increased among parents and professionals. While it is important not to over-diagnose every alteration of behavior as a sign of a psychiatric disorder, it is equally important not to dismiss valid psychiatric symptoms as 'epiphenomena' and 'chance findings.' When a teenager with autism starts having crying spells or other mood symptoms, or starts making suicidal comments, it is naive and unethical not to consider depression as a possible diagnosis and instead to assume that the symptoms are all 'part of autism.' What is required as a first step, therefore, is a fundamental change of attitude to the care of persons with autism spectrum disorders.

Second, the manner in which services are provided for persons with PDD needs to be revisited. In some countries, such as the US, there is an unfortunate division of services into the categories of mental illness and developmental disabilities. This division is not only flawed but also potentially harmful because mental illness and developmental disabilities often exist together, and should be treated as such. A psychiatric examination should form an integral part of the evaluation of a person with an autism spectrum disorder. This is especially true if the patient is an adolescent or if there are complicating medical conditions, such as epilepsy. Patients should also receive a detailed physical examination, including basic laboratory tests, such as the assessment of thyroid functions. Thus, the approach to a person with autism should be multidisciplinary in nature, and always include medical and psychiatric evaluation.

Third, the training needs of professionals should be re-examined. Autism is a childhood-onset disorder. For this reason, most cases are seen by child psychiatrists. However, autism does not disappear when the patient turns 18 years of age. Unfortunately, most 'adult' psychiatrists do not possess an adequate training or background in autism, and are likely to miss the disorder and its complications. The same applies to direct care workers who do not often have a background in the detection and assessment of psychiatric symptoms. While some professionals may not be aware of the psychiatric correlates and complications of autism, others may hesitate to give the diagnosis because of ideological reasons.

Fourth, there is an urgent need to investigate the true prevalence of psychiatric disorders in persons with PDD. The available evidence is based on clinic-based studies. What is needed is a systematic assessment of psychiatric disorders of persons with PDD living in the community because those who are referred to psychiatrists and other mental health professionals are likely to show increased rates. At the same time, it is important to compare the rates of psychiatric disorders in this population using suitable controls such as those with Down syndrome or those with speech and language disorders. Estimating the true prevalence of the disorder is essential in order to plan for services.

Fifth, changes need to be made in the methods of assessment and diagnosis. More information is needed about the manner in which psychiatric symptoms emerge and present in persons with PDD, especially in those who have significant language and intellectual deficits. Standardized interviews and ratings scales specifically for use with persons with autism spectrum disorders need to be devised. At present, the diagnosis of psychiatric disorders in this population is based on the usual DSM/ICD criteria which may not be applicable in all cases, especially in those who have low verbal skills. In some cases, existing criteria may need to be modified to apply to persons with PDD.

Sixth, newer methods of treatment should be explored. A combination of psychosocial and biological interventions should be regarded as the standard form of treatment for this population. Several misconceptions exist about the use of medications, ranging from lack of response and increased susceptibility to side-effects. No treatment, behavioral or otherwise, fits all cases of autism or Asperger syndrome. While no medication has been known to alter the core symptoms of autism, psychotropic drugs are often helpful in decreasing the behavioral symptoms and increasing the success of other forms of treatments.

Seventh, the effect of psychiatric comorbidity should be taken into account in research studies. While some reasons for the association of autism with psychiatric conditions may lie in pure chance factors, some others might suggest the existence of distinct phenotypes. For example, some patients within the autistic spectrum may be at an increased risk of developing psychotic disorders. Investigation of these potential subtypes can increase our understanding of the causes of autism and also help us devise more effective treatments.

Conclusion

Persons with autism spectrum disorders often present with a variety of behavioral symptoms such as hyperactivity, mood swings, and aggressive behavior, which may form the main reason for their referral to clinicians. In some cases, these symptoms are severe enough to cause significant distress not only to the affected person but also to the family and care-givers. It is important not to ignore them either as incidental findings or as part of the overall autistic syndrome. Instead, a systematic approach should be adopted to assess and diagnose them, and, where appropriate, to treat them aggressively. Several treatment methods should be used simultaneously, including medications and psychotherapy. Research focusing on the psychiatric comorbidity of PDD is still in its initial stages, and much remains to be done. Diagnosis and treatment of associated psychiatric symptoms and disorders contribute significantly to the long-term outcome of autism and Asperger syndrome; they also increase our understanding of the mechanisms that underlie these challenging conditions.

Subject Index

Note: page numbers in bold refer to information contained in tables and boxes, page numbers in italics refer to diagrams.

Author Index